The Transformation
of the Roman World

Published under the auspices of the
CENTER FOR MEDIEVAL AND RENAISSANCE STUDIES
University of California, Los Angeles

Contributions of the
UCLA CENTER FOR MEDIEVAL AND RENAISSANCE STUDIES

UCLA CENTER FOR
MEDIEVAL AND RENAISSANCE STUDIES
CONTRIBUTIONS: III

The Transformation of the Roman World

Gibbon's Problem after Two Centuries

Edited by

LYNN WHITE, JR.

UNIVERSITY OF CALIFORNIA PRESS
BERKELEY AND LOS ANGELES, 1966

University of California Press
Berkeley and Los Angeles, California
Cambridge University Press
London, England

In Antiquity the Capitoline Hill, the citadel of Rome and its chief shrine, could be approached only from the Forum, the center of the city's political and commercial life. During the Middle Ages little was done to alter this physical arrangement. In the 1530's, however, Michelangelo redesigned the Campidoglio, the piazza of the Capitoline, and what he did to it shows him to have been profoundly a man of the Middle Ages. Glorying in the magnificence of the ancient Roman tradition, nevertheless he drastically reoriented the Campidoglio away from its pagan past, the Forum to the east, toward Christianity, the shrine of St. Peter to the west. He removed to the Campidoglio the great equestrian statue of Constantine from the Lateran square (that in fact it represents Marcus Aurelius is irrelevant), and since then the first Christian emperor, turning his back upon paganism, has ridden majestically toward the Vatican, conducted on either hand by the Dioscuri, the symbols of the martyrs. To Michelangelo history was the pageant of salvation; man's destiny was the drama of Providence, a divine comedy.

During the next two hundred years the Christian view of the nature of history ceased to dominate the minds of educated men. In the late afternoon of October 15, 1764, Edward Gibbon, a rather conceited young Englishman on the grand tour, sat in St. Mary's in Aracoeli, a Christianized temple adjacent to the Campidoglio; but Michelangelo's symbols no longer spoke to him or for him. The church is somber at that hour save for slanting orange rays of the setting sun. In the gathering shadows, as he listened a bit contemptuously to the friars chanting vespers, it occurred to Gibbon that someone should investigate carefully what was to him a tragedy which he eventually phrased as the decline and fall of the Roman Empire. From that moment emerged the greatest single book of history.

Another two centuries have passed. In the spring of 1964 a group of historians connected with the Center for Medieval and Renaissance Studies of the University of California, Los Angeles, came together, very largely for their own delight, to see what has happened to Gibbon's problem in the interim, and why. They were joined by C. Warren Hollister of the University of California, Santa Barbara, and by Jeffrey B. Russell of the University of California, Riverside. The group expresses its appreciation to the University of California Extension at Los Angeles for arranging a series of lectures on the topic during the autumn of 1964, to the University of California Press for bringing these to a wider audience, and to Michael Schrader for preparing the index.

This symposium deals with three layers of human experience: first, what really happened, as we now see it, in the age of the Roman world's transformation; second, Gibbon, and why he saw these things as he did; third, ourselves, and why our angle of vision differs from Gibbon's. The study of history is chiefly a means of discovering ourselves as we are mirrored in our thoughts about the past. The contributors offer this volume as an aid to self-understanding.

LYNN WHITE, JR.
Director, Center for Medieval and Renaissance Studies

CONTENTS

viii   CONTENTS

The Transformation
of the Roman World

INTRODUCTION:
GIBBON AND THE ENLIGHTENMENT
Andrew Lossky

*O*UR WHOLE CONCEPT of the early Middle Ages has been colored by Edward Gibbon's *Decline and Fall of the Roman Empire*. Whether we open the pages of Mommsen, or Lot, or Pirenne, or Rostovtseff, or Baynes, to mention only a few eminent historians, we see them wrestling not only with "Gibbon's problem," but with Gibbon himself, sometimes by implication, but more often explicitly. "An Empire to endure a death agony of a thousand years must possess considerable powers of recuperation" —with this blast at Gibbon, Baynes opens his study on the *Byzantine Empire*. Why is it that Gibbon's ghost still stalks among us, while most of the other thinkers of the Enlightenment, men of no mean stature, have found their resting places, where they can be analyzed, categorized, and quietly left alone? [1]

Another question: why did Gibbon concern himself with the medieval world? This was a strange, almost inappropriate, occupation for an eighteenth-century gentleman conscious of his enlightenment. Gibbon's age had inherited from the sixteenth and seventeenth centuries a classification of European history into three parts: Ancient

---

[1] To this general observation there are several exceptions: for instance, Montesquieu continues to crop up in various disguises in the pages of de Tocqueville, Ortega y Gasset, and elsewhere, while Kant still exercises the ingenuity of the epistemologist.

History, toward the end of which men of letters wrote excellent Latin and knew Greek well; more recently, "the restoration of learning in Europe by Lorenzo de Medici" [2] ushered in Modern Times, when the use of good Latin and the knowledge of Greek were revived; in between lay a trough—the "Middle Ages." We still retain this periodization in our school curricula and in the periodical press, while conveniently losing sight of its basis, which is too embarrassing for the state of education in our age. In the first half of the eighteenth century there was no general agreement as to the duration of the Middle Ages. The French Academy in the first edition of its *Dictionary* in 1694, and several of the subsequent French dictionaries, define the Middle Ages as lasting "from the decline of the Roman Empire to about the tenth century," whereas Chambers' *Cyclopaedia* of 1753 states that they lasted "from Constantine to 1453." It is possible that we owe to Gibbon's influence the period "from 476 to 1453," though it is doubtful that Gibbon himself would have subscribed to such a division of history; for Gibbon the beginning of the Middle Ages was in the third century, while their core was "from the 7th to the 11th century"; [3] this makes Gibbon, in some sense, a precursor of Pirenne. Whatever the duration of the Middle Ages, it was a bad period, a "Gothic night," as Rabelais described it.

Gibbon's innermost reasons for choosing the Middle Ages for his province we may never know, and it is unlikely that he himself was conscious of them; yet he was acutely aware of the moment of conception of his grand

[2] D. M. Low (ed.), *Gibbon's Journal to January 28, 1763* (New York, 1929), p. 104.

[3] See Gibbon's preface (1782) to the first volume of *The History of the Decline and Fall of the Roman Empire*, ed. J. B. Bury (7 vols.; London, 1896–1900), I, viii. Unless otherwise noted, all citations to the *Decline and Fall* are to this edition, with chapter number given first, followed by volume and page numbers.

design. He recorded it in writing no less than four times: "It was at Rome, on the fifteenth of October, 1764, as I sat musing amidst the ruins of the Capitol, while the bare-footed fryars were singing Vespers in the temple of Jupiter, that the idea of writing the decline and fall of the City first started to my mind." [4]

This famous passage evokes a mood of brooding over the passing of the glories of ancient Rome; it also contains an innuendo: the "barefooted fryars" seem to be in some way connected with this sad event. Yet one may well ask why Gibbon did not choose to dazzle us with the glories of ancient Rome rather than dwell upon the decay of the City. Is this morbid taste? Or does he tell us a cautionary tale? Neither of these explanations is satisfactory, and we must look for Gibbon's inspiration elsewhere. I shall attempt to show that, while each of the ingredients of Gibbon's thought clearly belongs to the eighteenth century, his idiosyncrasy is not typical of his age. Gibbon's lasting contribution to history, and his peculiar fascination, may be largely attributed to this altogether original constitution of his mind. But, before embarking on a discussion of Gibbon's originality, it is necessary to give a rough sketch of some typical acts of faith and idiosyncrasies of his contemporaries; then Gibbon's place among them will stand out more clearly.

In contrast with the effervescence of the sixteenth century and the rugged genius of the seventeenth, the eighteenth century appears to be an age of the systematizer, the

---

[4] John Murray (ed.), *The Autobiographies of Edward Gibbon* (London, 1897), p. 302 (Memoir E). For the other versions see *ibid.*, pp. 270 (Memoir C), 405 (Memoir D); see also the concluding sentence of the *Decline and Fall.* We gather from Memoirs C and D that Gibbon was inside the church of the Zoccolanti (Santa Maria in Aracoeli) when he experienced his moment of truth "in the gloom of the evening."

standardizer, and the popularizer. Perhaps the most un-
complimentary thing that can be said about the eighteenth
century is that a majority of its thinkers seem to rest without undue discomfort on the Procrustean bed on which I
am about to present them. All, or nearly all, the major
thinkers of that age believed that "Nature" and the "Law
of Nature" are the measure of the supreme good. Beyond
this, however, their unanimity ceases, and a vast majority
of them fall into one of two categories, depending on their
definition of Nature: those who believe in "Nature-as-it-
ought-to-be," that is, Nature as a system of norms ultimately established by the Deity; and those who believe in
"Nature-as-it-is" in an uncorrupted state, and which can
sometimes be observed in operation. The former I call
"classicists"; the latter, for want of a better term, "proto-
romantics." The classicists predominated in the first half
of the eighteenth century; the proto-romantics became an
important force in the second half.[5] Among the classicists
we can count the Cartesians, Locke, the Newtonians
(though hardly Newton himself), Voltaire, d'Alembert
and most of the French Encyclopedists (with the possible
exception of Diderot), Jovellanos, and Beccaria. We would
include among the proto-romantics the followers of
Fénelon, Defoe, the Free Masons, the Physiocrats, Condorcet, Rousseau, Adam Smith, and Herder.

The chief assumption of the classicists is that the Law of
Nature prescribes universal norms equally applicable in all
places and at all times. Human nature remains always and
everywhere the same. The task of every government is to

---

[5] I venture to uphold this oversimplification as a crude rule of
thumb, in spite of the works of Paul Hazard and Daniel Mornet. These
two scholars have conclusively shown the sturdy growth of proto-
romantic thought in the early eighteenth century and even earlier; but
their reader is likely to forget that they are dealing, for the most part,
not with the usual and dominant modes of thought, but with important exceptions to them.

divine the norms of the Law of Nature, if need be with the aid of the philosophers, to translate them into positive laws, and then to ram these laws down the throats of the subjects without regard for historical precedent or for the special rights and liberties of the privileged orders of society. A government guided by wisdom and inspired by virtue may thus drill some decency into mankind, which is, on the whole, a sorry crew. Physical nature is hideous unless it reflects geometric proportion, that is, if it is left to its own devices. The Alps, for example, can boast of no beauty to delight the senses of a cultivated gentleman; they are but a frightful barrier lying athwart his route to the promised land of Italy, to be crossed as quickly and as painlessly as possible. The canons of art likewise rest on the principles of simple Euclidean geometry and of symmetry. Hence, all medieval art, whether Romanesque or Gothic, is primitive, or barbarous, or both.

History, according to a classicist, should concern itself mainly with Periclean Athens, Augustan Rome, Renaissance Italy, and the Age of Louis XIV, which brings forth the glorious Age of Reason of the present. Its chief function is to uncover the universal mainsprings of human action in civilized society and to determine the social laws that govern human society, disregarding the individual peculiarities, the accidental, and the bizarre. All other history is the story of deplorable deviations from the norms of Nature-as-it-ought-to-be and is best mercifully forgotten. It can furnish the lawyer the materials with which to build his petty claims, claims based on barbarous customs bequeathed by the past, which it is the duty of civilized society to change. At best, it provides a field of innocuous and useless diversion for the antiquarian "erudite," a person to be pitied for his dim lights and misdirected energies.

The classicist believes in the devil in history: enthusiasm, which can be exorcised only by the light of "sweet reasonableness." Obviously, "enthusiasm" does not mean all purposeful and strenuous endeavor, but only a passionate espousal of a cause without rational and rigorous examination of its merits. Because of its very nature, such an examination can be undertaken only by an unagitated mind, and the serenity of the examiner can almost be taken as a pledge of the truth of his conclusions. Every strong emotion that puts out the light of reason threatens to deliver its victim into the hands of "the prince of darkness." [6] An "enthusiast" is thus a man possessed, one to be shunned by all right-thinking people. There was some historical justification for this view of the eighteenth-century thinkers, especially in England, France, Germany, and the Netherlands; looking back at the tremendous upheavals of the past two centuries, with their attendant cruelties and bloodshed that had made the life of man "nasty, brutish, and short," they could plausibly ascribe these calamities to unbridled passion, and especially to religious passion. To put the reins of reason on human passion had been a matter of urgent and practical concern for every classicist from Grotius and Descartes down.

Quite different were the presuppositions of the protoromantics. They believed in the regenerative forces of simple "Nature" as it had existed in a pristine form, or as it

---

[6] See John Locke, *An Essay Concerning Human Understanding* Book IV, ch. 19: "Of Enthusiasm." See also David Hume, *Essays Moral, Political, and Literary,* Essay 10: "Of Superstition and Enthusiasm" (which Hume dubs "the corruptions of true religion"). Cf. Henry Fielding (whom Gibbon liked very much), *Joseph Andrews,* Book I, ch. 17: the good parson Adams says, "But when he began to call nonsense and enthusiasm to his aid . . . I was his friend no longer." For many more examples of the use of the term "enthusiasm" in a pejorative sense by eighteenth-century English writers (John Wesley among them), see J. A. H. Murray, *A New English Dictionary on Historical Principles* (commonly known as the *Oxford English Dictionary*), Vol. III, Pt. II (Oxford, 1897), pp. 215–216.

could still be observed in places where it had not been corrupted by luxury and the complexities of human society. The chief task of government was to "console the sufferers," but also to clear the way for an untrammeled operation of the forces of nature, thus providing the necessary conditions for the betterment of mankind; in its extreme form this last doctrine was found, toward the end of the eighteenth century, in Condorcet and Adam Smith. The proto-romantic mood contributed to a revival of the cult of the "noble savage," whether of the American Forest or of ancient Germany.[7] It was not long before the proto-romantics discovered that one need not travel quite so far in space or in time to find the noble savage: he was available closer to home in the guise of an honest peasant, or of a provincial nobleman preserving his rustic and military virtues on his estate and refusing to be corrupted by the blandishments of court life. It is worth noting that, at least in its earlier stages (for instance, in Fénelon and Montesquieu), this revived cult was nearly always connected with a professed or implied preference for aristocratic values and for "natural" government, that is, government by natural leaders of society, the independent and uncorrupted nobility. If we scrub a noble savage, he usually turns out to be an aristocrat. By the time of Rousseau and Herder, however, the noble savage was divested of his aristocratic quality, and his cult led to a glorification of folkways in the present and in the past, and to the science of ethnography.[8]

For a proto-romantic, feeling and even emotion were legitimate and respectable manifestations of the human

[7] Like most significant intellectual currents, the cult of the noble savage has a long pedigree going back to ancient Greece; in modern times it received a considerable impulse from the Jesuit missionaries of the seventeenth century.

[8] An inquiry into this social degradation of the noble savage would be highly enlightening; I am not aware of any such study.

spirit, and so were individual differences and peculiarities. He discovered the beauty of physical nature both in its rugged and in its placid aspects, divorced from mathematical formulae and untouched by human hand.[9] Human art had to follow, to bring out the essential, unique, and unrepeatable features of this nature. A proto-romantic could appreciate both the realism and the majesty of a Gothic edifice. Romanesque, or Byzantine, art, charged with symbolic intellectual content, was, however, alien to him, and he considered it primitive in a bad sense, that is, showing a lack of skill. Above all, he was sensitive to the mood of the place and of the moment, and it is these moods or brooding ruminations that are responsible for his inspiration and his keenest insights.

There are several major thinkers of the Enlightenment who do not fit into either of the categories described, or who seem to fall into both. The most notable of these are Newton, Montesquieu, Goethe, Kant, and Gibbon. Newton was really a seventeenth-century giant, disfigured by his followers during the Enlightenment when he was shorn of his Christian mysticism. About Goethe, suffice it to say that he was a conscious eclectic and a far greater poet than theoretical thinker. Kant's peculiarity lies in his epistemology with its synthesis of rationalism and empiricism, which puts him beyond the divisions between the two groups we have discussed. But Montesquieu and Gibbon were two kindred, yet different, spirits. Both of them dealt with the problem of the decadence of Rome: Montesquieu

---

[9] Gibbon remarked that the fashion of "climbing the mountains and viewing the glaciers" in search of "the sublime beauties of nature" was common in the 1780's but had been notably absent in the 1760's; see *The Autobiography of Edward Gibbon,* ed. Dero A. Saunders (New York, 1961), p. 103. The text of this edition is far more complete than that of the "official" autobiography of Gibbon edited by Lord Sheffield, yet it is more manageable for the reader than the critical edition of the various drafts edited by John Murray in 1897. In subsequent footnotes, the Saunders edition is referred to as *Autobiography.*

in his *Considérations sur les causes de la grandeur des Romains et de leur décadence* (1734; revised edition in 1748), and Gibbon in the *History of the Decline and Fall of the Roman Empire* (1776–1788).

Montesquieu, in spite of, or, I prefer to say, because of his incisive penetration into the structure of human society, often confused the concepts of Nature-as-it-ought-to-be and Nature-as-it-is. Hence arose that peculiar duality of his system, stressing, on the one hand, the universal aspect of human nature and of the laws of society, and, on the other hand, the uniqueness of each particular society. Montesquieu's Nature-as-it-ought-to-be operated differently in different parts of the earth and in different groups; it was thus individualized for each society and for each body politic and was made dependent, in some respects, on Nature-as-it-is. An inquiry into the local traditions or institutions of feudal France or of the tribes in the forests of Germany thus became a worthy endeavor for an enlightened gentleman. Yet Montesquieu was not a historian, but a social scientist. History, for him, was mainly a reservoir of material for the discovery of the "laws of history." For an *érudit,* concerned primarily with gathering accurate factual information, he had contempt. Occasionally he would indulge in flights of imagination unsupported by factual data, and for this Gibbon, who had a profound admiration for Montesquieu, would take him to task in his footnotes: Gibbon's ideal was a "philosophical historian," with equal weight assigned to either part of this dual title. But before embarking on a discussion of Gibbon, the "philosophical historian," we should say a few words about Gibbon, the man, for some of the circumstances of his life and traits of character deviate from the norms of the eighteenth century.

Edward Gibbon was born in 1737 of a substantial old English family in the border group between the landed gentry and the upper middle class. Gibbon himself was even more proud of his status as a gentleman than of his claim to literary distinction. Financially, the Gibbons had had their ups and downs: the historian's grandfather had been one of the directors of the South Sea Company; in the mid-eighteenth century, their family affairs were in a rather precarious condition, largely owing to irresponsible management by Gibbon's father. As a child, Gibbon suffered from frail health, with the result that his formal education was desultory. From childhood, however, he was a voracious and indiscriminate reader, "and the only principle that darted a ray of light into the indigested chaos was an early and rational application to the order of time and place." [10] The study of maps and chronology was an early avocation with Gibbon; later it developed in him a respect for precise factual erudition. It was also at this tender age that he acquired a taste for Homer, or rather for Pope's verses apropos of Homer.

Shortly before his fifteenth birthday Gibbon was sent to Oxford as a gentleman-commoner, there to spend "the fourteen months the most idle and unprofitable of my whole life." "The monks of Oxford," steeped "in port and prejudice" and contriving "to unite the opposite extremes of bigotry and prejudice," left little impress on Gibbon's mind.[11] Leaving the question of the justice of these strictures aside, let us note that at Oxford Gibbon had every facility to pursue his indiscriminate reading. It was not any direct personal influence or contact, but the reading of Bossuet that inspired his decision to reconcile himself to the Church of Rome in 1753. According to the rigor of the law, the offense amounted to high treason. Although in eighteenth-century England the religious culprit would not have lost his life or limb, he was liable to forfeit his

[10] *Autobiography*, p. 67.
[11] *Ibid.*, p. 72, 82, 110.

civil and property rights. In the age of the Duke of New-
castle, such "honest sacrifice of interest to conscience" [12]
was not a common occurrence in England; the generation
of the Younger Pitt had not yet arrived on the scene to
make it fashionable.

The doors of Oxford being closed to Gibbon, his father
promptly dispatched him to Lausanne, where he was
placed in the family of the Calvinist minister Pavillard. It
was at Lausanne, in the course of the next five years, that
Gibbon's mind was cast in the mold familiar to the readers
of the *Decline and Fall of the Roman Empire*. Under the
guidance of Pavillard, Gibbon embarked on a systematic
study of the Latin authors, learned Greek, and read modern French literature. For a while he followed a course in
mathematics, but, having grasped its principles, he abandoned it: ". . . nor can I lament that I desisted before my
mind was hardened by the habit of rigid demonstration, so
destructive of the finer feelings of moral evidence." [13]
Pascal's *Provincial Letters* enthralled him. Gibbon would
reread them almost every year, and, by his own admission,
he learned from Pascal "to manage the weapon of grave
and temperate irony." [14] The other authors who marked
him profoundly were Cicero, Virgil, Tacitus, and Montesquieu. Later on, before he turned to writing in English
(for his first compositions had been in French), Gibbon
also studied the style of Swift and Addison and of the other
English writers since the Glorious Revolution who
breathed "the spirit of reason and liberty." [15]

At Lausanne Gibbon was also introduced to the works
of the French *érudits* of the past hundred years, so much
despised by the *philosophes* of the Enlightenment. Most of

[12] *Ibid.*, p. 86
[13] *Ibid.*, p. 102.
[14] *Ibid.*, p. 103.
[15] *Ibid.*, p 122.

these men had been ecclesiastics, working either independently or under the auspices of institutions like the Abbey of St.-Germain-des-Près, or, later, the Académie des Inscriptions. Picking up the legacy left by Erasmus and the scholars of the late Renaissance, they had perfected the canons and the tools of critical evaluation of sources and were thus the progenitors of the modern "scientific" historical method. Far from despising them, Gibbon was provoked into his first independent literary effort, the *Essai sur l'étude de la littérature*,[16] by a desire to defend them from the attacks of d'Alembert and the other Encyclopedists. Later, Gibbon was to study the works of Tillemont, La Bletterie, Mabillon, Spanheim, and many other "antiquaries" with ever increasing assiduity and admiration. His early propensity for "rational application to the order of time and place" kept reasserting itself.

In 1758 Gibbon returned to England and shortly thereafter entered the Hampshire militia. The Seven Years War was entering its decisive phase; there was some fear of a French invasion, and the militia was called out. For two and a half years (1760–1762) Gibbon was engaged in "bloodless and inglorious campaigns," moving about with his battalion along the south coast of England. The service made him "an Englishman and a soldier." We may well question the latter quality in a man who asserted that he had never handled a gun; yet Gibbon claimed to have received from his service "a clearer notion of the phalanx and the legions, and the captain of the Hampshire grenadiers . . . has not been useless to the historian of the Roman empire." [17] However that may be, the assurance of an armchair tactician is all too evident in Gibbon's de-

[16] Written in 1758–59 at Lausanne and in England; first published in 1761.
[17] *Autobiography*, pp. 132–134.

scription of battles, movements of troops, and military organization.

No sooner was Gibbon relieved from the militia than he embarked on a grand tour of the Continent. He stayed several months in Paris, then in Lausanne, and from there he proceeded on his fateful pilgrimage to Italy. Nearly four years were to pass, however, from the memorable day in October 1764 before Gibbon finally turned to his great work. The first volume of the *Decline and Fall* appeared in 1776 and was an immediate success with the public, most of whom had had no prior inkling of Gibbon's literary or historical talent; so secretive was he of his work. The second and third volumes appeared in 1781. After some hesitation and the interval of a year, Gibbon began to prepare the last three volumes, covering the period from the abdication of Romulus Augustulus in the West to the fall of Constantinople in the East. The whole work was completed on June 27, 1787, and published in the following year.

In 1774, while he was still engaged in writing the first volume of his *History*, Gibbon was elected M.P. for Linskeard in Cornwall through the influence of his kinsman, Lord Eliot. He sat in the Commons until 1783 as a "mute" member, consistently voting for the government and for his friend, Lord North, whom he sincerely admired, and to whom, in effect, he later dedicated his magnum opus.[18] Summing up his parliamentary experience, Gibbon wrote that "the eight sessions that I sat in Parliament were a school of civil prudence, the first and most essential virtue of an historian." [19] Apart from his silent vote, Gibbon's participation in politics included the preparation of a state paper in 1779 in rebuttal to the French manifesto on that

[18] See Gibbon's preface to Vol. IV of the *Decline and Fall* (1788).
[19] *Autobiography*, p. 174.

kingdom's intervention in the War of American Independence. In the same year he was made a Lord Commissioner of Trade and Plantations, a sinecure that in no way interfered with his work and which added between 700 and 800 pounds to his yearly income. But the Board of Trade was abolished in the general collapse of 1782–83. Partly for reasons of economy, partly from sentimental attachment, Gibbon decided to settle at Lausanne, sharing a house with an old friend, Georges Deyverdun. It was there that the second half of the *Decline and Fall* was written. In 1793 he went to England to console Lord Sheffield, his friend and future literary executor, whose wife had recently died. During this visit to England, the hydrocele that had afflicted Gibbon for several years became worse, and he died on January 16, 1794.

From his late twenties on, Gibbon's slight frame had to support a very corpulent body. Almost in the middle of a disproportionately large face was a small rotund mouth. At social gatherings Gibbon's typical posture was to sit in a chair, his bulky figure inclined slightly forward, his forefinger stretched out, as he would tap his snuffbox and purse his lips preparatory to delivering in mellifluous tones a Ciceronian period that had taken shape in his head. In the course of his life Gibbon met many notable figures. In the late 1760's he entered a Masonic lodge in London, and in 1774 he became a member of Dr. Johnson's club. He knew almost all the literary and political celebrities of Britain: Johnson, Burke, Garrick, Goldsmith, Sheridan, Adam Smith, Hume, Chesterfield, Horace Walpole, to mention only a few; with Sir Joshua Reynolds his relations seem to have been closer than with most of the others. He was simultaneously a good friend of Lord North and of Charles James Fox. In Lausanne and later at Ferney he had dealings with Voltaire. During his several visits to Paris, he got to know d'Alembert, Diderot, d'Holbach, Helvétius (who took a special interest in him), the Abbé de la Bletterie, Bougainville, Mirabeau, Madame Geoffrin, Madame du Bocage, and many others; but it was Buffon who attracted Gibbon most, probably because in him Gibbon sensed a philosophical naturalist, something akin to a "philosophical historian." However, Gibbon's really intimate friends in Paris were the Neckers. Gibbon was more or less in love with Madame Necker—a romance that had started when she was still the penniless Mademoiselle Suzanne Curchod at Crassy, near Lausanne. Yet, for all his wide circle of acquaintances, Gibbon was not gregarious: "I might say with truth that I was never less alone than when by myself." [20] He never showed his writings to anyone, and they went directly from him to the printer. Gibbon was self-sufficient and self-satisfied; as a lover he was shabby. All his life he preferred to be a distant observer rather than a close witness, much less a participant, in the drama of history. As he contemplated the possibility of the French Revolution spilling over into Lausanne, he declared that "the first stroke of a rebel drum would be the signal of my immediate departure." [21]

From early youth Gibbon had "aspired to the character of an historian." [22] He toyed with many projects: the campaigns of Charles VIII of France in Italy, the Third Crusade, the baronial wars in thirteenth-century England, the life of the Black Prince, of Montrose, of Sir Walter Raleigh. Many of these themes were taken from the later Middle Ages, which would have been strange if Gibbon had been a simple dyed-in-the-wool classicist. It is also worth noting that in nearly every instance Gibbon seemed to fix his attention on colorful individuals, though it is

[20] *Ibid.*, p. 119.
[21] *Ibid.*, p. 204.
[22] *Ibid.*, pp. 137–141.

difficult to tell whether he thought of them as unique personalities or as classic Cartesian types. After discarding all these projects, Gibbon began to work on a *History of the Liberty of the Swiss*, but, having drafted the first book, he abandoned the story whose materials were "fast locked in the obscurity of an old, barbarous German dialect." A history of the Florentine Republic under the Medicis attracted him next; he wished to examine the interaction between political institutions and culture, as well as the role of Savonarola's enthusiasm in opposition to both. In short, in these early gropings of Gibbon we see the emergence of the philosophical historian who was not unprepared for the experience of October 15, 1764.

We can judge of Gibbon's taste by his disparaging remarks about Gothic art, as well as about the Arch of Constantine. In France, while darting a "contemptuous look . . . on the stately monuments of superstition," he proclaimed the church of St. Sulpice to be "one of the noblest structures in Paris." [23] Anyone familiar with this vacuous edifice knows that it is nothing but an exercise in elementary symmetry and geometric proportion. We would thus appear justified in putting Gibbon among the classicists. And yet, it was in these words that Gibbon described his passage of the Mt. Cenis Pass in 1764: "The most lovely sunshine in the world gilded this romantic scene, and gave it a sombre colouring which disposes the soul to an agreeable melancholy." [24] No out-and-out classicist would have written such words; nor would he have been carried away by the mood of the moment and the surroundings as he was amid the ruins of the Capitol on October 15. To realize Gibbon's

[23] *Ibid.*, p. 143; see also Murray, *The Autobiographies of Edward Gibbon*, p. 263. For comments on the Arch of Constantine, see *Decline and Fall*, ch. 14:I, 423–424.

[24] Diary entry for April 24, 1764, quoted in D. M. Low, *Edward Gibbon, 1737–1794* (New York, 1937), p. 170.

extraordinary sensitivity to surroundings, it is enough to read that page in his memoirs where he recounts without a trace of repentance his "several days of intoxication," amounting to "enthusiasm" (!), when he first saw Rome.[25] As he was beginning to come out of his intellectual inebriation, Gibbon wrote to his father, "I am really almost in a dream. Whatever ideas books may have given us of the greatness of that people, their accounts of the most flourishing state of Rome fall infinitely short of the picture of its ruins. I am convinced that there never, never existed such a nation, and I hope, for the happiness of mankind, there never will again." [26] Clearly, Gibbon stood beyond the division between classicism and romanticism, a tense man in whom these opposite tendencies lived together.

We tread on even trickier ground in dealing with Gibbon's religious views, where the issues have been obscured by controversy. Gibbon's view of Christianity is treated in Professor Ladner's chapter; for my part, let me merely point out that those of Gibbon's contemporaries and later critics who imputed atheism to him were wide of the mark. By his own admission, in his early youth he had been "fond of religious disputation"; during his first sojourn at Lausanne, however, he suspended his "religious inquiries, acquiescing with implicit belief in the tenets and mysteries which are adopted by the general consent of Catholics and Protestants"; from this position he later evolved into a religious pyrrhonist, like his avowed models, "Chillingworth and Bayle, who . . . emerged from superstition to skepti-

---

[25] *Autobiography*, p. 152. Cf. Gibbon's comment on Emanuel Chrysoloras, the Greek "father of the Italian schools," beholding Rome in the beginning of the fifteenth century: ". . . to the eye of liberal enthusiasm, the majesty of ruin restored the image of her ancient prosperity" (*Decline and Fall*, ch. 67: VII, 132).

[26] Letter of Oct. 9, 1764, in J. E. Norton (ed.), *The Letters of Edward Gibbon* (3 vols.; New York, 1956), I, 185.

cism." [27] It would be more precise to say that Gibbon became a deist agnostic, not unlike Voltaire, whom he did not hold in high esteem. Though he was no enemy of the Divine Logos and no ignoramus in theology, as any reader of his *History* will readily see, Gibbon looked with profound suspicion on any system of positive theology.[28] At best, it was a useless exercise of human ingenuity; at worst, it fomented senseless and pernicious divisions in the body politic and fanned the flames of bigotry and enthusiasm.

Gibbon's barbs directed at the Church as a human institution in history are well known. What he disliked in Christians and Jews was bigotry, zeal, and enthusiasm, this "fever of the mind"; he singled out the monks and the martyrs as being especially susceptible to these vices. It would be fair to say that Gibbon's preconceptions made him blind to some significant areas of religious life; nowhere is this more evident than in his sweeping condemnation of monasticism. But at least Gibbon was consistent in his dislikes, for he was equally caustic in his remarks about the opposite faction: ". . . nor could I approve the intolerant zeal of the philosophers and Encyclopaedists, the friends of Holbach and Helvétius; they laughed at the skepticism of Hume, preached the tenets of atheism with the bigotry of dogmatists, and damned all believers with ridicule and contempt." [29] And yet, on occasion, Gibbon would draw a sympathetic portrait of people who stood

[27] *Autobiography*, pp. 82, 86, 97.

[28] Gibbon believed that "the knowledge that is suited to our situation and powers" is "the whole compass of moral, natural, and mathematical science" (*Decline and Fall*, last paragraph of ch. 13:I, 392). Metaphysics and theology were thus beyond man's ken.

[29] *Autobiography*, p. 145; see also *Decline and Fall*, ch. 67:VII, 139, n. 15: "In his way, Voltaire was a bigot, an intolerant bigot." Cf. *Essai sur l'étude de la littérature* (London and Paris, 1762), p. 102: "... l'Ignorance a deux filles: l'Incrédulité et la Foi aveugle."

for everything he chose to abhor: William Law, the rigorist, nonjuring, Anglican divine; Miss Hester Gibbon, the historian's saintly aunt and disciple of William Law; or St. Athanasius, whom he admired for his pluck. He had nothing but praise for the learned Benedictine monks of the Congregation of St. Maur, or for the Jansenist Tillemont "whose inimitable accuracy almost assumes the character of genius." [30]

Of Gibbon's political affiliation we know that he sided with the Tories in the House of Commons. But as a historian he attacked clerical establishments; nor did he embrace the interests either of the small landed gentry or of the royal prerogative. His heart was definitely with the hereditary aristocracy, and he was thus much closer to the Whig tradition and to Montesquieu than to the orthodox Tories. Gibbon's famous encomium of the five good emperors, from Nerva to the Antonines, might lead one to believe that he espoused the cause of enlightened despotism. [31] This appearance, however, is deceptive, for the greatest glory of these emperors was that they "delighted in the image of liberty." Throughout his *History* Gibbon consistently sides with the senatorial party, however weak or discredited. Perhaps the greatest crime of Constantine, Gibbon's bête noire, was his failure "to form a body of nobles, whose influence may restrain, while it secures the authority of the monarch." [32] Many more examples can

[30] *Autobiography*, pp. 42–45, 165; *Decline and Fall*, ch. 21:II, 330 ff.

[31] "If a man were called to fix the period in the history of the world during which the condition of the human race was most happy and prosperous, he would, without hesitation, name that which elapsed from the death of Domitian to the accession of Commodus. The vast extent of the Roman empire was governed by absolute power, under the guidance of virtue and wisdom" (*Decline and Fall*, ch. 3:I, 78).

[32] *Ibid.*, ch. 17:II, 165.

be found of Gibbon's advocacy of hereditary temperate monarchy, "independent of the passions of mankind," and circumscribed by intermediate powers.[33]

Aristocratic values are menaced not only by despotic royal power, but also by "the mean and promiscuous multitude" whose resolutions "generally depend on a moment." "Popular innovation" is apt to injure the constitution, for, under a "democratical government," the powers of sovereignty "will be first abused, and afterwards lost, if they are committed to an unwieldy multitude." [34] One of the contributing factors in the decline of Rome was that "the noble art [of jurisprudence], which had once been the sacred inheritance of the patricians, was fallen into the hands of freedmen and plebeians, who, with cunning, rather than with skill, exercised a sordid and pernicious trade." [35] Small wonder, then, that Gibbon recoiled with disgust from the French Revolution, which he dubbed "the French disease," and that he subscribed to the reflections of his former political opponent, Edmund Burke.[36]

As a cultivated gentleman, Gibbon could not fail to cherish "civilization," by which he understood the cutural physiognomy of the upper classes in the Greco-Roman world of the classical period and in modern Europe. The first step in the acquisition of civilization is the use of letters, which is "the principal circumstance that distinguishes a civilized people from a herd of savages, incapable of knowledge and reflection." The barbarians can be likened to a modern illiterate peasant, who "surpasses but very little his fellow-labourer the ox in the exercise of his mental

[33] See, for example, in *Decline and Fall*, the opening paragraphs of ch. 7:I, 167 ff., or the discussion of Septimius Severus at the end of ch. 5:I, 120 ff., or of Mamaea's government in ch. 6:I, 149 ff.

[34] *Ibid.*, ch. 2:I, 33–34, 40; ch. 6:I, 156 and *passim*; see also *Autobiography*, pp. 90, 178, 184, 202.

[35] *Decline and Fall*. ch. 17:II, 174.

[36] *Autobiography*, pp. 202–204.

faculties." The barbarians are fierce and live in "a state of ignorance and poverty which it has pleased some declaimers to dignify with the appellation of virtuous simplicity." [37] We have nothing to learn from these people, and Gibbon can well afford to toss off his contemptuous remark about the pre-Islamic Arabs: "I am ignorant, and I am careless, of the blind mythology of the barbarians." [38]

But civilization, too, brings unavoidable dangers in its train; the first of these is corruption. Gibbon describes both the Greeks and the Persians of the third century A.D. in identical terms: ". . . long since civilized and corrupted." At the same time, the elegance of Italy and of the internal provinces of the empire had become "feeble" and incapable of nurturing the profession of arms. [39] Gibbon often sighs for the primitive martial virtues of the early Romans, who, during the first four centuries of their history, "in the laborious school of poverty had acquired the virtues of war and government." [40] Strangely enough, it was during the happy age of the Antonines that long peace and uniform government had "introduced a slow and secret poison into the vitals of the empire. The minds of men were gradually reduced to the same level, the fire of genius was extinguished, and even the military spirit evaporated." [41] Less than thirty years after the death of Marcus Aurelius, Gibbon compares "the untutored Caledonians, glowing with the warm virtues of nature, and the degenerate Romans, polluted with the mean vices of wealth and slavery." [42] The poverty of the German barbarians "se-

[37] *Decline and Fall*, ch. 9:I, 218.
[38] *Ibid.*, ch. 50:V, 327.
[39] *Ibid.*, ch. 2:I, 38; ch. 8:I, 195; ch. 12:I, 332.
[40] *Ibid.*, ch. 7:I, 194.
[41] *Ibid.*, ch. 2:I, 56.
[42] *Ibid.*, ch. 6:I, 130. The fact that this passage is predicated on the authenticity of *Ossian* is irrelevant for this argument; what matters for our purposes is that the savages are endowed with "warm virtues of

cured their freedom, since our desires and our possessions
are the strongest fetters of despotism." [43] In the end, "the
Roman world was indeed peopled by a race of pigmies,[44]
when the fierce giants of the north broke in and mended
the puny breed. They restored a manly spirit of freedom
and, after the revolution of ten centuries, freedom became
the happy parent of taste and science." [45] In all these
praises of the barbarian, Gibbon comes dangerously close
to being the "declaimer" whom he treated with such irony
in the passage quoted earlier. He is in flat contradiction
with his own classicist self, but he is in agreement with
Montesquieu, who also thought wistfully about the prime-
val forests of Germany. Both Gibbon and Montesquieu had
a profound respect, bordering on tender veneration, for
Tacitus. This attraction for the Roman historian was not
accidental. Tacitus was a polished gentleman who prided
himself on being an "arbiter elegantiae," and who, in the
course of exquisite banquets in the midst of refined company, would dream about the manly virtues of the barbarians of the forest, and about austere, simple, and rustic life,
which contained the fountainhead of wisdom and virtue.

In his youthful essay on the study of literature, Gibbon
had formulated the concept of a "philosophical historian";
the *Decline and Fall of the Roman Empire* was, in a sense,
a realization and a development of this idea. Of Gibbon's
models only Tacitus lived up to the mark.[46] Livy was a
historian, hardly a philosopher, while Montesquieu was a

nature." Cf. *Autobiography*, pp. 161–162, where Gibbon remarks,
apropos of the Sixth Book of the *Aeneid*, that Aeneas and the Sybil
traveled "from the dreams of simple nature to the dreams, alas! of
Egyptian theology and the philosophy of the Greeks."

[43] *Decline and Fall*, ch. 9:I, 223.

[44] In a moral, not in an ethnic sense.

[45] *Decline and Fall*, ch. 2:I, 58.

[46] See *ibid.*, ch. 9:I, 213. Tacitus is described as "the first of historians
who applied the science of philosophy to the study of facts"; cf. *ibid.*,
ch. 12:I, 319 ff.

philosopher rather than a historian. The chief characteristic of a "philosophical historian" is that he can penetrate intuitively to the "general causes" and can relate them to particular situations. These "general causes," of which Gibbon does not give any precise definition, operate mainly through the mores, religion, and "all that is subject to the sway of opinion"; slowly, but surely, they "change the face of the earth." [47] A study of thought, literature, manners—in short, "cultural history"—thus gives us one of the main clues to understanding the meaning of human events. The basic general cause, human nature, remains constant—"the human heart is still the same" [48]—and Gibbon seems to agree with Hume that the feelings and motives of the ancient Greeks and Romans can be studied in modern Englishmen and Frenchmen. Climate constitutes a special type of general cause, for it leaves a seemingly indelible imprint on character. The *Decline and Fall* is full of references to this formative role of climate.[49] Nevertheless, in the notes for a revision of the second edition of his *History*, Gibbon wrote, "The distinction of North and South is real and intelligible. . . . But the difference between East and West is arbitrary and shifts round the globe. As the men of the North, not of the West,

---

[47] See *Essai sur l'étude de la littérature*, pp. 131–133, 138–140.

[48] *Decline and Fall*, ch. 15:II, 43 n. 115.

[49] See, for instance, *ibid.*, ch. 6:I, 156: The virtues and vices of Elagabalus and Alexander Severus "contracted a tincture of weakness . . . from the soft climate of Syria," where these two princes, who had no resemblance to each other, had passed their boyhood. Cf. ch. 15:II, 14: ". . . the warmth of the climate [of Syria and Egypt] disposes both the mind and the body to indolent and contemplative devotion." Cf. ch. 42:IV, 341: ". . . the climate of Asia has indeed been found less congenial than that of Europe to military spirit." A history of the obsession with climate as the chief formative influence in human affairs, from the Greeks to the present day, would make a fascinating study, and would bring out strikingly contradictory views that have been held on the subject.

the legions of Gaul and Germany were superior to the *South*-Eastern natives of Asia and Egypt. It is the triumph of cold over heat; which may, however, and has been surmounted by moral causes." [50]

The last admission is of paramount importance for an understanding of Gibbon. His pure "philosopher" would have hardly tolerated such tinkering with his "general causes." Not only can one general cause counteract another, but, operating below them, is a vast array of particular causes, often working at cross-purposes, modifying one another and the general causes, and producing the intricate and rich chaos of human life. This hierarchy of particular causes is what a good "erudite" historian usually investigates with the aid of a minute and accurate inquiry into the facts. Without such labor the structure of the philosopher would be chimerical, or, at best, vitiated by flights of uncontrolled imagination and by rash conclusions, of which even Montesquieu is occasionally guilty. Therefore, Gibbon takes up arms in defense of the *érudits*—the Académie des Inscriptions, Tillemont, Spanheim, La Bletterie, and many others—against the eighteenth-century *philosophes*. Among the latter it was d'Alembert who provoked him especially when he extolled imagination above memory and advocated that at the end of every century all facts should be sifted, and those found unworthy of preservation expunged from the record. Gibbon argued that even the most "sickly" (*chétif*) fact, in the hands of a Montesquieu, may become a clue to uncovering one of the mainsprings of human action,[51] thus leading us back to the "general causes" of a philosophical historian.

The self-contradictions in Gibbon's system of history are easy to find. In fact, it is hardly a system at all, but an attempt to comprehend the infinite complexity of human

[50] *Decline and Fall,* Introduction: I, xxxvi.
[51] *Essai sur l'étude de la littérature,* pp. 134–135.

life without renouncing some of the shibboleths of the eighteenth-century classicists. This is what lends elasticity to his overall view; there is room enough not only for the "trends and forces," but also for the life of institutions and of classes, for the individual, and for chance. The role of the camel in Arab economy, the senate or the lawyers in the body politic, the character of a prince, or the loss of a horseshoe nail all claim his attention; however "in human life the most important scenes will depend on the character of a single actor." [52] In short, Gibbon is more flexible than either Montesquieu or Toynbee. For instance, Montesquieu's principle of decay is embedded in the very cause of Rome's growth to greatness. Gibbon, while agreeing with Montesquieu, escapes his determinism through the stress he lays on multiple causes. We can disprove some of the facts in Gibbon's *History* and reject some of his assumptions, but the rest of his intricate and magnificent structure will withstand our assaults. True enough, Gibbon's *History* is not so comprehensive, either geographically or socially, as the twentieth-century historians understand this requirement;[53] but, even in this point, Gibbon has a lesson to teach us: to be truly "comprehensive," history must treat not only of cabbages, but also of kings.

According to Gibbon, the Roman Empire reached its zenith in the age of the Antonines, after which the decline set in; such an interpretation was in harmony with the classicist compartment of Gibbon's mind. In contrast, the Rome of Montesquieu, erected on the single principle of military virtue, was already in precipitate decline in the age of Cicero. Later, however, Gibbon modified his view; in revising his work toward the end of his life, he wrote, "Should I not have given the *history* of that fortunate pe-

[52] *Decline and Fall*, ch. 65:VII, 78, a discussion of the role of the Turkish sultans in building up the Ottoman Empire.
[53] This theme is developed in Lynn White's conclusion.

riod [A.D. 98–180] which was interposed between two iron ages? Should I not have deduced the decline of the Empire from the Civil Wars that ensued after the Fall of Nero, or even from the tyranny which succeeded the Age of Augustus? Alas! I should: but of what avail is this tardy knowledge?" [54]

Apart from the many subsidiary causes (the license of the praetorian guards and of the legions, heavy taxation, the expense of blood and treasure, the maxims of Septimius Severus, the personal character of many emperors, etc.), Gibbon finds four main reasons for the fall of Rome. The principal of these is "immoderate greatness"; the others are wealth and luxury, the deluge of barbarians, and the spread of Christianity.[55] The deluge of barbarians comes as a *deus ex machina* to expose the inner decay of the Empire and to precipitate the catastrophe. The other three causes have the nature of "general causes." Let us examine them briefly. "The decline of Rome was the natural and inevitable effect of immoderate greatness. Prosperity ripened the principle of decay; the causes of destruction multiplied with the extent of conquest; and, as soon as time or accident had removed the artificial supports, the stupendous fabric yielded to the pressure of its own weight." The collapse of Rome was thus inevitable, because Rome had overstepped the limits that it is safe for a body politic to observe. In the implied doctrine of the optimum size of the state we can detect overtones of Montesquieu and his spiritual ancestors going back to the Greeks. Likewise, the connection between wealth and decay is very old, and, again, no one expressed it more forcibly than Montesquieu, who

[54] *Decline and Fall,* Introduction: I, xxxv.

[55] These observations appear in "General Observations on the Fall of the Roman Empire in the West," appended to ch. 38 of the *Decline and Fall,* IV, 160 ff. Unless otherwise indicated, quotations in this paragraph and the next are taken from this section.

devoted many pages to the proposition that all riches corrupt and that immoderate riches corrupt absolutely.

The role of Christianity in the decline of Rome was complex. "The introduction, or at least the abuse of Christianity had some influence on the decline and fall of the Roman empire." The "doctrines of patience and pusillanimity" undermined public virtue. The effete were all too prone to cover their cowardice and indolence with the cloak of religion, and "the last remains of the military spirit were buried in the cloister"; we know what Gibbon thought of the monks. After Constantine, theological factions in the Church became political factions in the commonwealth and needlessly swelled the number of the enemies of the state. At the same time, however, ecclesiastical organization was a cohesive force in the Empire, though its beneficial effects were confined to the orthodox. "But the pure and genuine influence of Christianity may be traced in its beneficial, though imperfect, effects on the Barbarian proselytes of the North. If the decline of the Roman empire was hastened by the conversion of Constantine, his victorious religion broke the violence of the fall, and mollified the ferocious temper of the conquerors." It is in this rather intricate context that we should interpret the famous sentence: ". . . in the preceding volumes of this History I have described the triumph of barbarism and religion." [56]

How did Gibbon envisage the scope and purpose of his *History?* The entire work, he said, "would connect the ancient and modern history of the World" by unfolding the

[56] *Ibid.*, ch. 71:VII, 308. In this section Gibbon discusses the pilfering and destruction of the buildings and monuments of ancient Rome, and exonerates both the Christians and the barbarians from most of the blame.

story of "the memorable series of revolutions, which, in the course of about thirteen centuries, gradually undermined, and at length destroyed, the solid fabric of human greatness"—"a revolution which will ever be remembered, and is still felt by the nations of the earth." [57] Gibbon's enterprise was the first major attempt to examine the Middle Ages as a whole, without tying them to any specific national kingdom in western Europe. Bossuet, indeed, had vaguely planned something of the sort in his *Discours sur l'histoire universelle,* but did not go beyond writing a few sketchy pages on the period between Constantine and Charlemagne. Gibbon, unlike Bossuet, could not use the Divine Providence to hold his structure together. Instead, he had to rely on acts of faith of the eighteenth-century Enlightenment, however unorthodox might be his use of them. This was not conducive to any sympathy on the part of Gibbon for the medieval ethos, either in the West or in the East; herein lies his greatest weakness as a historian and the chief source of his blindness with respect to the Byzantine Empire, whose sins were that much less pardonable insofar as it claimed to be the Roman Empire. Throughout his writings he calls the Middle Ages "dark" or "an age of ignorance." What mattered to Gibbon most was a philosophical historian's link between the ancient world and the modern across the chasm of the Middle Ages. But he was too great a historian to be wholly consistent in the application of his views, and rays of understanding frequently enlighten the scene, even when his mind refuses to follow up his involuntary discovery.

It remains to ask the question whether Gibbon's *History* is a cautionary tale intended to warn of the dangers besetting the civilized world. To this question Gibbon himself provides an emphatic answer in the negative. Of late, the rule of reason has arrived for good, and its continued sway

[57] Gibbon's Preface to *ibid.,* I, v, vii, and ch. 1:I, 1.

is assured by Europe's being organized as "one great republic," consisting of many independent states "whose various inhabitants have attained almost the same level of politeness and cultivation." This civilized republic knows, or controls, nearly the whole earth, and "the reign of independent barbarism" has been contracted to "the remnants of Calmucks and Uzbecks." It is, of course, possible that some people, now "scarcely visible in the map of the world," may arise to threaten our repose, should another Muhammad breathe "the soul of enthusiasm" into them. Gibbon does not believe in the possibility of a "relapse into original barbarism." [58] Little did he dream when he published these reflections in 1781 that only a few years later the French Revolution would open the gates to a flood of a new kind of barbarism, which would eventually engulf not only all of Europe, but the entire globe, and whose end is not yet in sight.

There have been many historians of the later Roman Empire; not a few of them have left an honorable mark in historiography. Most of them, however, were children of their own age; as such, they become dated, and, with the passing of ages, gradually sink into oblivion. But a historian of genius, like any other genius, is never just a child of his age; he towers above it, though he may participate in its life, its ideas, and its hopes. No matter what his weaknesses may be, his "writings will instruct the last generations of mankind." This remark, which Gibbon made about Tacitus, can, with equal justice, be applied to Gibbon himself.

[58] These reflections are found in the "General Observations" appended to ch. 38 of the *Decline and Fall.*

I

THE CRISIS OF THE THIRD CENTURY

Mortimer Chambers

$\mathcal{E}$DWARD GIBBON did not write a history of Rome. We know from his other writings that he cared little for democratic revolutions; he would not have enjoyed narrating the careers of popular leaders such as the Gracchi or Caesar. He preferred to begin his mighty work at the summit of Roman statecraft, when the Empire's frontiers were "guarded by ancient renown and disciplined valour," and when "the gentle, but powerful, influence of laws and manners had gradually cemented the union of the provinces." [1] He considered the Empire a harmonious work of art, an enlightened system later weakened by Christians and barbarians. He shared the eighteenth-century vision of the perfectibility of man. Therefore his chronicle begins with the most nearly perfected age of Rome: the Antonine period of the second century A.D., when the Roman Empire still stood gleaming in the late afternoon sun. From this pinnacle the path led only downhill, a path that Gibbon followed with worldly irony toward the point from which he had started—the ruins of an ancient Roman temple where he conceived his task on an October evening two hundred years ago. [2]

Gibbon opens his history with three chapters Herodo-

[1] *Decline and Fall*, ch. 1:I, 1.
[2] Cf. J. J. Saunders, "Gibbon in Rome 1764," *History Today*, 14 (1964), 608–615.

tean in scope, Tacitean in sentiment. Here he analyzes the solidity of the Empire and praises the wise Antonine rulers whose reigns "are possibly the only period of history in which the happiness of a great people was the sole object of government."[3] An even higher compliment is his famous remark: "If a man were called to fix the period in the history of the world during which the condition of the human race was most happy and prosperous, he would, without hesitation, name that which elapsed from the death of Domitian to the accession of Commodus"[4] (96–180). We might challenge Gibbon, as the American historian Tenney Frank did, by pointing to the relative poverty of the Antonine age in literature, philosophy, and art;[5] and the plague that accompanied the troops returning from the East, in the late 160's, must have had serious consequences which unfortunately cannot be expressed in statistical form.[6] Yet, on the whole, historians do not quarrel radically at this point with Gibbon's judgment. Marcus Aurelius, who alone incarnates Plato's philosopherking in Roman history, will retain his high reputation.

Not long after the benign administration of the Antonines, the gathering storm burst upon the Empire. The third century, as all admit, was the moment of challenge. In many respects it marks the beginning of the Middle Ages, and especially of the Byzantine segment of the Middle Ages. But what was the third century? Depending on the view we take of certain reigns, we might date the start of the third century in 211 with the death of Septimius Severus, or in 235 with the death of Alexander Severus, the

[3] *Decline and Fall*, ch. 3:I, 76.

[4] *Ibid.*, ch. 3:I, 78.

[5] Tenney Frank (ed.), *An Economic Survey of Ancient Rome* (Baltimore, 1933–1940), V, 296–304.

[6] Note, however, that J. F. Gilliam, "The Plague under Marcus Aurelius," *American Journal of Philology*, 82 (1961), 225–251, does not consider the plague a serious cause of the decline of Rome.

last ruler of the Severan dynasty. But it seems better to go back to 193, immediately after the murder of Commodus on December 31, 192. The reign of the detestable Commodus was scarcely philosophic, but at least it continued that of his father, Marcus Aurelius. The lower end of the third century might be fixed at May 1, 305, with the retirement of Diocletian; but the long rule of this dynast rather seems to terminate the era of crisis at 284. Thus the third century, for our purposes, ran from 193 to 284.

At the end of this epoch we find a far different kind of Roman Empire from the civilized system of Antoninus Pius (138–161) and his successors. Diocletian had greatly strengthened the bureaucratic element in the government, which was now frankly a monarchy. The traditional institutions of the Principate, as they were established by Augustus, counted for little, and Rome was so close to the Byzantine Empire that some Byzantine historians would date the beginning of their special period to 284. Speaking of this change in the Empire, Gibbon says, "The senate of Rome, losing all connexion with the Imperial court and the actual constitution, was left a venerable but useless monument of antiquity on the Capitoline Hill." [7] And he strikes home with an essential point: "Like Augustus, Diocletian may be considered as the founder of a new empire." [8]

The work of Diocletian was decisive, heroic, and ruthless. Almost by an act of will he stabilized the Empire, truncated the age of anarchy, and installed the monarchy that did not end until 1453. But Diocletian's system took root in a historical context and emerged from a historical background. If we are to understand the evolution of the Empire between the time of Marcus and that of Diocletian, we need to examine the intervening century. The

[7] *Decline and Fall*, ch. 13:I, 380.
[8] *Ibid.*, ch. 13:I, 351.

issue is how Roman society was being altered during this period and how the way was prepared for the new "Byzantine" order that began in 284.

Gibbon's approach to this period was almost entirely political and military. His chapters 5 through 13 are a thorough review of wars, rebellions, and conspiracies, with a secondary place allowed to changes in imperial administration. Partly because Gibbon and his predecessor, Tillemont, have done their work so well, we may assume that the general course of these affairs can be followed in such standard narratives as the *Cambridge Ancient History,* volume 12, or in any reliable textbook. None of these supplant Gibbon's own narrative.

The overall political picture is vexatious and confusing. For a few decades the dynasty of the Severi, which ruled nearly continuously from 193 onward, gives at least some measure of order to the era 193–235. Beginning in 235 the Empire plunged into its supreme crisis. At the lowest possible count, 20 men claimed the title of emperor within the next 50 years; but they were only temporary heads of armies, which in turn were the true ruling power. The lowest point was reached about 260 under the reign of Gallienus. The frontiers were lacerated with invasions, and even Gaul threw off her loyalty and set up the independent state known as the Imperium Galliarum. A ray of light shone in 269, when Claudius won a timely victory over the Goths. Aurelian, his successor, subdued the rebellious city of Palmyra in the East. After another dozen years, history salvaged Rome at last with Diocletian; but henceforth it was a new kind of Rome.

Rather than retrace these paths made familiar by Gibbon, let us leave the dreary record of successive wars and murders by seeking methods of inquiry that were not fashionable in his day. Only false modesty would assert that we have made no progress in historical thinking since Gibbon.

I therefore propose to examine three related subjects during the century of crisis: the state of the economy, of administration, and of religion. Each of these areas of life suffered changes during the third century that pointed the way toward the Byzantine state.

Roman economy could not weather the years of anarchy with any prosperity. Its weakness was beyond the reach of any administrator or government. As a result, some third-century emperors receive the blame for repressive actions that were practically forced on them. Ancient economy was agricultural to a degree scarcely comprehensible in the modern Western world. But rural life leaves behind few spectacular traces. We today focus attention on an occasional surprising commercial find, such as the brand-new Gallic pottery sealed under the eruption of Vesuvius in A.D. 79, evidence that demonstrates the Roman importing of Gallic ware in preference to Italian.[9] Such remains tell their own story, and we must not neglect them. Yet they are, as it were, only the exposed tip of the iceberg. The submerged mass was a mute and largely unrecorded farming economy that, like the life of the masses generally, we historians perceive less often.

It is therefore a serious error, and one that Gibbon did not make, to imagine the Empire as a full-fledged capitalistic system with large interdependent classes of entrepreneurs, bourgeois, and so on. Industry, exports, and trade were incidental and did not furnish the real basis for the life of the Empire. As for invested wealth which grows through the labor of others, it too had to rest mainly on land. Pliny the Younger, an experienced civil servant and a man whose financial acumen carried him to an early con-

[9] D. Atkinson, "A Hoard of Samian Ware from Pompeii," *Journal of Roman Studies*, 4 (1914), 27 ff.

sulate under Trajan, placed nearly all his wealth in land.[10]
He also considered land the best investment when looking
around for a gift that would bring security to his old
nurse: he bought her a farm.[11]

As the Empire developed, it was able to extend prosperity to more people. Indeed, the provinces soon outstripped
Italy in economic strength. Spanish wine, for example,
captured the Italian market. This is shown most economically by the excavation of the huge pottery dump along
the Tiber near Rome known as Monte Testaccio, in which
Spanish wine jars predominate beginning in the second
century.[12] Industry, too, began to shift its center of gravity to the provinces. The artifact made in greatest quantity (apart from officially controlled coins) was the humble
pot. The success of Gallic pottery, already noticed at
Pompeii, is further shown by the willingness of Italians to
move to Gaul and set up factories there; this was done, for
example, by some of the family of one Cn. Ateius.[13] Gallic
pottery in due course even took over the market at the
Claudian colony of Camulodunum in Britain. We assume
that the purchasing agents were under no pressure to buy
Italian products, and so naturally they bought Gallic pottery, which was cheaper than Italian.[14]

Yet the spreading prosperity in agriculture and, to a
lesser degree, in industry across the Roman world was not
caused by a true breakthrough in technology, nor did it

[10] C. Plinius Secundus *Epistulae* 3.19.8: "sum quidem prope totus in
praediis."

[11] Pliny *Ep.* 6.3.

[12] Frank, *op. cit.*, p. 272.

[13] *Ibid.*, pp. 192–193.

[14] The decline in the export of Italian pottery is evident from the
excavations at Camulodunum (Colchester). See C. F. C. Hawkes
and M. R. Hull, *Camulodunum: First Report on the Excavations at
Colchester* (Oxford, 1947), pp. 189–191, where the authors conclude that Arretine pottery was not imported to that site after about
A.D. 45.

herald a notable increase in the distribution of goods. We see little more than the carrying on of the same kind of activity by more people; and this was the only way (except through such devices as water-driven mills) of multiplying productivity. In fact, the vast difference in per capita production between ancient and modern technology has been cited as the main reason why we find it difficult to "apply" the lessons of ancient economic history.[15] Agriculture had not really improved its methods; and industry had not developed to the point where it could resist serious strain or a high degree of physical destruction.

The instability of ancient commerce was compounded by the lack of such modern devices as token money. The government could issue coinage only so long as the supply of silver held out, and this supply was finite. The effects of a shortage in silver are visible from a pathetic step taken by Marcus Aurelius. He had inherited a large surplus from his predecessor, Antoninus; but to meet expenses during the Marcomannic wars (*ca.* 170) Marcus was reduced to selling the royal jewels and wardrobe.[16] The absolute dependence on a physical supply of silver is also attested by the insecurity of those who hid their money in the numerous coin hoards found within the Empire. This nervous action raised further difficulties for the government in its efforts to find enough silver for the needed coinage. Nor was the mere shortage of bullion the only problem, for we may assume that ancient Rome, like many another state, had no great surplus of income over expenses, and, during a period of constant warfare, her resources were stretched to the limit.

An economy of this kind was much more vulnerable to

[15] M. Hammond, "Economic Stagnation in the Early Roman Empire," in *Tasks of Economic History,* supplement to *Journal of Economic History,* 6 (1946), 63–90, esp. p. 90.

[16] *Scriptores Historiae Augustae* (hereafter cited as SHA), *Marcus Antoninus* 17.4.

shocks than a modern one. In the absence of (so to speak) an economic cushion to fall back on, a change for the worse could occur more rapidly. The precise effects on the various kinds of people in the Empire must be to some degree uncertain, and it is probable enough that the extremely wealthy landowners were somehow able to remain wealthy. It would be an exaggeration to speak of the population of the Empire as if everyone were immediately made penniless.[17] On the other hand, some large fortunes, legacies from the prosperity of the late Republic and early Empire, had already been raided by the confiscations of first-century emperors such as Vespasian.[18] Some, at least, of the upper class must have suffered as their wealth was diverted to paying for wars; probably the middle class felt the pressure even more keenly. As purchasing power was threatened during the anarchy, there was less and less demand for goods above an ordinary standard of craftsmanship.

Such, in general, was the economy that was now called on to finance nearly uninterrupted wars and grandiose building schemes. As if that were not enough, some emperors realized that their only security lay in the army and acted accordingly. Caracalla (211–217) seems to have taken seriously the alleged dying words of his father, Septimius Severus: "Enrich the soldiers, despise the rest." [19] He sharply raised the soldiers' pay, perhaps after all a necessary step in view of the prolonged wars that he had to fight against Germanic tribes on the Danube and even farther north.[20] Numerous donations to the soldiers are also

[17] For the view that many inhabitants of the empire could make some kind of economic adjustment to the new conditions, see A. H. M. Jones, *The Later Roman Empire, 284–602* (Oxford, 1964), I, 28 ff.

[18] C. Suetonius Tranquillus *De vita Caesarum, Vesp.* 16, *Domit.* 12.

[19] Cassius Dio 77.15.2.

[20] *Cambridge Ancient History* (Cambridge, Eng., 1923–1939), XII, 725.

recorded during his reign, while the still surviving Baths of Caracalla attest the expense of his building program.

To obtain the money needed for these purposes, Caracalla adopted the direct method of taxing those who had money and could not, by relying on their position in the state, avoid paying. He legalized his robberies by such devices as the extraordinary tax for the so-called *aurum coronarium*.[21] This gold was originally demanded by triumphing generals to provide crowns for their processions. Caracalla's ordering it for his budgets pointed the way for others. Elagabalus (218–222) continued to exact this tax and also made what invasions he could on the remaining wealth of the populace.[22]

A characteristic act of Caracalla's financial policy was his raising the tax on manumissions of slaves and on inheritances from 5 to 10 percent.[23] But this mere doubling of the inheritance tax evidently did not suffice. Perhaps in 212 Caracalla passed his famous enfranchising act by which he gave Roman citizenship to every free man living within the Empire (except the class of the so-called *dediticii* whose identity is uncertain).[24] We are seldom well informed about the motives of ancient statesmen, and we do not know why he took this seemingly modern and liberal view of the nature of man. Probably the Greek historian Dio hit the mark in stating that Caracalla enfran-

[21] Cassius Dio 78.9.2.

[22] *Oxyrhynchus Papyri* 1441 (crown tax under Alexander Severus), 1659 (under Elagabalus).

[23] Cassius Dio 78.9.4.

[24] Cassius Dio 78.9.5. The date 214 is given by F. Millar, "The Date of the *Constitutio Antoniniana*," *Journal of Egyptian Archaeology*, 48 (1962), 124–131, who discusses P. *Giessen* 40, the papyrus preserving the edict (or something much like it); but see also J. F. Gilliam, "Dura Rosters and the *Constitutio Antoniniana*," *Historia*, 14 (1965), 74–92. The identity of the *dediticii* is treated by H. J. Benario in *Transactions of the American Philological Association*, 85 (1954), 188–196, and by J. H. Oliver in *American Journal of Philology*, 76 (1955), 279–297.

chised all his free subjects because only citizens paid inheritance taxes.[25] This may indeed be no more than Dio's inference, and possibly several converging motives inspired the Emperor; but Dio's explanation makes sense against a background of clear financial crisis.

When Caracalla and his successors had exhausted the ordinary and traditional means of raising money, they turned to other expedients. The purpose of collecting funds was to support the army on its campaigns. This economic purpose could also be achieved, at least in part, by recognizing that money was becoming hard to raise and by exploiting the system of contributions in kind. These exactions from the people were allegedly to be reimbursed by the state; but the unmistakable tone of protest in various sources reveals that payment was not always made. Nearly every kind of goods was requisitioned for the army, the largest consumer of wealth.[26] Soldiers were often quartered in homes, despite the protests of their hosts and victims.[27] The results of this system are clear: the burden fell again and again on those found able to bear it, until they too sank into poverty.

The other device used by the third-century emperors was tampering with the currency. The silver content of Roman coins was often debased. In a modern state, where coins are normally token money, it matters less of what material they are composed; but since Rome did not use token money, the debasement of silver could have serious

---

[25] Cassius Dio 78.9.5.

[26] Copious evidence for exactions in kind is assembled by M. Rostovtzeff, *Social and Economic History of the Roman Empire* (2d ed.; Oxford, 1957), II, 721 n. 45.

[27] On quartering troops in private houses in the time of Caracalla, see Cassius Dio 78.3.4. On the economic parasitism of the soldiery, see Rostovtzeff, *op. cit.*, II, 723 n. 46; cf. the recent collection by N. Lewis, *Leitourgia Papyri: Documents on Compulsory Public Service in Egypt under Roman Rule* (Philadelphia, 1963).

consequences. By the time of Septimius Severus, the debasement was evidently as much as 40 percent.[28] Caracalla sought to rescue coinage from complete depreciation by using such silver as was available to strike larger coins. He introduced the coin called (by modern writers) the Antoninianus, which was probably worth two denarii, the denarius being the standard silver coin. But the new coin could not be maintained at the proper weight of silver, and by 260 the Antoninianus had become little more than so-called billon, that is, silver highly adulterated with copper. This worthless money led to an inflation that further threatened the solvency of the state.[29]

The way in which Diocletian and his colleagues dealt with their problems indicates the results of these troubled economic conditions in the third century. The two main reforms of Diocletian went hand in hand. These were a general reform of the currency and his famous edict on prices. In fact, it was the failure of the currency reform that made the edict appear necessary. For Diocletian grasped the essential point that the existing currency commanded no confidence because of its poor material. He was fortunate in being able to lay his hands on a supply of precious metals, probably from the East, where his restoration of Rome's military position was thus especially important.[30] But we may guess that he too was unable to hold down the inflation. Experts conjecture that his gold and silver coins retained their value but that his bronze ones could not be traded at the fixed or announced price. Therefore prices soared again. This time Diocletian used a more authoritarian method. In his edict (best consulted in the edition in Tenney Frank's *An Economic Survey of Ancient Rome,* volume 5) dating from 301, he made a dicta-

---

[28] H. Mattingly, *Roman Coins* (2d ed.; London, 1960), p. 124.
[29] *Ibid.,* p. 125; cf. Jones, *op. cit.,* I, 26–32.
[30] Mattingly, *op. cit.,* pp. 211–212, 250.

torial attempt to lay down prices that could not be exceeded. The edict shows in what detail the Emperor tried to solve the problem; and this solution had at least the merit of an experiment. But its evident failure is shown by the fact that Diocletian later had to allow it to lapse.[31]

The verdict of historians on Diocletian's work is confirmed by a look at his manner of grappling with the economic situation. He did little more than extend and rationalize the existing practices, sealing them in by imposing a more efficient system of bureaucratic control. He by no means abandoned the system of collections in kind, despite his promising start in reforming the currency. By a complex scheme he divided the Roman world into units for taxation.[32] Assessors then visited these units and fixed the amount due from each of them. It was difficult to get one's assessment reduced, but sometimes landholders could convert their obligations into cash payments by the process known as *adaeratio*.[33] History seems to show that Diocletian made this crushing system work, but its establishment attests the new rigidity that was necessary if the Empire was to emerge from the third century in any kind of working order. Thus, at one step, we feel we are leaving the world of Rome and entering that of Byzantium, where monarchy was accepted without ideological misgivings.

Gibbon devoted no particular chapter to the changes in government and administration during the third century. Perhaps the problem could not be discussed in his time since he lived before the nineteenth-century historians who elevated the study of Roman government and law into a science. Barthold Georg Niebuhr, the founder of the

[31] Lactantius *De mortibus persecutorum* 7.

[32] For a description of this system, see Jones, *op. cit.*, I, 62 ff.; cf. E. Stein, *Histoire du Bas-Empire* (Paris, 1949–1959), I, 74 ff.

[33] This process is mentioned in *Cod. Theod.* 7.4.28.

modern discipline of history, was born in 1776, when Gibbon issued the first volume of the *Decline and Fall;* and Theodor Mommsen completed his great study of the Roman constitution, the *Römisches Staatsrecht,* precisely a century after Gibbon's last three volumes appeared in 1788. Yet Gibbon could not and did not overlook the direction in which Rome's government was moving. Within the first two centuries, as he states, "The successors of Augustus exercised the power of dictating whatever laws their wisdom or caprice might suggest; but those laws were ratified by the sanction of the senate." [34] But now, in Diocletian's time,

> In the exercise of the legislative as well as of the executive power, the sovereign advised with his ministers, instead of consulting the great council of the nation. The name of the senate was mentioned with honour till the last period of the empire; the vanity of its members was still flattered with honorary distinctions; but the assembly, which had so long been the source, and so long the instrument, of power, was respectfully suffered to sink into oblivion.[35]

The main trend in third-century administration is simply described: it was toward more and more control by the emperor and his circle of trusted servants. True, even by the time of Hadrian and the Antonines the Senate had lost most of its traditions of independence and authority; and Gibbon's picture of the Senate acting as an ultimate referee over the legislation of the first two centuries is deliberately anachronistic. The Senate, as a body, had made few crucial decisions since the days of Caesar or even earlier. However far back we begin the enfeeblement of the Senate, the movement was accelerated by Septimius and his heirs. Probably this policy was forced on the Severi and the other third-century emperors by overpowering circum-

[34] *Decline and Fall,* ch. 13:I, 380.
[35] *Ibid.*

stances. The Empire had to become militarized or succumb totally. Yet the administration found it expedient to seek an ideological basis for this new principle. For example, the judicial theorists whose work finds its way into the *Digest* were concerned to legitimize the custom by which the emperor issued laws. They solved this problem to their satisfaction by deciding that, since the emperor clearly possessed imperium, or a general power to command, he also had the power to legislate.[36] We could probably find flaws in this doctrine, but it is more to the point to observe the grim historical circumstances in which it was produced. Since absolutism was a necessity at the moment, the jurists had little choice but to interpret the law accordingly.

One sign of the lower prestige of the Senate under Septimius was his refusal to continue the tradition by which the command of Roman legions was normally restricted to senators.[37] He placed three new legions under the command of the next highest class, the equestrians.[38] This act is also a sign of the continuous rise of the equestrians within the third century. Any powers they gained were additional to the considerable scope they already possessed. Their most important single post was that of the commander (prefect) of the Praetorian Guard, the body that had often thrown its support decisively behind one or another candidate for the throne. While the equestrians were gaining increased stature by commanding legions, they also advanced to important civil commands. Septimius picked up a useful idea from Augustus and began stationing equestrians as governors of provinces. Augustus

[36] *Digest* 1.4.1.

[37] Note, however, that even in Augustan times the equestrian prefect of Egypt commanded legions.

[38] These were the Parthian legions. For their equestrian commanders, see H. Dessau, *Inscriptiones Latinae Selectae* 1356, 2771 (hereafter cited as *ILS*); *SHA, Caracalla* 6.7.

had done this in Egypt; that nation was customarily in charge of a handpicked prefect, and perhaps we should not reckon it as a province at all but rather as a private possession of the emperor. The province of Mesopotamia now received an equestrian prefect as its governor in place of the usual legate drawn from the Senate.[39] By a corollary of the same principle, Septimius made a change among the governors of the Imperial provinces, the ones assigned to the emperor's administration and normally governed by senators whom he appointed. Septimius turned some of these provinces over to equestrians holding the title of procurator, a name used in earlier times to denote a reliable agent of the emperor.[40] Here, too, the Senate sank further into an ineffectual role.

This movement continued throughout the century, even though it was slow to reach its destined end, the total exclusion of senators from responsible posts. Gallienus, about 260, made his contribution to the further dishonor of the Senate by removing senators from legionary commands.[41] From this time onward legionary commanders were equestrians with the title of prefect (*praefectus legionis*). In this way, the emperor could reward his loyal followers among the army and bring them into the governing circle. As we would expect, Diocletian carried this process further and formally divided the military authority from the civil authority in the provinces; he sent out civilian governors, called judges (*iudices*), and along with them military commanders (*duces*).[42] Gone, therefore, were the days in which a Caesar was the sole and supreme

[39] For a prefect of Mesopotamia, see *Corpus Inscriptionum Latinarum* 6.1642 (hereafter cited as *CIL*).

[40] For a procurator in an imperial province, see *CIL* 3.1625.

[41] Aurelius Victor *De Caesaribus* 33.34.

[42] For this division between military and civil authority, see Jones, *op. cit.*, I, 43 ff.

commander of all Roman forces in Gaul, fighting his campaigns in the summer and holding trials in the winter.[43]

This matter of trials takes us deeper into some changes made in the third century. Long before, Aristotle rightly observed that "when the people gain control of the votes in a jury, they gain control of the state." [44] That is another way of saying that popular control of juries and justice is the one essential mark of a democracy. The mere existence of juries is no guarantee of popular sovereignty, since a monarch can always create an elegant set of juries and then simply staff them with his favorites. In Republican Rome, one of the most controversial political issues was the control of the jury that sat over cases of alleged extortion. Depending on which faction controlled the state at a given moment, the precious seats were handed out to senators, or equestrians, or a mixture of both. This court, in turn, was only one of the "permanent juries" (quaestiones perpetuae) in the Republic; and their dissolution would be a sign that the state was drifting away from such democracy as Rome enjoyed.

Now, apparently under Septimius, these juries were dismissed and their powers were turned over to the prefect of the Praetorian Guard or to the prefect of Rome (praefectus urbi).[45] Here is another step toward the nearly Byzantine monarchy of the late third century. The more important position now accorded to the Praetorian prefect is always connected with the personality of Plautianus, a trusted adviser of Septimius. At the same time, the prefect became responsible for administering the military treasury; in less discreet language, he took charge of the forced

[43] Caesar Gallic War 1.54.
[44] Constitution of Athens 9.1.
[45] Th. Mommsen, Römisches Strafrecht (Leipzig, 1899), pp. 219–221.

contributions in kind and the outright confiscations needed to maintain the army.[46] Before we criticize the Romans for installing this military despotism, let us again
recall that at every moment Rome was fighting for her life
against invaders on the frontiers; under such unpleasant
conditions any genteel respect for tradition had to give
way.

Along with the increased power of the equestrian prefect, another movement appears, a tendency toward making decisions in a meeting of oligarchs who were usually
called "friends" (*amici*) of the emperor.[47] Modern scholars (but no ancient writers) call this group the *consilium
principis*. Anyone familiar with administration knows that
a group of a few men always arises and either initiates new
ideas or guides the thinking of others. In the Rome of the
period in question, the emperor sought to establish himself
as the admitted source of law; and he was aided, as we have
seen, by his constitutional theorists. The "friends" met,
gave advice, and assisted the emperor in proclaiming his
decrees. The final step was taken by Constantine, who recognized and welcomed this practice. He formalized the
circle of friends, gave it the name of *consistorium,* and so
completed the work set in train by Hadrian and furthered
by Septimius.

A particularly difficult problem of administration arose
for the Romans in the field of religion, a treacherous bat-
tleground where lances and swords are sometimes shattered
against an idea. In exploring the tension between Roman
paganism and Christianity, we may find it difficult to
state, as the Romans also did, the precise reasons for the

[46] O. Hirschfeld, *Die kaiserlichen Verwaltungsbeamten* (2d ed.;
Berlin, 1905), p. 246.

[47] For a complete discussion of the council of "friends," see J.
Crook, *Consilium Principis* (Cambridge, Eng., 1955).

long conflict between Rome and the Church. Rome, down into the third century at least, had no official state religion, and her attitude toward the various faiths and cults was often surprisingly tolerant. Indeed, there is some pagan evidence showing that Christianity was practiced side by side with paganism. For example, Alexander Severus is said to have maintained a statue of Christ in his chapel, along with images of the deified emperors, Abraham, Orpheus, and other worthies.[48] If we like, we may approach such seemingly contradictory evidence with caution; but whether or not Alexander practiced this bizarre custom, the anecdote apparently did not seem incredible to the writer in the *Augustan History*.[49]

On the pagan side itself, there was a notable lack of religious purism. Long ago Rome had more or less officially worshiped the Romanized gods of the Olympic pantheon, Jupiter, Juno, and the rest; and at all times Romans worshiped local gods, deities of the household and of the country. Yet, from early times, we may also trace that importation of foreign (especially Eastern) gods that confused ancient paganism and may have diluted its strength for the fight against Christianity. An outstanding example is the official admission of the cult of the Great Mother (Magna Mater, or Cybele) with her consort, Attis, from Phrygia in 204 B.C.[50] This orgiastic cult, with its six-day-long festival, its flagellations and castrations, seems hardly Roman; one might suppose that religious indiscipline had already overtaken Rome by the second century before Christ. In fact, however, the Romans still held to their pragmatic view of religion as an adjunct to politics. They imported this cult strictly in answer to a political problem, namely

[48] *SHA, Alex. Sev.* 29.2.

[49] That this passage in the *SHA* is a forgery is argued by J. Straub, *Heidnische Geschichtsapologetik in der christlichen Spätantike* (Bonn, 1963), p. 166.

[50] Livy 29.14.5–14; 29.37.2.

how to expel Hannibal from Italy in 205 B.C. The Sybilline books, a source of prophetic wisdom, recommended the use of this new cult, and the King of Pergamum was kind enough to transfer to Rome the black stone housing the goddess. The Romans installed the cult, duly defeated Carthage, and kept up the festival; but they did so in a dignified and sanitary manner. Only Phrygians could be eunuch-priests of Cybele, and the cult was under the supervision of a special board.[51] Rome had committed herself to tolerate this feverish cult, but her general suspicion of such things is shown by the famous decree of the Senate, suppressing a suddenly discovered group of Bacchic enthusiasts in 186 B.C.[52] No more Eastern cults were imported for some time.

By the time of the Empire, Rome had come once again to allow more scope to foreign deities. Unsuccessful attempts had already been made to introduce the worship of the Egyptian goddess Isis. She was now definitively accepted under the reign of Caligula (37–41), who probably built the temple to Isis in the Campus Martius.[53] His successor Claudius (41–54), perhaps by way of reasserting the rights of an older and by now traditional cult, granted further dignity and recognition to the ritual of Cybele. He removed the restriction that had barred Roman citizens from serving as priests to the Great Mother; but he continued to discourage castration among Romans by decreeing that the priests were no longer to be eunuchs.

[51] A. D. Nock, *Conversion* (Oxford, 1933), pp. 68–69. For the prohibition against Romans' acting as priests, see Dionysius of Halicarnassus *Antiquitates Romanae* 2.19.4; for the prohibition against castration, see Valerius Maximus 7.7.6.

[52] Livy 39.8 ff.

[53] According to Josephus, Caligula took part in a ceremony in honor of Isis dressed in women's clothing (*Antiquitates Judaicae* 19.30).

Claudius also established a series of festival days running intermittently from March 15 through March 27.[54]

This acceptance of Egyptian and Phrygian deities was typical of the tolerant, even fascinated, attitude of Rome toward these enthusiastic cults. During later eras such religions sank their roots deeper in Roman life. One famous rite was known as the *taurobolium;* this ceremony was held in honor of several deities, but originally it belonged to Cybele. According to taste, one may consider it wickedly inspiring or downright revolting. A platform was erected and a bull led onto it. Underneath in a pit the initiate awaited the slaughter of the beast. Then, as we learn from the Christian poet Prudentius, he allowed the blood dripping through the platform to bathe his body, his face, his mouth, and his eyes. He was then presented to the crowd of spectators as one who had imbibed the potency of the deity and had been absolved of his sins by this crimson baptism.[55] Our first evidence for a *taurobolium* in the West comes from A.D. 134;[56] the rite endured into the fourth century.

But within the third century this long-established cult was challenged by another that had the advantage of official imperial sponsorship. This was the cult of the god Elagabalus, and the same name was assumed by the effeminate emperor who reigned from 218 to 222. His grandmother, Julia Maesa, was from a family of Emesa that had long enjoyed a hereditary priesthood of this god. When Elagabalus became emperor, he had the black stone that supposedly housed the deity brought from Emesa to Rome.

[54] F. Cumont, *The Oriental Religions in Roman Paganism*, Eng. trans. (Chicago, 1911), p. 56.

[55] For this classic description of the rite, see Prudentius *Peristeph.* 10.1011 ff.

[56] *ILS* 4271.

The *Augustan History* tells how he transferred the stone to the Palatine Hill, built a temple in its honor, and tried to combine under one roof such disparate rites as those of Vesta, of the Jews, of Christianity, and, indeed, of all gods.[57] Gibbon's picture of this worship demands quotation.

> In a solemn procession through the streets of Rome, the way was strewed with gold dust; the black stone, set in precious gems, was placed on a chariot drawn by six milk-white horses richly caparisoned. The pious emperor held the reins, and, supported by his ministers, moved slowly backwards, that he might perpetually enjoy the felicity of the divine presence. In a magnificent temple raised on the Palatine Mount, the sacrifices of the god Elagabalus were celebrated with every circumstance of cost and solemnity. The richest wines, the most extraordinary victims, and the rarest aromatics, were profusely consumed on his altar. Around the altar a chorus of Syrian damsels performed their lascivious dances to the sound of barbarian music, whilst the gravest personages of the state and army, clothed in long Phoenician tunics, officiated in the meanest functions, with affected zeal and secret indignation.[58]

A further step along the same path was taken by Aurelian in the 270's. For some time, as images on coins amply prove, the sun or Sol had been respected in Rome.[59] Now Aurelian formalized the cult of Sol Invictus (the Invincible Sun). The gods Bel and Helios were transferred from Palmyra in Syria to a temple in Rome; there they were worshiped by official Roman priests.[60] Two Eastern cults above all might have become universal religions: the worship of Isis, imported from Egypt, and that of Mithras,

[57] *SHA, Elagabalus* 3.4–5.

[58] *Decline and Fall*, ch. 6:I, 145, based on Herodian 5.5.7–10.

[59] The evidence is spread through *The Roman Imperial Coinage*, ed. H. Mattingly and E. A. Sydenham (London, 1923——), esp. vols. 4, 5. See also Mattingly, *op. cit.*, p. 157.

[60] Zosimus 1.61.2; Cumont, *op. cit.*, p. 252.

from Persia. As we have seen, Rome accepted Isis in a permanent temple under the reign of Caligula; under the Flavian dynasty of Vespasian and his sons, Egyptian deities appear on Roman coins, and Domitian (81–96) rebuilt the temple of Isis and her companion Sarapis.[61] Later, Commodus became a devotee of Isis.[62] He also practiced Mithraism, which was the most popular religion among the Roman army in the more heavily armed provinces. We find shrines of Mithras, caves with a relief of the god at one end, far and wide, but they were not built by municipalities or official bodies.[63]

One common feature united, to some degree, the Eastern religions. Their gods were worshiped with considerable mystery, otherworldliness, and spiritual enthusiasm. This marked an important change from the matter-of-fact style of traditional Roman worship, and the atmosphere of sanctified mystery surrounding the Eastern cults partly laid the way for Christianity.

The Romans' tolerance of exotic cults only sharpens the puzzle in their relations with the nascent Christian church. Apparently they knew little of the mild doctrines of Christianity; a religion sponsoring an ethical life and devotion to God would not have inspired ferocious persecutions. The offense of the Christians lay elsewhere. First, they were a secret group, unsociable and self-contained. Tacitus reports that the Romans thought the Christians "hated mankind," [64] and by their own profession they ate the flesh and drank the blood of their savior. Again, Christians publicly defied the traditional gods of Rome and refused to sacrifice to the health of the emperor. Not that Rome insisted that her subjects must perform some strictly

[61] Eutropius 7.23.5.
[62] *SHA, Commodus* 9.4.
[63] Nock, *op. cit.*, p. 132.
[64] Tacitus *Annales* 15.44: "odio humani generis convicti sunt."

defined ritual like the Catholic mass; all the same, there was a flexible but still recognizable set of deities which the Christians rejected wholly.

In effect, their program amounted to civil disobedience. As Gibbon saw and firmly pointed out, the Christian church set itself up as a state within a state. The members distinguished sharply between the community of the faithful and the general community. This distinction itself would have been difficult, if not impossible, for an ancient pagan to draw. Worse than that, the Church developed a network of bishops communicating with and assisting each other. A Roman might have described this movement as a Christian secession; and it seemed especially intolerable during the third century when invasion and anarchy had already attacked the Empire at its foundations.

When Christians were punished, it was often because in their brave devotion they had compelled Roman magistrates to punish them whether the magistrates were sadistic or not. The most famous testimony to the frustrated reluctance of a magistrate confronted with defiant Christians is the letter of Pliny the Younger to his emperor, Trajan.[65] Pliny here explains that when Christians are brought before him he offers them three chances to recant. If they do not do so, he orders them to be punished. Trajan approves his practice and adds that Pliny is to refrain from hunting down Christians or listening to anonymous accusations. Now Pliny was an unusually scrupulous magistrate, and Trajan was a fair-minded administrator; but, as recent research has indicated, even the average civil servant made no particularly strenuous efforts to find and murder Christians.[66]

The testimony of Pliny (which Gibbon duly exploited)

[65] Pliny *Ep.* 10.96. See also *Decline and Fall*, ch. 16:II, 92.

[66] For this conclusion, see G. E. M. de Ste Croix, "Aspects of the Great Persecution," *Harvard Theological Review*, 47 (1954), 75–113.

comes from the early second century. During the third century Rome was not so forgiving of her critics. The state, frustrated by war and economic strangulation, began to lash out at the Christian community that refused to pay the required tribute to the public gods. Intermittent persecutions darken this period, and they did not cease until the edict of toleration issued by Galerius in 311. Yet there was no permanent official policy enjoining persecution. As a secret society, the Christians were subject to the laws against such societies, but it is significant of the wavering attitude of Rome that these laws could be relaxed. For example, Septimius Severus instructed provincial governors to allow charitable collections among the poor, provided that the societies in question did not meet more often than once a month; his fear was that more frequent meetings might transform these beneficent clubs into centers of political agitation.[67]

Septimius did give way, at times, to the spirit of persecution that often alternated with a spirit of tolerance. Probably in 202 he issued a decree forbidding anyone from being converted to Christianity.[68] This act of repression led to such persecutions as the one directed by Scapula, the governor of proconsular Africa. An interesting sidelight on this persecution is the letter addressed to Scapula by the church father Tertullian.[69] The letter attempts to divert the persecution by pleading; and, in its course, Tertullian gives us some historical material of high value as he cites some examples of leniency shown to Christians by earlier Roman magistrates. He also testifies to some mildly tolerant acts of Septimius (any contradictions in Septimius' policy are surprising only to those who expect the Romans to be consistent): "Even Severus himself, the father of

[67] Justinian *Digest* 47.22.1.
[68] *SHA, Severus* 17.1.
[69] Tertullian *Ad Scapulam.*

Antonius [i.e., Caracalla], cared for Christians; for he sought out the Christian Proculus . . . , whom he kept in his palace until his death." And later, "Severus, knowing that men and women of the highest rank belonged to this sect, not only refrained from injuring them, but favored them with his testimony and restored them to us openly from the angry populace." [70]

In the middle of the third century the emperor Decius launched the first general and serious persecution.[71] Nor is it accidental that the Empire chose this moment, one of extreme danger, to turn its vindictive anger on the Church. Evidently Rome associated Christianity with many of its troubles, as St. Augustine practically tells us. He tries to show, in the opening pages of his *The City of God,* that Christianity was not in fact the cause of the catastrophes into which Rome seemed to be sinking.

We who know the end of the story realize that the persecutions were to fail, owing to the inspired defiance of the martyrs. Nonetheless, the Decian persecution had considerable temporary effect. This is admitted by St. Cyprian in his *De Lapsis* ("On the Apostates").[72] Human ingenuity could sometimes defeat the challenge. Some Roman magistrates permitted the sale of certificates, called *libelli,* falsely attesting that the bearer had complied with the requirements of Roman religion.[73] Gibbon, commenting on this practice with the expected irony, observes that timid Christians could "reconcile, in some measure, their safety with their religion. A slight penance atoned for this profane dissimulation." [74] The story of the *libelli* does more than merely reveal how one might survive the Decian and

[70] *Ibid.,* 4.

[71] On the Decian persecution, see J. Lebreton and J. Zeiller, *A History of the Early Church,* Book III, ch. 6 (New York, 1962).

[72] See especially ch. 28, and cf. Jones, *op. cit.,* I, 33–35.

[73] For examples of *libelli,* see *Oxyrhynchus Papyri* 658, 1464.

[74] *Decline and Fall,* ch. 16:II, 107.

other persecutions. It touches one of the main factors in the inevitable defeat of paganism. Roman religion, in its official public form, consisted entirely of mechanical cult acts, while Christianity was based, to the true believer, on inner conviction and well-nigh helpless commitment.

Further waves of persecution dashed over the Church, especially during the reign of Valerian, beginning in 257. This movement, in turn, was canceled by Valerian's son Gallienus. In 260 he issued an edict of toleration. The text of this document is lacking, but from a passage in Eusebius we can read Gallienus' instructions advising that places of worship were to be open for use by any groups at their pleasure.[75] There is no reason to think that Gallienus' action proceeded from a more relaxed political situation or from any series of reassuring Roman victories. On the contrary, 260 was the lowest point reached in the third century by the suffering Roman Empire; a state of imminent ruin seemed indicated by the secession of Gaul, where the rebellious governor, Postumus, established an independent state. Amid all this trouble, Gallienus' edict was a surrender on another front, a first admission that Christianity could not be halted.

Some forty years of peace and expansion followed for Christianity. Diocletian, who was concerned to restore and steady the tottering Empire, tried, as part of his effort, to recall Rome to her ancestral religion. He did this especially by circulating images and titles of the old Roman gods on his coins; Jupiter and Hercules appear most prominently.[76] We need not be surprised at this movement, nor was it explicitly anti-Christian; it was rather a patriotic reaffirmation of the idea of Rome. Diocletian furthered the same movement by designating himself "Jovius" while his colleague Maximian took the name "Herculius." These

[75] Eusebius *Historia Ecclesiastica* 7.13.
[76] Mattingly, *op. cit.*, pp. 238 ff.

titles were meant to show that the rulers were under the
protection of Jupiter and Hercules. Representations of the
rulers often portray them in glorious vestments, but Diocletian and Maximian were not worshiped as actual gods
while they lived.

Later in his reign, from 303 onward, Diocletian allowed
another persecution of Christians; this one, the last, is also
called the "great" persecution. Historians agree that the
prime mover behind this persecution was Galerius, one of
the four rulers of Rome under the later system of Diocletian. This at least is the view taken by two ancient
sources, Eusebius and Lactantius.[77] If we combine their
opinion with the implication of Lactantius that Diocletian's wife Prisca and his daughter Valeria had all but
embraced Christianity,[78] we may be able to guess why
Diocletian held his hand for so long and did not make persecution one of his policies when he began his campaign in
favor of the Roman gods. The great persecution had its
effects, but in the end it too had to yield to the new idea. In
311 Galerius called off the persecution with his edict of
toleration, an edict that echoes and confirms that of Gallienus.[79] Christianity did not become the official religion
of the state until the reign of Theodosius I (378–395); its
victory is cynically described by Gibbon in chapter 28.
But the third century had closed with a final unsuccessful
attempt to arrest Christianity. Even in the failure we find
what we are looking for: evidence about the shifting
movement within the Roman Empire, about its change
from one thing into another.

[77] Eusebius *Historia Ecclesiastica* 8.4.; Lactantius *De mortibus
persecutorum* 10.
[78] Eusebius *Historia Ecclesiastica* 8.1; Lactantius *De mortibus
persecutorum* 15.
[79] Eusebius *Historia Ecclesiastica* 8.17; Lactantius *De mortibus
persecutorum* 34.

Only with Diocletian and his successors can we see what the third century meant to the Empire; only with the end of the process can we trace back and understand the changes. The pattern of the third century was one of more and more centralization, intolerance, lack of experiment, and neglect of human liberty. We may agree that this portion of history was deplorable, but in the same breath we must admit that it was contributing to the formation of the Byzantine state. This state, in turn, lasted for another thousand years after the traditional date for the "fall of Rome" in the West, a dubious term for a historical metamorphosis.[80]

Byzantium preserved Greek literature and thought in her libraries and collections until Greek manuscripts at last began to make their way back into the Western world, fertilizing it once more through the libraries of humanists and their patrons. On this view, we can hardly overstate the cultural importance of the ancient Greek town renamed in his own honor by Constantine. But Edward Gibbon found little to praise in Byzantine history. Only after Gibbon and his successors had mapped out virtually every feature of the classical period did others advance systematically to explore the Eastern Empire.

The work of these pioneers has therefore done much to place the third century in its proper historical setting. Indeed, a modern Gibbon might replace the poetically tragic title of the eighteenth-century masterpiece with a more prosaic one, denoting the transformation, not the fall, of an empire. We believe we understand better than anyone could have understood in Gibbon's day how the Empire suffered in the third century during its change into the long-lived Byzantine Empire. We can also see how its

[80] For a collection of essays about the fall of Rome, its causes, and its significance, see M. Chambers (ed.), *The Fall of Rome: Can It Be Explained?* (New York, 1963).

economy was developing features that would persist in the early Middle Ages. Government took the only way open to it and became despotic and even more centralized. And the tenacious new faith from the troublesome province of Judaea was winning the ultimate victory, a victory within the minds of men. The third century, for all its anarchy and turmoil, stands as one of the turning points in European history. It looms larger as we see the past more clearly.

II

THE IMPACT OF CHRISTIANITY

Gerhart B. Ladner

$\mathcal{S}$EVERAL YEARS before Edward Gibbon began to contemplate and describe the spectacle of *The Decline and Fall of the Roman Empire,* he wrote a curious sentence:

> The history of empires is that of the misery of man; the history of the sciences [and here he means all classes of knowledge, not only the natural sciences] is that of his greatness and happiness. . . . This reflection . . . should render this latter branch of study very dear to every lover of mankind.[1]

Thus begins his *Essay on the Study of Literature,* his first published work which appeared in French in 1761.

There can be no doubt that what Gibbon so often calls the "melancholy" character of historical events remained a concept essential to him as a historian throughout his life.[2] The peculiar blend of praise and censure of Christianity in the *Decline and Fall,* which at times represents the attitude

---

[1] The French text of the *Essai sur l'étude de la littérature* (hereafter cited as *Essai*) in John Lord Sheffield's edition of Gibbon's *Miscellaneous Works,* III (Basel, 1796), 141, reads as follows: "L'histoire des empires est celle de la misère des hommes. L'histoire des sciences est celle de leur grandeur et de leur bonheur. Si mille considérations doivent rendre ce dernier genre d'étude precieux aux yeux du philosophe, cette réflexion doit le rendre bien cher a tout amateur de l'humanité."

[2] Cf. *Decline and Fall,* ch. 15:II, 2, 19; also ch. 14:I, 410, and ch. 16:II, 106, 138.

of a haughty rationalist, often is animated by the serious and sympathetic ethos of a philanthropist or, to use Gibbon's term, an *amateur de l'humanité*, who possessed a sharp eye for not a few of the tragic failures as well as for some of the characteristic achievements of Christianity and for the effects of both upon the race of men.

It seems to me that Gibbon saw more than is generally recognized of the radical newness of Christianity and that he penetrated more deeply into its meaning than might be expected from his background. I am far from denying Gibbon's limitations in the understanding of many phenomena crucial to Christianity. He did after all live in eighteenth-century England with its mixture of an Anglican version of deism and of the doctrinaire rationalism of the Enlightenment, tempered though it might be by protoromantic trends and by the long tradition of natural and empirical checks and balances of English society. As a result, Gibbon was often led from a genuine show of sweet reasonableness to an unjust—and, to use one of his favorite expressions, "specious"—denunciation of superstitions, where we would rather speak of specific forms of religious sensibility and belief.

In spite of these time-bound limitations, Gibbon did have a sense and discernment of the melancholy or tragic element in history, and, in particular, of the unique concatenation of the tragic and the redeeming elements in Christian history.[3]

Gibbon speaks only rarely of the great Greek or Roman tragedians, though he had them all in his library from an early period of his life onward[4] and most probably had read them all. It would seem, though, that it was chiefly

[3] This has been recognized to some extent by G. Giarrizzo, *Edward Gibbon e la cultura europea del settecento* (Naples, 1954), pp. 206, 310 f.

[4] Cf. G. Keynes, *Edward Gibbon's Library* (London, 1940).

Homer, Virgil, and the great Roman historians who expressed for him the tragic and heroic sense of ancient myth and history.[5] This was more than enough to impart to him a stimulus that was a powerful influence in lifting his account of the tragedy of the Roman Empire far above that of his predecessors in Renaissance and baroque historiography, who, since Flavio Biondo, had tried to delineate Roman imperial decline.[6]

Perhaps it is possible to define classical tragedy, however imperfectly, as a parable of man's relation with the gods, in which his liberty is more than precariously balanced against the interplay of superior powers. In a remarkable passage of his *Essay*, Gibbon posits the underlying problem quite clearly when he declares that the ancients "saw everywhere the actions of gods, who inspired the weak mortals with virtue or vice, [mortals] who were incapable of escaping their will," and that in pagan Antiquity "a god was in charge of each event of life, each passion of the soul, and each division of society." [7]

Gibbon treats ancient polytheism throughout as a superstition.[8] Moreover, he denies the validity of classical historical determinism, and, while allowing for "general causes" in history, refuses to "reject design and accident." [9] He, of course, does not believe in the power of the ancient gods, or even of blind fate, and yet he cannot eliminate the tragic conflict between the intentions of the individual and suprapersonal forces.

[5] Cf. *Essai*, pp. 190 f., 164 ff., 177 f.
[6] For the historiographical tradition that leads from Flavio Biondo (d. 1463), *Historiarum ab inclinatione Romanorum imperii decades* (from 472 to 1440), to Gibbon, cf. C. Dawson, "Edward Gibbon," *Proceedings of the British Academy*, XX (London, 1934), 163, 173 f.
[7] *Essai*, p. 191.
[8] Cf. *Decline and Fall*, ch. 28:III, 188, 205; *Essai*, pp. 180–195.
[9] Cf. *Essai*, p. 195: "... pour peu qu'une action paroisse compliquée admettons y les causes générales, sans rejeter le dessein et le hasard."

This is perhaps why Gibbon does not give a comprehensive explanation or clear-cut reasons for the decline and fall of the Roman Empire. There were, to be sure, the decay of military virtue, the loss of political liberties, the increasing burden of taxation, and the deleterious effect of irregularly scattered luxury upon the economy and the morality of the Empire, and, finally, the substitution of the Church for the State as the principal object of loyalty for a new elite. Yet, which of these phenomena were more important than others, and how were general causes related to the actions of the individual protagonists in the great drama? Here Gibbon cannot give a simple answer any more than a dramatist can transform the course of a human tragedy into an argument of ineluctable logic.

Gibbon's famous conclusion that "the decline of Rome was the natural and inevitable effect of immoderate greatness" [10] has nevertheless more depth than Voltaire's dictum: "This Empire fell because it existed, for it is after all a fact that everything must fall." [11] It has more depth precisely because the concept of "immoderate greatness" has more specific connotations of tragedy than Voltaire's mere assertion of mutability. For Gibbon tries to explain how those same victorious legions that conquered the world for Rome could not resist the enervating effects of prolonged peace, the temptations of military power, and the influx and influence of potentially or actually hostile barbarian mercenaries and invaders.[12] More important, he shows how dearly the pacification of the Empire and the golden age of the Antonines were bought at the expense of

[10] Cf. *Decline and Fall*, "General Observations on the Fall of the Roman Empire in the West," following ch. 38:IV, 161.

[11] "Cet empire est tombé parce qu'il existait. Il faut bien que tout tombe," quoted by Dawson, *op. cit.*, p. 177, from Voltaire, *Dictionnaire philosophique*, ed. R. Naves and J. Benda, I (Paris, n.d.), 260.

[12] Cf. *Decline and Fall*, ch. 7:I, 194; also "General Observations," IV, 161–162.

free institutions of government.[13] Finally, and perhaps most importantly in the context of early Christian history, he makes us understand how new and peculiar elements of tragedy developed in imperial Rome from the sovereign and untrammelled individualism embodied in the emperors who had assumed the privileges and burdens of a godlike condition. The lives and reigns of a Commodus, a Caracalla, and a Heliogabalus, but also of a Constantine and a Constantius, as retold by Gibbon,[14] may be compared with Seneca's tragedies, of which, incidentally, Gibbon's library contained several copies.[15] This is a type of tragedy in which the drama is no longer primarily in the conflict between man and the gods or fate, as it was in Greek tragedy, but rather in the boundless hybris or the autocratic will of man himself who thinks himself as great as the gods or at least considers himself as the infallible interpreter of the divine will.[16]

I believe then that Gibbon really understood the tragic spirit of Greece and Rome, not only as expressed in literature, but also as manifest in historical events, and that when he speaks of the "melancholy" character of this or that phase of the decline and fall of Rome he is, if not always consciously mindful of tragedy, at least subtly influenced by his realization of it.

But when a historian of the Roman Empire reaches the moment in which the effect of Christianity upon the course of events cannot be overlooked, he is confronted by

[13] *Ibid.*, ch. 3:I, 59 ff.

[14] For Commodus, Caracalla, and Heliogabalus, cf. *ibid.*, ch. 4:I, 84 ff.; ch. 6:I, 131 ff., 144 ff.; though Gibbon used the *Historia Augusta* and Cassius Dio uncritically, it can hardly be said that he overly distorted the characters of these emperors. For Constantine the Great and Constantius, cf. ch. 18:II, 202 ff.; ch. 21:II, 359 ff.

[15] Cf. Keynes, *op. cit*

[16] Cf. the excellent introduction by T. Thomann to the Latin and German editions of Seneca's tragedies (Zurich and Stuttgart, 1961).

an altogether new problem with regard to the tragic or melancholy character of history, and it is part of Gibbon's greatness that he did not shirk the problem, though he did not do it full justice.

On the one hand, in the Christian view of things, the coming of Christ had once and for all overcome the tragic course of human history by lifting the destiny of man out of the range of those suprahuman or infrahuman forces symbolised or represented by the gods or by fate or by hybris, forces with which he could no longer cope by himself. On the other hand, even those who had responded to the new chance given to mankind, that is to say, the Christians, had not lastingly or not fully responded to it and had thus caused a new and, in a sense, worse tragedy than that of pre-Christian history. To Gibbon, and not to him alone, the tragedy of Christian history is that of a great promise only partially fulfilled.

Let us listen to Gibbon himself at the beginning of his famous fifteenth chapter on "The Progress of the Christian Religion":

> A candid but rational inquiry into the progress and establishment of Christianity may be considered as a very essential part of the history of the Roman Empire. While that great body was invaded by open violence, or undermined by slow decay, a pure and humble religion gently insinuated itself into the minds of men, grew up in silence and obscurity, derived new vigour from opposition, and finally erected the triumphant banner of the Cross on the ruins of the Capitol. . . .
>
> But this inquiry, however useful or entertaining, is attended with two peculiar difficulties. The scanty and suspicious materials of ecclesiastical history seldom enable us to dispel the dark cloud that hangs over the first age of the Church. The great law of impartiality too often obliges us to reveal the imperfections of the uninspired teachers and believers of the Gospel; and, to a careless observer, their faults may seem to cast a shade on the faith which

they professed. But the scandal of the pious Christian, and the fallacious triumph of the infidel, should cease as soon as they recollect not only by whom, but likewise to whom, the divine revelation was given. The theologian may indulge the pleasing task of describing religion as she descended from heaven, arrayed in her native purity. A more melancholy duty is imposed on the historian. He must discover the inevitable mixture of error and corruption, which she contracted in a long residence upon earth, among a weak and degenerate race of beings.[17]

To this text one of Gibbon's editors, the well-known Anglican divine H. H. Millman, adds the following comment: "Divest this whole passage of the latent sarcasm betrayed by the subsequent tone of the whole disquisition, and it might commence a Christian history, written in the most Christian spirit of candour."[18]

I must say that I do not find much latent sarcasm here, nor do I believe that Gibbon, out of prudence or fear of ecclesiastical persecution, dissembled his true feelings about the Christian religion when he remarked on the lofty character of early Christianity or on its later contributions to civilization. Had he been afraid or prudent, he would never have affected the ironical, sarcastic, even hostile tone that he did indeed use toward Christianity and Christians on many occasions.[19]

The main problem, then, confronting the historian who wants to understand the innovating power of Christianity

[17] *Decline and Fall*, ch. 15:II, 1 f.

[18] H. H. Milmann's edition of *Decline and Fall*, II (Paris, 1840), 44n.

[19] Regarding this whole matter see also Gibbon's *Vindication of Some Passages in the Fifteenth and Sixteenth Chapters of the Decline and Fall of the Roman Empire* (*Miscellaneous Works*, V [Basel, 1797]); cf. D. M. Low, *Edward Gibbon* (New York, 1937) p. 262. The most comprehensive account of Gibbon's hostility toward many aspects of the Christian religion is that of S. T. McCloy, *Gibbon and His Antagonism to Christianity . . . and the Discussions That It Has Provoked* (New York and London, 1933), ch. i.

in ancient and later history can be stated in terms that I think are not alien to Gibbon: If the essence of Christianity was tragically diminished by events of Christian history, what was its lasting newness, its actual greatness?

Gibbon himself discusses five characteristics of early Christianity which, according to him, made up the newness and the greatness that led to its success: the zeal of the Christians, their doctrine of a future life, their miracles, their pure and austere morality, and, finally, the development of hierarchical government in the Church concurrently with the decline of political government in the state, or to use Gibbon's own words, "the union and discipline of the Christian republic, which gradually formed an independent and increasing state in the heart of the Roman Empire." [20] Obviously, these five points, in spite of their significance, do not suffice to define the tremendous and truly decisive change that Christianity brought about in the world.[21]

Among the foremost idiosyncrasies that caused Gibbon to slight essential aspects of Christianity were his contempt for theology [22] and his hatred of monasticism.[23] As a result, he did not see that the meaning of Christianity for the late Roman Empire cannot be intellectually grasped if there is no clear understanding of who and what Christians of that time believed Christ was; he therefore underestimated the religious and intellectual importance of the trinitarian and Christological disputes of the first four

[20] *Decline and Fall,* ch. 15:II 2, 54.

[21] A good, comprehensive view of the newness of Christianity in the midst of its historical surroundings is given by K. Prümm, *Christentum als Neuheitserlebnis* (Freiburg im Breisgau, 1939).

[22] Cf. especially *Decline and Fall,* ch. 21:II, 335 ff.; e.g., 341, on Trinitarian disputes: "These speculations, instead of being treated as the amusement of a vacant hour, became the most serious business of the present, and the most useful preparation for a future life."

[23] Cf. especially *ibid.,* ch. 37:IV, 57 ff.

general councils. Nor did he recognize that the monks were the greatest fighters against that recurrent contamination of Christianity by the worldliness he so deplored: he failed to appreciate that monasticism was an attempt to establish a purer form of the Christian life than that which could be expected from the whole Church once it had become very large and very mixed. One might go even further and assert that Gibbon, great historian though he was, did not fully understand the new dimensions that the concepts of time and history had received in Christian thought through the coming of Christ and the phenomenon of the Church.

In the following discussion of Christianity I omit two of the elements Gibbon considered essential: the belief in a future life and the belief in miracles. It is true that the Christians developed these beliefs in a very special way,[24] but, even though Gibbon is right in assuming that they greatly contributed to the success of the Christian religion,[25] they were and are to be found also in various forms outside Christianity. It is different with Gibbon's three remaining reasons for the victory of the Christians over the pagans. We may use them as starting points for the investigation of the innovating force of Christianity if we

[24] Thus, for instance, the Judeo-Christian emphasis on the resurrection of the body differs from the Hindu and Greek emphasis on the immortality of the soul.

[25] In this connection, it is interesting to note, Gibbon seems to admit with some sincerity the occurrence of miracles at least for the life of Jesus and for apostolic times, if not for the whole span of the first two or three centuries of the Christian era. He is puzzled about where to draw the chronological line between the ages in which miracles occurred and in which, according to him, they no longer occurred. Cf. *Decline and Fall*, ch. 15:II, 30 f., with Pascal's famous chapter on miracles in his *Pensées*, ed. L. Brunschvicg, reprint, Collection Internationale (Garden City, N.Y., 1961), e.g., no. 852, p. 254: "Les miracles sont plus importants que vous ne pensez: ils ont servi à la fondation, et serviront à la continuation de l'Eglise."

somewhat widen their scope. What Gibbon calls zeal—and his feeling about zeal and zealots was, to say the least, ambivalent [26]—was really a new attitude to truth based on the event of the Incarnation; what he calls pure and austere morality involved a new approach both to ethics and to asceticism, culminating in the triumph of the monastic ideal; and what he considers the growth of an ecclesiastical state within the political state was, in fact, only one aspect of the life of the Christian Church which saw itself peculiarly suspended between heaven and earth, between eternity and time, and thus, among other things, produced a new conception of history.[27]

Let us then first look at Christianity's new attitude toward truth. It was, above all, an exclusive attitude; it was an exact opposite of the pluralistic conception of religion prevalent in the Greco-Roman—oriental milieu of late Antiquity into which Christ was born. I need hardly recall how amicably Isis, Mithras, the Great Mother, the Invincible Sun, and other deities were associated in the Pantheon of the Roman Empire with the Olympian gods and the cult of Roma and the Emperor and how amazed and indignant the Romans were when they discovered that the Christians did not recognize any god except their own. But Christians had no choice in the matter if they wanted to be faithful

[26] Cf., for instance, *Decline and Fall*, ch. 21:II, 340, 343, 353, 390 f.

[27] I should like to thank Professor Lynn White, jr., chairman of the "Gibbon Lectures," for his felicitous suggestion that it might be well to center this paper on the Christian attitudes to truth and morality and on Church-state relations, and thus to make a judicious choice among the many "novelties" of the Christian religion. Cf. also C. Schneider, *Geistesgeschichte des antiken Christentums*, II (Munich, 1954), 274, 308 ff., 314 ff., 332 ff., for the renovating effects that the "absolute" claims of the Christian faith and its uncompromising ethical postulates had on the late ancient world, notwithstanding the dangers of intolerance, bigotry, and anxiety which were gradually to emerge, as they are bound to do in all associations of human beings.

to their Master, who, according to the Gospel of St. John, had said: "I am the Way, and the Truth, and the Life" (John 14:6).

There seem to be three important exceptions, however, to the novelty and uniqueness of the Christian attitude toward truth. These are the Greek, the Jewish, and the Buddhist attitudes. A very brief discussion of each will help us to understand Christianity better.

First, the deep and admirable search for supreme and even divine truth in Greek philosophical thought from Socrates to Plotinus, while it had never revoked its dedication to reason, had nevertheless not been lacking in religious elements. Yet, the ultimate quasi-religious realities of the classical conception of truth had remained in the realm of poetic myth as in Plato, or of cosmic intuition as in Aristotle, or of mystic speculation as in Plotinus, whereas the Christians believed and claimed that the truly divine had entered into experienced history, into verifiable reality. This, according to Christianity, was what happened in the Incarnation.

As Professor Harry Wolfson has so clearly shown in his books on Philo [28] and on the philosophy of the Church Fathers,[29] the meeting of the Judeo-Christian religious revelation with the Greco-Roman habits of rational thought produced a new kind of theological philosophy or philosophical theology, which is one of the great achievements of the human mind, though this achievement carries with it great problems of its own. The historical, as well as metahistorical, character of the New Testament religion forced the mind of Christians to come to terms that were rational and at the same time "binding" with events and phenomena, such as the Incarnation and the Church,

[28] H. A. Wolfson, *Philo* (Cambridge, Mass., 1947).
[29] H. A. Wolfson, *The Philosophy of the Church Fathers*, I (Cambridge, Mass., 1956).

which to them were both actual and transcendent. For the Greeks to learn how to *know* truly had been a sure way to become good or even godlike. For the Christians, the situation was somewhat different: Christ himself was the ultimate truth, and he had entrusted it to his Church. Not to know, or not to accept, this truth seemed incompatible with true goodness. Heresy was considered a moral defect because it was a lack of love for the Church of Christ, a Christ who had become incarnate and a Church in which he continued to live on mysteriously. The certainty of possessing the truth eclipsed the religious pluralism of late Antiquity, and only very slowly was this Christian certainty to learn how to respect religious dissent.

It is because of the Jewish refusal to accept the Christian view of Christ Incarnate that the second apparent exception to the novelty and uniqueness of the Christian attitude toward religious truth is no real exception either. On Christian premises, Jewish faith in the one true God was incomplete if compared with the corresponding Christian belief, except in so far as it prophesied and foreshadowed the coming of a God-Man and His universal role as the bringer of supreme truth to all men. And it radically differed from the Christian faith in so far as it wanted to keep the one God and the Messiah the property of the Jewish people alone. Moreover, Christ himself had strongly asserted his divine sonship, whereas the Jews thought of the Messiah as a God-sent but otherwise merely human being.

How much the Christian attitude to truth is centered in the person of a divine Christ can be seen if we compare the two accounts of creation found in the first chapter of the Book of Genesis and in the prologue to the Gospel of St. John, respectively. The book of Genesis begins with the words: "In the beginning God created heaven and earth. And the earth was void and empty, and darkness was upon the face of the deep; and the Spirit of God moved over the waters" (Gen. 1:1 f.). This means that God created both heaven, which is spiritual, and earth, which is material. This conception was an advance over those old oriental, and especially Babylonian, dualistic creation accounts, according to which the spiritual powers of heaven had to overcome preexistent material and chaotic forces, so that the cosmos, an ordered universe, could emerge. In the Gospel of St. John, however, the traces of the old dualism have become even more subordinate: "In the beginning was the Word, and the Word was with God, and the Word was God. . . . All things were made by Him: and without Him was made nothing that was made. In Him was life and the life was the light of men. . . . That was the true light, which enlighteneth every man that cometh into this world." Here creation is clearly from nothing and the spiritual and unique character of the creational act has become even more explicit through the fact that creation is carried out by God's own Word, the Logos, Christ, who is also His Divine Son.

The Christian conception of truth then is rooted in a God who is both a Creator-God and God Incarnate. And this brings us to the last of the three attitudes to truth which at first glance seem to compete with the Christian one, the Buddhist attitude. The Buddha certainly came to teach religious truth, above all the four holy truths of his Sermon of Benares, which are concerned with suffering and the overcoming of suffering. Yet the content of Buddhist truth taken as a whole is quite different from that of Christian truth taken as a whole. The Buddha himself never claimed that he was in any way connected with the creation of this world or that he was the Son of God, God Incarnate. Even when Mahayana Buddhism conceived of a succession of Buddhas, in all of whom an ultimate divine reality or truth was embodied, this belief was not so much one of Incarnation in the Christian sense of the term as one of reincarnation. The Buddhas have passed through many deaths and reincarnations before achieving Buddhahood. Bodhisattvas or future Buddhas may stand at the threshold of Buddhahood, capable of entering Nirvana if they so choose, but may nevertheless submit to further reincarnation for the benefit of mankind.

Such pluralistic views of reincarnation differ greatly from basic Christian assertions of incarnational and redemptional belief such as St. Augustine's statement in his *City of God:* "Christ died once and for all for our sins." [30] Here everything is centered on the uniqueness of the deity's entry into our world; furthermore, in the radically sacrificial character of this divine intervention, the effectiveness of which could be real, however, only if Christ was in truth God and Man.

The novel Christian conception of truth is therefore based on the belief that a man, Jesus, was himself the Supreme Truth, in other words, that he was truly God. How exactly could this be possible? The two general councils of Ephesus and Chalcedon in 431 and 451 attempted to answer this question in their debates and decisions against heretics who stressed either the humanity of Christ at the expense of his divinity, or his divinity at the cost of his humanity. The first of these two councils was directed against Nestorius of Constantinople's teaching about the Incarnation, in which, according to his opponents, he overemphasized Christ's humanity. It may hold our attention for a moment, for, among all general councils of the Church, it is one of the most "melancholy" in Gibbon's sense of the term, and nevertheless it succeeded in defending one of the most essential tenets of Christianity. Nestorius' chief antagonist, the Patriarch Cyril of Alexandria,

---

[30] *De civitate Dei* XII 14, ed. B. Dombart, I (Leipzig, 1908), 532.

is the crucial figure in both respects.[31] He used dubious and perhaps reprehensible means to reach his goal, the condemnation of Nestorius, who had good reasons for writing a book entitled *Tragedy* about his experiences.[32] Gibbon is rightly indignant about the way in which Nestorius and his Antiochene friends were treated and rightly censures the intrigues, briberies, and violence of Cyril and his followers. He allows that "humanity may drop a tear on the fate of Nestorius"[33] (in spite of the latter's own inhumanity in the prosecution of heretics). Yet even though we may well be repelled by Cyril's methods[34] and even if Nestorius really was condemned unjustly or for the wrong reasons,[35] such considerations cannot, I think, alter the fact that it was Cyril and not Nestorius who asserted and saved the core of Christian religiousness. This core was the belief that the divine Logos, the Word of God, had become flesh and that therefore in the union between the divine and the human nature which exists in Christ Incarnate, the divine Logos Himself had remained the unifying subject, as it were, rather than being only one of the two natures present in the union.[36]

[31] Gibbon deals with Cyril, Nestorius, and the Council of Ephesus in *Decline and Fall*, ch. 47:V, 107 ff.

[32] Only fragments survive; cf. F. Loofs, *Nestoriana* (Halle, 1905).

[33] *Decline and Fall*, ch. 47:V, 121.

[34] Cf. the balanced account of Cyril's life by G. Bardy, "Cyrille d'Alexandrie," *Dictionnaire d'histoire et de géographie ecclésiastiques*, XIII (Paris, 1956), 1169 ff., and the less balanced, but still instructive, studies by E. Schwartz, "Zur Vorgeschichte des ephesinischen Konzils," *Historische Zeitschrift*, CXII (1914), 237 ff., and "Cyrill und der Mönch Viktor," *Sitzungsberichte der Akademie der Wissenschaften in Wien, Philosophische-historische Klasse*, CCVIII (1928), 4.

[35] Cf. M. V. Anastos, "Nestorius Was Orthodox," *Dumbarton Oaks Papers*, XVI (1962), 119 ff.

[36] I may refer here to A. Grillmeier, "Das Scandalum oecumenicum des Nestorius," *Scholastik*, XXXVI (1961), 332 ff.; T. Camelot, "De

The safeguarding of the doctrine of Christ's full divinity by Cyril corresponded to one of the deepest concerns of the Christian, and especially of the Greek Christian, soul: the desire for deification, for godlikeness even in this life.[37] Only if the Christ who walked on this earth as a man was at the same time truly a divine being could man hope to be deified to the extent of his capacity.

Western Christendom was to express assimilation to God, imitation of Christ, more in terms of sanctification than of divinization; the idea of holiness as well as that of godlikeness had been inherited by Christianity from Judaism, but the former idea seems to have remained less susceptible to Greek philosophical influence than the latter. However this may be, in terms of sanctity, too, only the fullest conceivable, that is to say, truly divine, holiness of Christ could form the presupposition for the achievement of sainthood by man, which again is ultimately his union with God.[38]

Cyril's mystical theology certainly continued the best

Nestorius à Eutyches," in *Das Konzil von Chalkedon*, I (Würzburg, 1951), 213 ff.; C. J. Hefele and H. Leclercq, *Histoire des conciles*, II, pt. 1 (Paris, 1908), 247. Cyril's is a doctrine of the *person* of Christ (cf. Camelot, *op. cit.*, pp. 230 f.), whereas Nestorius' is one of *natures*, which was influenced by the Aristotelian and Stoic trends of the School of Antioch (cf. *ibid.*, p. 228; also E. v. Ivanka, *Hellenisches und Christliches im frühbyzantinischen Geistesleben* [Vienna, 1948], pp. 84–92). It is the divine Logos Incarnate of the Council of Ephesus, of St. Cyril of Alexandria, and of the Council of Chalcedon who appears in the majestic Pantocrator images of Byzantine and Romanesque art. For the Athanasian, anti-Arian origin of the Christological Pantocrator title cf. P. Beskow, *Rex Gloriae* (Stockholm, 1962), pp. 295 ff.

[37] Cf. J. Liebaert, *La doctrine christologique de saint Cyrille d'Alexandrie avant la querelle nestorienne* (Lille, 1951), pp. 218 ff.: "La médiation du Verbe incarné," and 229 ff.: "La déification de l'humanité"; in general, cf. J. Gross, *La divinisation du chrétien d'après les pères grecs* (Paris, 1938).

[38] See also below, p. 76.

tradition of the spirituality of the Greek Christian East. It is all the more distressing for us, as it was for Gibbon, to see that high mystical thought could be joined to an unscrupulous ecclesiastical policy, which was largely governed by the long-standing rivalries between the patriarchal sees of Alexandria and Constantinople and, combined with monastic fanaticism,[39] could, after Cyril's death, lead to the regrettable events of the so-called Robber Synod of Ephesus of 449. Yet the melancholy moral deficiencies of some mystics and monks must not make one forget that mysticism and monasticism were in many ways the most sublime products of that great renewal of morality which was brought about by Christianity and which, according to Gibbon, was one of the reasons for its success.

"The pure and austere morality of the Christians," "the reformation of manners which was introduced into the world by the preaching of the Gospels," were inseparable in Gibbon's eyes "from the divine persuasion which enlightened or subdued the understanding." [40]

And, indeed, in Christianity the link between the religious and the moral sphere was unprecedented in closeness. That a man must strive for moral goodness in order to worship God effectively is not a commonplace in the history of religions. Christian morality was all the more novel in the late ancient milieu as it included sexual purity centered around virginity or around strict fidelity in monogamous marriage. In the ethical sphere, too, the New Testament message amounted to a great religious innovation, though the Old Testament had prepared the way.

In classical Antiquity, morality had, on the whole, been the domain of philosophy rather than of religion. The

---

[39] Cf., for instance, H. Bacht, "Die Rolle des orientalischen Mönchtums in den kirchenpolitischen Auseinandersetzungen um Chalkedon (431–519)," in *Das Konzil von Chalkedon*, II (Würzburg, 1953), 193 ff.

[40] Cf. *Decline and Fall*, ch. 15:II, 2, 32.

doings of the Olympian and non-Olympian gods were certainly no model of pure morals. On the other hand, Judaism, governed by legal as well as by ethical postulates, had
not so consistently set morality and its culmination in love
above the law as Christ was to do.[41]

Gibbon touches upon a very important point when he
links the Christian reformation of morality to repentance,[42] for repentance (*metanoia*), a complete change of
mind or heart, was exactly what Jesus demanded of those
who wanted to enter the Kingdom of God.[43] Yet Gibbon
rationalistically underestimates the range of the phenomenon of penitence. He has little more to say about it other
than that many a saint was first a sinner. But there was
considerably more to it. Gibbon does not sufficiently an-
alyze, because he does not sufficiently understand, Christian ethics, which is an ethic of spiritual perfection
modeled after a mediator between God and man, who was
morally, and in every other respect, a perfect man and the
divine Son of a perfect God. In Christianity the best way,
perhaps the only way, not to be a sinner is to strive to be a
saint, is to imitate Christ and thus to be united with God,
to be deified.[44]

[41] Later, when the Church had developed an elaborate legal system
of its own, it did not always follow Christ's example in this respect.
Nevertheless, in the classical canon law from the twelfth to the
fourteenth century the bond of love and the bond of law were not
mutually exclusive; justice and mercy did meet on the plane of law
(paraphrased from S. G. Kuttner, *Harmony from Dissonance: An
Interpretation of Medieval Canon Law,* Wimmer Lecture X [Latrobe,
Pa., 1960], p. 50).

[42] *Decline and Fall,* ch. 5:II, 32.

[43] Cf., for instance, Mark 1:15.

[44] Cf. above p. 74. Gibbon completely misunderstood the meaning of godlikeness and holiness in the Christian religion and the role
of the saints as models and intercessors for more ordinary Christians.
As he did so often, he saw here, too, only the excesses, and used a well-
worn cliché in labeling the Christian veneration of saints a renewal of
polytheism (cf. *Decline and Fall,* ch. 28:III, 212 f.). On the meaning

In the greatest document of Christian ethics, the Sermon on the Mount, Christ said to all men, "Be you therefore perfect, as also your Heavenly Father is perfect" (Matt. 5:48). To be a true Christian means to follow the commandments of this perfect God: "By their fruits you will know them" (Matt. 7:16) and "Not everyone that saith to Me, Lord, Lord, shall enter into the Kingdom of Heaven; but he that doth the will of my Father, who is in Heaven, he shall enter into the Kingdom of Heaven" (Matt. 7:21). Other scriptural texts, both in the Old and the New Testament, indicate, however, that perfection is not merely justice or righteousness; it is, above all, altruistic love as described in St. Paul's great hymn on charity in the First Letter to the Corinthians (ch. 13). Such love begins and ends with the love of God and includes depreciation of self-love in one's love for others. "Thou shalt love the Lord thy God with thy whole heart and with thy whole soul and with thy whole mind," and "Thou shalt love thy neighbour as thyself" (Matt. 22:37, 39; cf. Mark 12:31, Deut. 6:5, Levit. 19:18).

It is difficult to conceive of a higher goal of ethical perfection. Nevertheless, the qualms of a wealthy young man elicited from Christ an even more specific statement on what perfection is. This statement is known by an almost technical term as the counsels of perfection: "If thou wilt be perfect, go, sell what thou hast, and give to the poor . . . and come follow me." This text from Matthew 19:21 played a great role in that concentration of Christian virtue called monasticism.[45]

The origins of monasticism in the strict sense coincided

of sanctity for the early Christians, cf. H. Delehaye, *Sanctus* (Brussels, 1927), pp. 24 ff., and V. G. Bardy, *La conversion au christianisme durant les premiers siècles* (Paris, 1949), pp. 146 ff.

[45] There is no real evidence of dependence of Christian monasticism on pre-Christian monasticism, such as that of the probably Essenian sect of Qumran.

approximately with the moment in the history of the Church in which she was confronted by the new tasks and dangers resulting from her having become a power, not only in the spiritual but also in the material order; and, from that time onward, those who in one manner or another followed the monastic way of life were the principal agents of reform in the Christian world. The monks, however, went to the desert not only because they sought a moral perfection that was hard to attain in the world; this to them was only a stepping-stone to higher things. Their greatest desire was to anticipate on earth by their prayers the perpetual praise of God by the angels and saints in Heaven.[46]

As a group, the monks were the most spiritual Christians. They were the foremost witnesses for the so-called eschatological aspect of Christian existence, that is to say, through their constant prayers they prepared themselves and others for whom they prayed for the "eschata," the last things, the return of Christ as judge of the world. Wealth and sexual love therefore meant nothing to them; some, in fact, overreacted against the luxury and sexual excesses of late ancient society by practising eccentric forms of asceticism. No doubt monasticism in general tended to emphasize those relatively moderate dualistic and puritanical strains present in Christianity since its early days, especially with regard to sexuality. Yet the monks, in spite of their spiritualism, never went so far as the rigorously dualistic Gnostics and Manichaeans in rejecting and opposing the material and corporeal world: they supplemented rather than denied the validity of the latter.

Significantly, it was the liturgical worship of God in the

[46] For the early Christian conception of monasticism as an angelic life, cf., for instance, A. Lamy, "Bios Angelikos," *Dieu vivant*, VII (n.d.), 57 ff.

monastic community which made the spiritual and eschatological mentality of the monks manifest first in chanted
prayer and religious poetry and art and then in the transference of the monastic principle of ordered peace under
spiritual guidance to ecclesiastical life at large and more
generally to the life of Christian society.

The early history of monasticism was at times marred,
especially in the Christian East, by tragically un-Christian
narrow-mindedness and militancy, whether the monks
merely defended their own ideals or supported hierarchic
faction leaders. Yet Gibbon and like-minded critics were
greatly mistaken in seeing all asceticism and monasticism
as escapism or as fanaticism. On the contrary, the con-
structive contributions of monasticism were many and
varied, and the underlying ascetic spirit gave to the monastic and quasi-monastic communities a dynamic impulse
that did not remain limited to the search for individual
perfection, but enabled them to assume reforming and
innovating leadership in almost all crucial phases of late
ancient, medieval, and early modern Church history. The
monastic and religious orders were the spiritual avant-
garde in the Church's periodically repeated renewal.[47]

It is impossible to enumerate or discuss all monastic
accomplishments on this occasion. Let me mention only
two points. One is the combination of ascetic god-seeking
and of intellectual labor which one of the great Benedictine scholars of our own age, Dom Jean Leclercq, in the
title of a famous book, has characterized as "The Love of
Learning and the Desire for God." [48] We all owe very
much to the medieval monks' conviction that the pursuit
of both secular and sacred knowledge is a God-pleasing en-

[47] Cf. Gerhart B. Ladner, *The Idea of Reform* (Cambridge, Mass.,
1959), pp. 319 ff.

[48] J. Leclercq, *L'amour des lettres et le désir de Dieu* (Paris, 1957);
English trans. by Catherine Misrahi, *The Love of Learning and the
Desire for God* (New York, 1961).

terprise. On such grounds they not only preserved in their manuscript copies the Christian and pagan classics, but also, between the sixth and the twelfth century, developed a literature and art of their own which, in an intellectually and aesthetically inspiring way, blended mystical and humanistic elements.

The second point is the emergence of a new ethos of work even in occupations of a physical and menial kind. This new attitude was by no means exclusively Benedictine; it was part and parcel of the monastic outlook from the times of St. Pachomius, St. Basil, and St. Augustine to those of St. Bernard of Clairvaux and of St. Francis of Assisi.[49] The conception of work well done, a conception not altogether extinct in our civilization, is much indebted to this monastic ethos.

We now finally must fix our attention on that new and peculiarly Christian phenomenon known as the Church, whose constitution and government Gibbon both appreciates as a historian and dislikes as a devotee of the Enlightenment. His much discussed contention that Christianity, and especially the emergence of an organized Church, had a great share in the decline and fall of the Rome Empire,[50] because loyalty to the Church replaced loyalty to the State, is to a large extent refuted by the long continued existence of the Byzantine Empire and of its flourishing Greco-Roman–oriental Christian culture, of which Gibbon had only a dim conception. From this point of view, perhaps more than from any other, the grand formula he uses to summarize the conception of his work, "I have described

---

[49] Two references may stand here for many: St. Benedict *Regula* 48, ed. P. Schmitz (3d ed. and French trans.; Maredsous, 1962), pp. 140 ff.; St. Francis of Assisi *Testamentum* 5, ed. H. Boehmer, *Analekten zur Geschichte des Franciscus von Assisi* (Tübingen and Leipzig, 1904), pp. 37f.

[50] See especially *Decline and Fall*, "General Observations on the Fall of the Roman Empire in the West," IV, 162 f.

the triumph of barbarism and religion," [51] appears as false as it seems seductive. Whether in the West, too, the Empire could have survived, in spite of the more violent onslaught of the barbarians and the more serious socio-economic situation, if such great Christian leaders as St. Ambrose of Milan or St. Leo the Great had wholeheartedly served the state rather than the Church, is perhaps not an idle question, but one that hardly permits a sure answer. And even if an affirmative answer could be given to this question, it would only lead to another problem that involves a value judgment: whether an integral preservation of the Roman Empire and its culture would have been more desirable than the new way of life of Christianity, the new world of the Church. [52]

The novelty of the Christian Church was not absolute, but, nevertheless, it was very real. Even the most closely comparable pre-Christian religious community, the *sangha* of the followers of the Buddha, lacks not a few of the significant connotations of the Christian Church. In the Mediterranean world, at any rate, the emergence of the Church was in many ways unprecedented.

In Near Eastern and Greco-Roman Antiquity, religion had been primarily an affair of the state. [53] Personal and sectarian religiousness had not been lacking, but they did not form a comprehensive socio-religious community outside and beyond the political or ethnical sphere. Aristotle's postulate in the first book of his *Politics* was still valid at

---

[51] Cf. *ibid.*, ch. 71:VII, 308.

[52] Gibbon himself, "General Observations," IV, 163, seems to touch from afar the heart of the problem when he declares: ". . . but if superstition [he is speaking of monasticism, his pet abhorrence] had not afforded a decent retreat, the same vices [namely, servile and effeminate indolence] would have tempted the unworthy Romans to desert, from baser motives, the standard of the republic."

[53] See, for instance, the classic disquisition by N. D. Fustel de Coulanges, *La cité antique* (1864), English trans. by W. Small (1873).

the end of classical Antiquity: ". . . the state or political community, which is the highest of all and which embraces all the rest, aims at good in a greater degree than any other." [54] In contrast with this, consider a famous statement by St. Augustine: "Two loves have made two cities, love of self unto contempt of God the earthly city, love of God unto contempt of self the heavenly city." [55] For Augustine, the community that pursues the highest good, that is, God, is not a state but a suprapolitical, supranational, and supranatural society, mixed on this earth with the earthly or worldly society, but nevertheless extending beyond to embrace its members in heaven. This is the Augustinian City of God, which very largely overlaps with the concept of the Church; there does remain a distinctness between the two concepts [56] which does not, however, concern us here.

All great social concepts of Christianity, be it the Kingdom of God or the Communion of Saints, the Church or the City of God, were conceived as immanent in this world, as visible, struggling, and time-bound, and, at the same time, as transcendent, as invisible, as triumphant, and as eternal in the world to come. There was, then, a Church as the community of the faithful on earth and a Church as the congregation of the heavenly city consisting of its citizens, that is to say, the saints and the angels. It is one of the great paradoxes of Christianity that such a concept as the Church can appear under these two aspects and nevertheless be ultimately one. For even though the many evil men who are part of the visible Church will never be found in its heavenly counterpart, the terrestrial and the celestial Church are seen as identical because only the good

[54] Aristotle *Politics* I. 1. 1252a.

[55] Augustine *De civitate Dei* XIV, 28, ed. B. Dombart, II (Leipzig, 1905), 56.

[56] Cf. Ladner, *op. cit.*, pp. 270–283.

and the reformable are believed to make up the *true* Church, either in this life or the next, either now or at the end of history.[57]

The general tension between the divine and the human element in the organism of the Church repeats itself in different forms on two more particularized levels: in the tension between the clergy and laity, or, to be more exact, between the hierarchy and the community of the faithful, and in the tension between the spiritual and the temporal concerns of the Church.

The Church, according to the developed doctrine of the Middle Ages,[58] is, on the one hand, the community of all believers who, in a mysterious way, have, according to St. Paul (I Cor. 12:12 ff.), become the body of Christ on earth and all of whom possess, according to St. Peter (I Peter 2:5, 9), a certain priestly character. On the other hand, the Church is in a very special way represented by the corporation of the hierarchy, that is to say, by the ordained bishops and priests who alone are able, again in a mysterious, though real, way to call the celestial body of Christ down upon the altar in the great sacramental act of worship called the eucharistic sacrifice or the Mass.

The hierarchical aspect of the Church had been decisive for the relationship between Church and state since the time of Constantine the Great, if not earlier. Since Pope Gregory VII in the eleventh century, the clerical hier

----

[57] Cf. Augustine *De civitate Dei* I, 35, ed. Dombart, I, 51, about evil men in the City of God "who are connected to her through the communion of the sacraments, but will not be with her in the eternal lot of the saints."

[58] The literature on the subject is enormous. For a brief survey, cf. Gerhart B. Ladner, "The Concepts of 'Ecclesia' and 'Christianitas' . . . , *Sacerdozio e Regno* . . . , Miscellanea Historiae Pontificiae, XVIII (Rome, 1954), 49 ff.; also F. Merzbacher, "Wandlungen des Kirchenbegriffs im Spätmittelalter," *Zeitschrift der Savigny-Stiftung für Rechtsgeschichte*, Kanonist. Abteil. XXXIX (1953), 274 ff.

archy, explicitly concentrated toward the papal office, became even more important in political-ecclesiastical relations. In Catholic countries this has remained so, at least in
principle, through early modern times. Not surprisingly,
such a development was accompanied by a corresponding
rise of hierarchical power, and it is easy enough for Gibbon
to present the history of the ecclesiastical hierarchy as the
history of ecclesiastical power politics.[59] It was that, but it
was not only that. It is hardly necessary to recall how hierarchs such as St. Athanasius, St. Basil, and St. Ambrose
defended the liberty of the Church and through it the
freedom of the spirit against the brute political power of
the state, which, though Christianized, had nevertheless
not quite given up the ancient and ever-tempting fusion
and confusion of the religious and political spheres. It was
probably unavoidable that the supremacy of the spiritual
order which the Church claimed against the material order
of the world, would gradually come to mean that the
Church itself could exercise its, by then considerable, material power, and even coercive material power. It would
do so in the Middle Ages and early modern times whenever
its own spiritual mission in the world with regard to Christian doctrine and morals was directly or even indirectly
involved.

A temptation to transgress limits, a temptation different
but hardly less dangerous than that inherited from Antiquity by the state, did in certain periods lead the hierarchical Church toward an undifferentiated spiritualism [60] that

[59] *Decline and Fall*, ch. 15:II, 39 ff. and *passim*.

[60] Concerning the existence of this "spiritualism" in the medieval
and early modern theories of papal direct or indirect power in temporal matters, cf. J. C. Murray, "St. Robert Bellarmine on the Indirect
Power," *Theological Studies*, IX (1948), 491 ff.; F. Kempf, "Die
päpstliche Gewalt in der mittelalterlichen Welt," in *Saggi Storici
intorno al Papato*, Miscellanea Historiae Pontificiae, XXI (Rome,
1959), 146–153, and "Die Katholische Lehre von der Gewalt der
Kirche über das Zeitliche," *Catholica*, XII (1958), 50 ff. Cf. also
p. 85, below.

could become a pretext for the overextension of the exercise of material power. At the same time and despite the warnings of far-seeing hierarchs such as Pope Gregory the Great, the hierarchy, while claiming material power on spiritual grounds, would rarely attempt to improve fundamentally those depressed material conditions of the majority of mankind which made a healthy spiritual life difficult.[61] Simplistic spiritualism of this kind was altogether harmful to the dignity of the full human person when it placed the whole field of manual work, including all economic and technological activity, on a low level in the scale of values.[62] Such attitudes, on the whole, were not shared by the monks, but rather were characteristic of certain hierarchs. The hierarchical office had been founded as a ministerial office, above all for the sake of the humble and the poor, above all for those who toiled and suffered under the material pressures of this world. Yet the record of the hierarchical Church with regard to the practical aspects of social-economic justice, though great at certain times and in certain places, has been far from coherent.

For instance, the ancient and medieval Church, while treating individual slaves and serfs in a spirit of brotherly love and while considering their freeing as a work of Christian charity, rarely challenged the institutions of slavery and serfdom.[63] Patristic-scholastic thought saw

---

[61] For Gregory the Great, cf., for instance, *Regula Pastoralis* II, 7 (Migne, *Patrol. Lat.* LXXVII, 41A f.), where the Pope tells bishops that "almost rightly . . . does the mind of the 'faithful turn away from absorbing what is preached if the care of external assistance is neglected by the pastor."

[62] Cf. L. White, jr., "The Changing Canons of Our Culture," in *Frontiers of Knowledge in the Study of Man* (New York, 1956), pp. 310 ff.

[63] In general, cf. R. W. and A. J. Carlyle, *A History of Mediaeval Political Theory in the West* (New York, Edinburgh, and London, 1909), II, 117 ff. This whole matter needs further investigation, especially in relation to medieval serfdom. For slavery, cf. C. Verlinden, *L'esclavage dans l'Europe médiévale* (Bruges, 1955), with bibli-

them as a consequence of original sin, on the same level as other consequences, such as coercive government and just or defensive war, equally regrettable and equally irremediable in this world.[64] It is true that a thorough reversal of the ancient and medieval attitude toward slavery and serfdom, and of the socially and economically depressed condition of slaves and serfs, on grounds of Christian morality would have been exceedingly difficult, and probably impossible, before economic and social conditions had begun to change radically in the later Middle Ages under secular rather than ecclesiastical pressures and under the impact of

ography also for Christian Antiquity; the lexicon articles by J. Dutilleul in *Dictionnaire de théologie catholique* (Paris, 1913), XV, 457 ff., s.v. "esclavage"; R. Naz, in *Dictionnaire de droit canonique* (Paris, 1953), V, 448 ff., s.v. "esclave"; C. Augrain, J. Weeger, and A. Derville, in *Dictionnaire de Spiritualité* (Paris, 1960), IV, 1067 ff., s.v. "esclave (spiritualité de l')"; K. Witte, in *Die Religion in Geschichte und Gegenwart* (2d ed.; Tübingen, 1931), V, 576 ff., s.v. "Sklaverei und Christenheit"; and H.-D. Wendland, in the third edition of the same work (1962), VI, a different article on the same subject, with recent literature. For serfdom, in addition to Verlinden, *op. cit.*, see, for instance, M. Bloch, "Liberté et servitude personelle au moyen âge, particulièrement en France," *Anuario de historia del derecho español*, X (1933), 31 f. n. 31; 74 n. 142, 79 f. See also the interesting recent article by S. Epperlein, "Die sogenannte Freilassung in merowingischer und karolingischer Zeit," *Jahrbuch für Wirtschaftsgeschichte*, 1963, Part IV, pp. 92 ff., where the author convincingly shows that the early medieval Church, while playing an important role in the transition from slavery to serfdom, only rarely granted serfs full freedom, because this would have deprived her of workers, indispensable to her as a great landowner within the manorial-feudal system. The greatest, though socially and economically only partly effective, factor in the achievement of liberty was the removal of city life; in this area ecclesiastical opinion remained for a long time divided: hostile where it identified itself with the feudal order, more friendly in Church reform milieus, such as eleventh-century Lombardy under Patarene influence or eleventh-century central and southern France under "Cluniac" influence.

[64] On these matters, cf. the classical account in R. W. and A. J. Carlyle, *op. cit.*

technological and organizational innovations.[65] But even then the dead weight of tradition in matters of servitude and economic subservience continued for a long time to influence the attitude of the Church. Christianity's relative lack of sensibility in matters of social-economic justice was a melancholy, a tragic aspect of Christian history which remained more or less hidden until more recent times when excesses and remedies matured, as it were, as a result of industrial and political revolutions. In this respect, even today Christian renewal urgently needs to be further developed and completed.

The tension between the spiritual and the material power of the Church, and especially of the papacy, was and is often conceptualized in the terms "direct power in spiritual things" and "indirect (spiritual) power in temporal things." The term "temporal" in this antithetical formula is not so obvious as it might seem. It is connected with the development in the ecclesiastical and political theory of the Middle Ages of the metaphor of the spiritual sword and the material sword, the latter concept often being widened to that of the secular or temporal sword from the early thirteenth century onward. The term "temporal" was substituted in this area of thought for the term "material" at a

[65] The early Church did institute a vast system of almsgiving and of pious bequests, centered on the so-called quota for the soul (cf. E. F. Bruck, *Kirchenväter und soziales Erbrecht* [Berlin, Göttingen, Heidelberg, 1956], but it did not consider it its task to concern itself with the socioeconomic presuppositions of poverty. Schneider (*op. cit.*, I, 519 f.; II, 328 f.) points out very well how helpless early Christian morality was before the economic system it confronted. It mitigated the system, but did little to change it. Cf. also the (slightly optimistic) views of B. Tierney, *Medieval Poor Law* (Berkeley and Los Angeles, 1959), pp. 22 f., with regard to the medieval canonists: "The real reason that such gifted thinkers did not condemn the whole established organization of society is the rather obvious one that, on the whole, in that particular historical and economic context, the existing hierarchical structure was the best adapted to promote the general welfare and to sustain the complex and brilliant culture of the high Middle Ages,"

relatively late date.[66] Nevertheless, this substitution is highly significant, for it is a logical consequence of the Christian view of time which was not only a *novum* in the world into which Christianity entered, but also continued to be of great importance for the civilization shaped by the Christian religion, and quite especially for Western civilization.

In pre-Christian Antiquity, speculation on time had been based on the belief in the perpetual cyclical recurrence of identical or similar situations and events. This belief is rooted in a widespread archaic mentality that attempts to deny the relentless deathbound course of time by the assumption of ever new cosmic or, at least, ever new biological beginnings.[67] With Christianity, all this changed

and p. 144 n. 4, with regard to the poverty of the serfs due to periodical crop failure: "The only eventual solution lay in the development of agricultural technology and communications."

[66] The most famous formulation of the metaphor of the spiritual and temporal swords is that in Pope Boniface VIII's bull *Unam Sanctam* (for instance in H. Denzinger, *Enchiridion Symbolorum*, ed. 21–23 [Freiburg im Breisgau, 1937], p. 219). Cf. in general R. Castillo Lara, *Coaccion eclesiastica y Sacro Romano Imperio* (Turin, 1956), pp. 224, 240 ff., a work that continues the well-known important studies of A. M. Stickler, who has shown that the metaphor of the two swords, based on an allegorical interpretation of Luke 22:38, at first did not concern the relationship between the spiritual and the temporal order, but between spiritual punishment (excommunication, etc.) and material coercion (especially capital punishment, war, etc.) Cf., for instance A. M. Stickler, "Il 'gladius' negli atti dei concilii dei RR. Pontefici sino a Graziano e Bernardo di Clairvaux," *Salesianum*, XIII (1951), 414 ff., and "Der Schwerterbegriff bei Huguccio," *Ephemerides Iuris Canonici*, III (1947), 281 ff. For the complex connections existing since the late thirteenth century between the "two swords," the "spiritual" and the "temporal" in Christian society, and the "direct" and the "indirect" power of the papacy, cf., for instance, John of Paris, *Tractatus de postestate regia et papali*, written *ca.* 1302–1303, c.X, ed. J. Leclercq (Paris, 1942), pp. 197–201.

[67] Cf., for instance, M. Eliade, *The Myth of the Eternal Return*, trans. from French by R. Trask, Bollingen Series (New York, 1954).

or received a new meaning. Past and future, extending from Creation to the Last Judgment, were seen with reference to the one principal historical fact of the coming of Christ. All past history led up to this event; all future history would be deeply influenced by it. The Christian view of time and history, then, is unilinear rather than cyclical. Moreover, this linear extension has not only a beginning and an end, but also a privileged focal point along the line, the event of Christ's coming, whereas eternally recurrent cycles have no meaningful center.[68]

On Christian terms, unilinear time is for man the necessary, the one and only, road to eternity. Thus, for instance, in St. Augustine's profound philosophy of time and history, time, it is true, dissolves the unity of God's eternity into multiple succession, but it also instills a first element of order into the otherwise directionless and chaotic flux of all things. In conjunction with man's memory of the past and anticipation of the future, time gives him leeway and guidance to reform himself and the times—ransoming the time, St. Paul called it (Eph. 5:15 f.)—and through this effort to win eternity.[69]

It has often been observed that Christians, and especially Western Christians and those influenced by them, are much more involved in time and history than, for instance, the ancient Greeks or Indians had been. The Christian position on time, like so many other Christian positions, was ambivalent and even paradoxical. On the one

---

[68] Cf. O. Cullmann, *Christ and Time*, trans. from German by F. V. Filson (London, 1962).

[69] Cf. Ladner, *The Idea of Reform*, pp. 203 ff. It may be noted that St. Augustine uses the term "temporal" also in speaking of secular government and power in this world (*rerum temporalium gubernatio*), a power that for him is provisional (*pro tempore*); cf. *Expositio quarumdam propositionum ex epistola ad Romanos* 72 (to Rom. 13:1 ff.), Migne, *Patrol. Lat.* XXXV, 2083. I am indebted for this interesting text to my assistant, Mr. Anthony Gagliano.

hand, Christians must not become too involved in temporal events; on the other hand, the latter are not without value or purpose. The temporal sphere is not a mere Indian *sansara*, no mere seductive and deceptive illusion. Once more we are brought back to the crucial fact that Christ himself has entered the temporal and historical world.

No doubt the relatively affirmative Christian conception of time is one of the reasons why the Church, especially in the West, felt entitled and constrained to apply its spiritual and, in one sense, timeless principles so energetically to the existential and temporal realities of the world, an attitude that brought about, among other things, the papal hegemony of the central part of the Middle Ages. That the tension between the spiritual and the temporal spheres could lead to confusion, to some abuse of wealth and power on the part of the Church, and to a fierce and ultimately successful struggle of the political against the ecclesiastical order, is undeniable. But this need not lead the historian to Gibbon's conclusion that all ecclesiastical and hierarchical interventions in the temporal sphere were in themselves necessarily evil. In the actual history of the Church in time there have been deformations, but there also has come into operation the typically Christian temporal and historical category of reform. Reform avoids the automatism of eternal recurrence, be it cosmological or biological, and asserts the intentionality of the human spirit and its unique position in a world which is seen as both temporal and on the way to eternity.

To conclude, Gibbon, who wanted to be a philosophical historian in the spirit of Montesquieu,[70] tried to establish the secondary causes [71] and effects of Christianity as of

[70] *Essai*, p. 177: "Si les philosophes ne sont pas toujours historiens, il seroit du moins a souhaiter que les historiens fussent philosophes." *Ibid.*, p., 179: "La théorie de ces causes générales seroit entre les mains d'un Montesquieu une histoire philosophique de l'homme."

[71] *Decline and Fall*, ch 15:II, 2: ". . . as the wisdom of Providence

other facts of history. His understanding of the Christian religion remained fragmentary, owing not so much to his dismissal of the first cause—this was, in part, the methodically sound bracketing of divine providence in a strictly historical inquiry—but instead to his failure to realize the full range of the religious motives of men and their results in history. Nevertheless, Gibbon did not lack all perceptiveness for the history of Christianity, especially not for its "melancholy" aspects. Church historians could learn from him to take seriously the many human imperfections, corruptions, and tragedies that are interwoven with the history of the Church. There are, it seems to me, far too few modern Church historians who have accepted and presented such facts in all their starkness and harshness. At the same time, there have been too many who have presented them with a hostile bias. A truly integral view of the complexities of Church history and of history in general would certainly not be satisfied merely with Gibbon's melancholy and skeptical resignation or with his scornful and cynical irony. For in such a wider view, which had been that of Giambattista Vico a generation before Gibbon, there is no fatal tragedy, no final decline; there are *corsi,* but there are also *ricorsi.*[72] Continual rebirth, reform, renewal are of the essence of the Christian religion and therefore also of Christian civilization and of its history.

frequently condescends to use the passions of the human heart, and the general circumstances of mankind, as instruments to execute its purpose; we may still be permitted, though with becoming submission, to ask not indeed what were the first, but what were the secondary causes of the rapid growth of the Christian Church."

[72] Cf. G. Vico, *Principii di Scienza Nuova* (1744), V, 1046 ff., ed. F. Nicolini, *Giambattista Vico: Opere* (Milan and Naples, 1953), pp. 835 ff.

III

HELLAS RESURGENT

Speros Vryonis, Jr.

*T*HE TITLE "Hellas Resurgent" will seem to some a euphemism, or perhaps a device intended to provoke a critical audience. Is it justified in the light of all that has been said about the chaos of the third century, that chaos which exposed classical civilization to a thunderous series of political, economic, spiritual, and intellectual shocks? Even superficial perusal of Gibbon leaves not the slightest doubt that he would have objected most emphatically, if not cholerically, to "Hellas Resurgent" as a label for Byzantine civilization.[1] There is no mistaking

[1] The only quandary in one's mind arises in determining whether scholars today will be more outraged by the first half of the title than Gibbon would have been by the second. The term "Hellas" is used in this chapter to indicate the Greek cultural tradition which remained strongest in classical and medieval times among the Greek and Hellenized populations of Greece, Anatolia, and a few isolated spots in Egypt, Syria, southern Italy, and Sicily. Whether the polyglot Byzantine empire was possessed of a culture that may be characterized as Greek has been occasionally and passionately debated. In terms of literary production, there is little question in this matter. The literary language was Greek, and the models of education and literary production were both classical and Christian. At the same time, disparate elements from various nonclassical traditions were absorbed into Byzantine culture. The single most important was the Christian religion, by origin Semitic and Monotheistic. By virtue, however, of the Christianization of the pagan world of the eastern Mediterranean, Christianity was itself Hellenized (see W. Jaeger, *Early Christianity and Greek Paideia* [Cambridge, 1961], p. 5). And so it was with

Gibbon's sentiments: there was no resurgence of Hellas or, indeed, of anything else. Gibbon's evaluation of Byzantine civilization becomes apparent, line after line, paragraph after paragraph, page after page, throughout his seventy-one chapters. He sees it as the story of a profound and un-relenting political and cultural decline, inseparably asso-ciated with a degenerate, orientalized, Christianized Greek nation.

In the preface of the first volume which appeared in February, 1776, Gibbon remarks: "The memorable series of revolutions, which, in the course of about thirteen cen-turies, gradually undermined, and at length destroyed, the solid fabric of human greatness, may, with some propriety, be divided into the three following periods." [2] These three periods are: (1) From Trajan to the sixth century; (2) from Justinian to 800; and (3) from 800 to 1453. From this periodization, one perceives that his history is one of colossal decline with a final and inexorable vengeance. Gib-bon devoted three ponderous tomes to the events of the first four centuries and one to the remaining 900 years. The reason for this seeming geometric disproportion he ex-poses at the beginning of chapter 48:

> I have now deduced from Trajan to Constantine, from Constantine to Heraclius, the regular series of the Roman emperors; and faithfully exposed the prosperous and ad-verse fortunes of their reigns. Five centuries of the decline and fall of the empire have already elapsed; but a period of more than eight hundred years still separates me from the term of my labours, the taking of Constantinople by the Turks. Should I persevere in the same course, should I observe the same measure, a prolix and slender thread

---

many other cultural phenomena. Though it is true that the Byzantine Empire, like the Roman Empire, was multinational, within the heartland of the Empire, the Greek peninsula and Anatolia, the predominating element was that of the Greek speakers.

[2] *Decline and Fall*, Preface: I, v–vi.

would be spun through many a volume, nor would the
patient reader find an adequate reward of instruction or
amusement. At every step, as we sink deeper in the decline
and fall of the Eastern Empire, the annals of each succeed-
ing reign would impose a more ungrateful and melancholy
task. These annals must continue to repeat a tedious and
uniform tale of weakness and misery. . . . The fate of the
Greek empire has been compared to that of the Rhine,
which loses itself in the sands before its waters can mingle
with the ocean. The scale of dominion is diminished to our
view by the distance of time and place; nor is the loss of
external splendour compensated by the nobler gifts of virtue and genius.[3]

After comparing these latter day Greeks with their classical ancestors, much to the disadvantage of the former, he
returns to the Byzantine Greeks:

> The subjects of the Byzantine empire, who assume and
> dishonor the names both of Greeks and Romans, present
> a dead uniformity of abject vices, which are neither sof-
> tened by the weakness of humanity nor animated by the
> vigour of memorable crimes. . . . From these considera-
> tions, I should have abandoned, without regret, the Greek
> slaves and their servile historians, had I not reflected that
> the fate of the Byzantine monarchy is passively connected
> with the most splendid and important revolutions which
> have changed the state of the world.[4]

Gibbon presents us with what he considers to be the unmistakable causes for and manifestations of this decline,
some of which have already been described in the preceding chapters. Preeminence among these causes and manifestations Gibbon assigns to the triumph of Christianity:
Christianity absorbed and distracted society with its useless and endless theological squabbles; it was responsible
for the rise of superstition so clearly visible in those emi-

[3] *Ibid.*, ch. 48:V, 169.
[4] In *ibid.*, ch. 48:V. 170–171, Gibbon has italicized the word "passively."

nently Greek phenomena within Christianity, iconolatry
and hagiolatry, and this superstition debased the spiritual
and intellectual standard of society; Christianity contributed to the degeneracy of the Greek nation by teaching
it abasement and passivity. Monasticism was complemen-
tary to this process, for it caused men and women to
renounce not only the pleasures but also the business of this
world. Thus, the world was deprived of the energies of
these "monastic saints, who," Gibbon writes, "excite only
the contempt and pity of a philosopher." [5] Christianity
created a state within a state and so helped to consume the
Empire in a parasitic manner.

Gibbon sees "orientalization," whatever this may have
meant to him, as a further contributing factor to this
degeneracy. In chapter 17 it is the vanity of the East manifest in court forms and ceremonies, and it has vanquished
Roman manly virtue. In speaking of the new "oriental"
forms of civil and military administration which Diocletian and Constantine introduced, he remarks that their
mere discussion will illustrate the Empire's rapid decay. In
the civil war between Constantine's two sons, Constans is
supported by the "martial nations of Europe" whereas
Constantius is at the head of the "effeminate troops of
Asia." Let me add that it was the latter, not the former,
who finally won. Gibbon's work bristles with literary
shafts hurled at the effeminacy of Greeks, at the malevo-
lence of eunuchs, and at the heroic hypocrisy of bishops.[6]

In chapter 53 he describes the state of the Empire in the
tenth century and presents a symptomatic comparison between the Greek character, on the one hand, and that of
the Latins and Arabs on the other:

[5] *Ibid.*, ch. 37:IV, 74.

[6] *Ibid.*, ch. 22:II, 396. Gibbon begins this chapter: "While the
Romans languished under the ignominious tyranny of eunuchs and
bishops. . . ."

Whatever titles a despot may assume, whatever claims he may assert, it is on the sword that he must ultimately depend to guard him against his foreign and domestic enemies. From the age of Charlemagne to that of the Crusades, the world (for I overlook the remote monarchy of China) was occupied and disputed by the three great empires or nations of the Greeks, the Saracens, and the Franks. Their military strength may be ascertained by a comparison of their courage, their arts and riches, and their obedience to a supreme head, who might call into action all the energies of the state. The Greeks, far inferior to their rivals in the first, were superior to the Franks, and at least equal to the Saracens, in the second and third of these warlike qualifications. . . . Whatever authority could enact was accomplished, at least in theory, by the camps and marches, the exercizes and evolutions, the edicts and books, of the Byzantine monarch. Whatever art could produce from the forge, the loom, or the laboratory, was abundantly supplied by the richness of the prince and the industry of his numerous workmen. But neither authority nor art could frame the most important machine, the soldier himself. . . . Notwithstanding some transient success, the Greeks were sunk in their own esteem and that of their neighbours. A cold hand and a loquacious tongue was the vulgar description of the nation. . . . What spirit their government and character denied, might have been inspired in some degree by the influence of religion; but the religion of the Greeks could only teach them to suffer and to yield.[7]

Though Gibbon reiterates the theme of Eastern martial degeneracy, he is quite ready to admit that the Empire's scientific skill, economic capacity, and the centralization of authority enabled it to compete successfully with both Latins and Arabs. The former are braver, but more anarchic in the arrangement of their energies. The latter are better than the Latins in ordering these same energies, but are still inferior to the Greeks whom they imitate.

[7] *Ibid.,* ch. 53:VI, 91, 95.

Gibbon continued the theme of orientalization as a factor in Byzantine decay in chapter 55, where he states that the conversion of the Slavs meant an advance for them from barbarism to civilization, but in a qualified sort of way: "It should appear that Russia might have derived an early and rapid improvement from her peculiar connection with the church and state of Constantinople which in that age so justly despised the ignorance of the Latins. But the Byzantine nation was servile, solitary, and verging to an hasty decline." [8] This oriental character is also present at the final siege of Constantinople by the Turks (a nation far more "oriental" than the one it vanquished!) in 1453. In describing the events of that dramatic battle, Gibbon cannot refrain from lavishing praise upon the greatly outnumbered Christian defenders, but he does so only after uttering the customary anathema upon the latter: "The nation was indeed pusillanimous and base; but the last Constantine deserves the name of an hero; his noble band of volunteers was inspired with Roman virtue; and the foreign auxiliaries supported the honor of western chivalry." [9]

These examples are only a few from the detailed catalogue of causes and manifestations of the Empire's decline which Gibbon presents. But he realized that though its decay was always in progress, it took a millennium for the Empire to fall. Therefore, he was on occasion forced to give reasons for the uncalled-for survival of Byzantium. More often than not, Gibbon's explanation of this longevity is negative. In the East it was the decadence of the Arab Caliphate and in the West the feudal chaos and anarchy, which, among other factors, brought respite to the Greek Empire. That is to say, Byzantium did not fall sooner because its internal decline was not so advanced as that of the

[8] *Ibid.*, ch. 55:VI, 166.
[9] *Ibid.*, ch. 68:VII, 177–178.

Arabs, and because its state of civilization was not so primitive as that of the West. But certainly this does not explain why it was that the Caliphate was more affected by internal decline, or why Byzantium was not in the state of chaos which the West experienced. It would be unfair to Gibbon to state categorically that he was not conscious of the necessity of supplying more positive reasons for Byzantine longevity. He recognizes the importance of the gifted individual in history, and such a person he considers Basil the Macedonian to have been. He comprehends the significance of technology and attributes the salvation of Constantinople from the Arabs to the invention of Greek fire. He comes closest, perhaps, to a positive explanation of Byzantium's endurance in chapter 53 where he speaks of centralized government, economic wealth, industry, and skills which the Greek Orient possessed in abundance. But by and large, Gibbon failed to come to grips with the problem of the unique length of the "decline."

How are Gibbon's evaluation and judgment of the Byzantine Empire to be explained? The remarks of Andrew Lossky and Gerhart Ladner have indicated the general nature of the answer. Though Gibbon was perhaps something more than a child of the Enlightenment, to the degree that he was its intellectual and emotional offspring, he was imbued with a corresponding distrust of and contemptuous disdain for organized hierarchical religions. This so prejudiced his view of history that he could not fully appreciate the historical role of religion in a period wherein religion dominated and colored every phase of life. His personal experience with religion, as well as with much of the literature that he read, contributed to the acerbity of his criticism of the Church. The unfortunate effect of Gibbon's blindness to the historical and cultural importance of religious matters was heavily compounded by his limited view of the historical unity of the subject he treated. He saw only two elements of continuity in his epic: the threadbare existence of that Empire that "dishonored the name of both Greeks and Romans," and, second, its uninterrupted millennial decline. He paid little attention to, and perhaps was incapable of comprehending, the larger historical process within which occurred the transmission of Greco-Roman civilization and its mutation into the Christian cultures of Byzantium and the West, entities simultaneously old and new, conservative and yet creative. As his history advanced through the centuries, Gibbon increasingly restricted the narrative to the surface of the Empire's life: the dark intrigues of the court and the bloody seditions of the armies. Rarely did he pierce beneath these superficial phenomena to the inner meaning of these events. There are times when, in the latter part of his narrative, Gibbon managed to break through this exterior and succeeded in finding something essential, indeed perhaps something he considered worthwhile. Invariably, this involved him in inconsistencies and outright contradictions until his personal tastes finally overcame his logic in the matter.[10]

The consequence of Gibbon's work for the study of

---

[10] Gibbon condemned the administrative reforms of Diocletian because they placed affairs in the hands of the eunuchs and courtiers and so relaxed the vigor of the state. A mere description of these institutions, Gibbon states, demonstrates the Empire's decay. But, at the very end of the same chapter (17), he suddenly reverses himself and declares that these reforms in government enabled the Empire to survive the barbarian invasions, to restrain the license of the soldiery, and to enjoy a continuity of its cultural life. In another realm, he traces the rise of superstition in the early Middle Ages to the spread of Christianity. Again, in one and the same chapter (28), he proclaims that the victors (Christians) were vanquished by the arts of their vanquished rivals (pagans). Thus he recognizes that much of Christian superstition already existed in the pagan world and simply penetrated the new religion as the latter absorbed the pagans. In spite of his insight into this matter, he continues to charge Christianity with the rise and spread of superstition.

Byzantium can be overestimated only with ingenuity. The *Decline and Fall* long placed the kiss of death upon Byzantine studies, even though these had already made remarkable progress in the seventeenth century. In fact, Gibbon's history, for much of the Byzantine period at least, would have been impossible without the earlier editions of the basic Byzantine historical texts and the remarkable works of Ducange. That it would take another century for Byzantine scholarship to revive is an unfortunate measure of Gibbon's greatness.[11] Contributing factors in the fame of the work were his greatness as a scholar, albeit one marred by heavy prejudice, and his superb style. His erudition and prejudice were rendered palatable not merely by his literary style; for even if one writes in the crispest fashion, nevertheless a wholesale narrative of wars, rebellions, court intrigues, and obscure religious controversies, compacted and squeezed into 2,500 pages, would soon exhaust the interest of the most scholarly reader. It is one particular element in his literary style, namely his ironic and sarcastic wit, which so greatly flavors the narrative as to relieve first the pain and then the exhausting fatigue of the reader's almost endless journey to 1453. Felicitous though this may be as literary anesthesia, the sarcasm and irony contribute seriously to the distortion of the picture of a whole society which Gibbon presents.

The morbid effects that Gibbon's pronouncements had on Byzantine studies are still discernable today among a very few of his more recent compatriots. It was the most distinguished of modern English Byzantinists, J. B. Bury, who published the critical edition of the *Decline and Fall*. In his edition, Bury takes more than sixty pages in the preface to indicate how outdated and insufficient Gibbon was on such basic matters as Justinian's reign, Constan-

[11] G. Ostrogorsky, *History of the Byzantine State* (New Brunswick, 1957), pp. 5–6.

tinopolitan topography, vernacular Greek, the Slavs, and so forth. Nevertheless, by his own explicit admission, Bury fell under the Gibbonian spell: "To attempt to deny a general truth in Gibbon's point of view is vain; and it is feeble to deprecate his sneer. We may spare more sympathy than he for the warriors and the churchmen; but all that has since been added to his knowledge of facts has neither reversed nor blunted the point of the Decline and Fall." [12] Because of his belief in the validity of Gibbon's point of view, Bury felt that the whole work could be brought up to date by the simple insertion of footnotes and appendices at the proper places, without changing the "point of view." More striking perhaps is the remark of Hugh Trevor-Roper, Regius professor of history at Oxford, in his preface to a recent paperback edition of an excerpted version of the *Decline and Fall*: "It remains a remarkable fact that anyone who wishes to study the later Roman or Byzantine Empire will still find Gibbon's Decline and Fall of the Roman Empire the best, as well as the most readable narrative of it. . . . Gibbon is the first great historian of a remote past whom the work of later centuries has not driven from the field." [13]

Though the Gibbonian judgment on Byzantium is still discussed, though many feel that Gibbon cannot be avoided, and there are even those who still feel that Gibbon was right, the results of scholarly research in the past three-quarters of a century have largely invalidated Gibbon, Trevor-Roper to the contrary notwithstanding. This is the result largely of a new scholarship inspired by the critical method of German classical philologists. This modern ap-

[12] *Decline and Fall*, Introduction: I, xxxviii.

[13] H. R. Trevor-Roper, *The Decline and Fall of the Roman Empire and Other Selections from the Writings of Edward Gibbon* (New York, 1963), p. vii. Those who concur might even emend Trevor-Roper's last sentence to read: "Gibbon is the first great historian of a remote past who has driven from the field the work of later centuries"!

proach, which gradually spread throughout Europe and to the United States, has disagreed with Gibbon in no uncertain terms. It has found that Byzantium was conservative, but that it was also creative. Indeed, it manifested innovative powers that left their indelible mark upon European civilization. Among the reasons for its conservatism were the burden and privilege of an illustrious inheritance. This inheritance, whether literary or political, had been canonized in late Antiquity, and one could do no better than to imitate this perfection. On the other hand, pressing necessity as well as new opportunities often forced or induced the Byzantines to seek new formulations and solutions. Thus, modern scholarship has revised the Gibbonian view in favor of a more nearly accurate judgment on Byzantine civilization.[14]

By examining the principal aspects of Byzantine civilization, that civilization which resulted from the fusion of Greek culture, Roman legal and administrative institutions, and Christian eschatology and ethics, one can discern to what extent there was a resurgence of Hellas. In the political realm, certainly one of the most important events of the late third and early fourth centuries was the removal of the imperial capital first to Nicomedia and then to Byzantium, both Greek cities in regions which had been Hellenized. The seat of imperium abandoned the Latin West and migrated to the Greek East even before the barbarian cataclysm of the fourth and fifth centuries. Following Rome's reduction of the Hellenistic monarchies, the Greek Orient had been subordinated in a provincial relationship to Rome, but as a result of the disorders of the third century, which the East was better equipped to resist, the situation of provincial subordination was suddenly reversed.

[14] Ostrogorsky, *op. cit.*, pp. 1–20, gives a brief and convenient survey of the history of Byzantine studies.

The vitality of the East is further demonstrated in the fact that the eastern half of the Empire survived the Germanic invasions, whereas the Latin West succumbed in the fifth and sixth centuries. This indicates that the East was now the more vital portion of the imperial organism, because, when the German crisis first burst, it came from the Gothic nation in southeast Europe. The Goths attempted, first in the third and then again in the late fourth and fifth centuries, to take over the Balkans, Constantinople, and parts of Asia Minor. But the effort proved beyond their capacities, and it was only after this failure that they were forced to move westward. The failure of the West to resist them is all too well known. It was a period in which there arose urban militias made up of citizens who effectively fought off barbarian attacks on their city walls.[15] In Constantinople, it was an aroused citizenry that helped to chase the Gothic soldiery from the city, killing many of them in the process. Simultaneously, a Greek intellectual from the province of Cyrene came to Constantinople and harangued the emperor on the evils of bringing Germans into the armies. Synesius warned the emperor that offices should be reserved for the citizens of the Empire, else one would be introducing wolves into the sheep fold. In Asia Minor the peasantry rose to defeat and slaughter the Gothic tribes when the latter had escaped the imperial troops as a result of the treachery of German officers. Then when the remnants of these Gothic tribes were settled in Asia Minor, they were eventually absorbed by Christianization and Hellenization, and so disappeared.[16] Is this not proof that there was a will to resist?

[15] G. Manojlović, "Le peuple de Constantinople," Byzantion, XI (1936), 617–716.

[16] E. Stein, Histoire du Bas-Empire (Paris, 1959), I, 234–237; A. H. M. Jones, The Later Roman Empire, 284–602, (Oxford, 1964), I, 178–179; P. Charanis, "On the Ethnic Composition of Asia Minor," in Prosfora eis S. P. Kyriakiden (Thessalonica, 1953), p. 141.

It is not mere chance that when once more the floods of Slavic tribal migrations and Arab military conquests threatened to destroy the Byzantine state, it survived. In the case of the former, it was the Latin-speaking parts of the Balkans, that is, the central and northern Balkans, which were permanently wrested from the Byzantines by the Slavs. In the East the Arabs were successful largely in the Armenian, Syrian, Egyptian, and African regions. Thus the Slavic and Arab high tides were reached when they washed against the Hellenized regions of the Balkans and Asia Minor. The Greek-speaking parts of the southern Balkans and Asia Minor displayed a remarkable vigor in surviving these great storms of the period of late Antiquity and of the early medieval world.[17] Given the magnitude of the threatening forces, this fact deserves careful attention and explanation. Moreover, under Justinian I the East destroyed both the Ostrogothic and Vandalic states; less than a century later, Heraclius virtually destroyed the Persian empire; and in the tenth century the Macedonian dynasty began the reconquest of large parts of the Slavic Balkans as well as parts of Muslim Mesopotamia, northern Syria, Crete, and Cyprus.

It is often the administrative or governmental institutions of a state which hold the balance of the state's fate, for it is through these institutions that the energies and resources of the state are mobilized. It is perhaps here, more than in any other respect, that Gibbon the political historian has failed to present a satisfactory analysis of Byzantine civilization. The successful modulation of flexible administrative institutions played a critical role in the Empire's ability to resist her powerful foes and then often to vanquish them. A state of such complexity and size

---

[17] W. M. Ramsay, "The Attempt of the Arabs to Conquer Asia Minor (641–694 A.D.) and the Causes of Its Failure," *Bulletin de la section historique de l'Académie Roumaine,* XI (1924).

could not attain satisfactory efficiency without centralization of authority and a great bureacracy obedient to the
will of the supreme ruler. Byzantium could not have been
run as was Athens, Republican Rome, or feudal Germany.
Inasmuch as Gibbon hated these institutions because he
felt that they had destroyed freedom, he gave insufficient
attention to the administrative reforms of Diocletian and
Constantine, and almost completely ignored the equally
important institutional arrangements of the seventh-
century rulers. By way of example, he despised the Dio-
cletianic separation of military and civil power (a separation deemed worthwhile in our day) in the provinces as
the artifice of eunuchs and courtiers who feared that provincial generals might march on the capital and so deprive
them of their sinecures. His obsession with eunuchs blind-
ed Gibbon to the basic fact that the principal danger to the
state in the late third century was not the barbarian threat,
but the all-powerful and covetous Roman generals in the
provinces. Quite rightly, Diocletian and Constantine, men
of more immediate experience in matters concerning both
eunuchs and ambitious generals, whittled down the
amount of power in any one man's hand. Civil and military functions were henceforth exercized by separate civil
and military officials, and the provinces were cut down in
size so that the effective power yielded by one man was decreased. So efficacious was this institutional reform that
Byzantium did not experience another third century for
many generations to come.

Even more glaring is Gibbon's failure to note adequately
the great administrative changes of the seventh century,
upon which the very fate of much of Europe depended
when, as a result of the invasions of the Slavs and Arabs,
prompt action was needed to save the state. Here again, in
the face of necessity, Byzantine statecraft devised a solution. Civil and military power were reunited in the hands

of the provincial generals, and their provinces were increased in size and decreased in number. The local peasantry was given plots of land, salaries, and tax exemptions in return for which it was to perform military service, and so henceforth a free peasantry came to constitute the backbone of the Byzantine military strength. It was this army of free peasant soldiers which saved the Empire from Arabs and Slavs and then went over to the offensive in the tenth century.[18]

The Byzantine institutions, which Gibbon so richly despised and so poorly comprehended, played a primary role in the political tenacity and periodic resurgence of Byzantium for eight centuries. In view of the overall political performance of Byzantium, Gibbon's judgment seems unfair. The Greek East attained a remarkable political achievement when in the late third and fourth centuries it donned the ponderous armor of the Roman Imperium, an armor which the Latin West could no longer support, and wore it successfully for so long.

The recuperative powers of medieval Hellenism are perhaps nowhere demonstrated so strikingly as in the important position Byzantium held in the economic life of the medieval world until the Crusades. As we have seen, the third century was a time of extensive economic woes. It was pointed out that the economy of ancient society was unable to sustain the shocks of this period, but the situation was worse in the West than in the East. Though the West declined economically to a state where a self-sufficient, natural economy played an increasingly great but not exclusive role, the East displayed remarkable economic recuperative powers. The troubles of the third

[18] G. Ostrogorsky, "Agrarian Conditions in the Byzantine Empire in the Middle Ages," in *Cambridge Economic History*, I (Cambridge, 1941), 196; P. Charanis, "Some Remarks on the Changes in Byzantium in the Seventh Century," *Zbornik radova vizantoloshkog instituta*, VIII (1963), 71–76.

century and later did not reduce its economy to the rude level of the economy of Western Europe. Its economy revived and developed in a comparatively vigorous fashion for almost 800 years.[19]

Though the manifestations of this economic vitality are clearly discernible, the causes are more tenebrous. Certainly one important factor in the economic stamina of the East was its survival of the barbarian invasions, though this is a circular argument inasmuch as its political survival cannot be separated from its economic strength. Conditions that favored industrial production and money economy included large population and a developed urban society.[20] As to size of population, the most recent study of ancient demography would have us believe that the eastern provinces were more heavily populated than the western.[21] The importance of towns for industry, commerce, and indeed for civilization as a whole is even

[19] The reader will find a very informative account in R. Lopez, "The Trade of Medieval Europe: The South," in *Cambridge Economic History*, II (Cambridge, 1952), 257 ff.

[20] F. Lot, *The End of the Ancient World* (London, 1931), pp. 69 ff.

[21] The most recent and detailed treatment of the population question is that of J. C. Russell, *Late Ancient and Medieval Population*, Transactions of the American Philosophical Society, Vol. XLVIII, pt. 3 (Philadelphia, 1958). His conclusions (pp. 71–87) on the populations of the Empire in the period prior to the great plague of 543, estimated in millions, are:

West		East	
Italy	4.0	Greece and Balkans	5.0
Iberia	3 to 4	Egypt	3.0
North Africa	2.5	Asia Minor	11.6
Gaul	5.0	Syria	4.3
Britain	0.5		23.9
	15 to 16		

Russell's figures are in keeping with the conservative estimates of J. Beloch, *Die Bevölkerung der griechisch-römischen Welt* (Berlin, 1886).

philologically self-evident. By and large, the East seems to have been possessed of larger numbers of towns and more vital cities, Asia Minor being perhaps the single most important province in this respect. Because of economic factors and its security from barbarian invasions, its towns continued a vital existence down to the eleventh and twelfth centuries at which time the Turkish invasions brought a partial disruption to their good fortune.[22] This urban vitality was crucial to the East's ability to withstand the economic and political vicissitudes of the transitional period. Urban continuity was important not only as a material factor: it was also essential to the survival of Christian Hellenism or Byzantine civilization. Without these cities the East would likewise have gone down.

The crafts, industry, and commerce had older and better established traditions in the East. Perhaps related to this are the findings of the pseudoscience of ethnic psychology, according to which Syrians, Greeks, Jews, and Armenians found commerce and the crafts more congenial than did the inhabitants of the Latin West in this early period of

[22] A. H. M. Jones, *The Greek City from Alexander to Justinian* (Oxford, 1940), deals masterfully with the history of the towns in the eastern Mediterranean during the first six centuries of the Christian era. The problem of the continuity of towns in Byzantium between the seventh and ninth centuries is presently the subject of debate. It seems highly probable that the continuity of urban centers in much of Asia Minor and the southern Balkans was not interrupted (G. Ostrogorsky, "Byzantine Cities in the Early Middle Ages," *Dumbarton Oaks Papers,* XIII [1959], 47–66; S. Vryonis, "An Attic Hoard of Byzantine Gold Coins (668–741) from the Thomas Whittemore Collection and the Numismatic Evidence for the Urban History of Byzantium," *Zbornik radova vizantoloshkog instituta,* VIII [1963], 291–300). A. P. Kazdan, *Derevnia i gorod v Vizantii IX–X vv* (Moscow, 1960), has maintained that these cities suffered a severe decline between the seventh and ninth centuries and then recovered. Of general interest is the fact that Russell's study, as well as that of Ostrogorsky, "Die Steuersystem in byzantinischen Altertum und Mittelalter," *Byzantium,* VI (1931), 233, indicates that population was expanding during this period.

history. This is another way of saying that historical and other environmental experiences had accustomed these Eastern peoples to commerce and artisanal enterprise. Much of classical Greek and Phoenician colonialism prior to the age of Alexander was commercial rather than imperial, and, in later times, the word "Greek" in central Europe very often came to connote any merchant from the Ottoman Empire. The capacity that Jews, Syrians, and Armenians have displayed in modern commerce is commonplace knowledge.

It is impossible to state precisely the causes for the economic superiority and revival of the East, but one can focus upon the manifestations of this vigor much more sharply. Though the examples of this stamina are both numerous and striking, a few cases will suffice to evoke a general picture. One of the most remarkable physical survivals of this prosperity is the still extensive number of Byzantine gold coins found today in museums, private collections, and also in the stalls of the money changers and jewelers in the streets of Athens, Thessalonica, and Istanbul. When Constantine the Great instituted the gold coin known as the solidus in the early fourth century, he inaugurated what has recently and felicitously been baptized the "dollar of the Middle Ages." [23] This gold coin remained relatively constant in weight and purity until the decline of the eleventh century. Down to the eighth century it was the principal money of international exchange, and after that time it shared the field only with the Arab gold dinar, itself inspired by and modeled on the solidus. Cosmas Indicopleustes, a sixth-century merchant

---

[23] R. S. Lopez, "The Dollar of the Middle Ages," *Journal of Economic History*, XI (1951), 209–234. On Byzantine money, see P. Grierson, "Coinage and Money in the Byzantine Empire, 498–c. 1090," *Settimane di studio del Centro di Studi sull' Alto Evo*, VIII, *Moneta e scambi nell' Alto Medievo* (Spoleto, 1961), 411–453.

from Egypt, noted the importance of this gold coin in the
emporia of southern India, and recent archaeological excavations have uncovered the Byzantine solidus in Chinese
tombs of the sixth and seventh centuries.[24] That this was
no mere occasional coinage intended solely to flatter the
prestige of the emperors emerges from the incidental information that around the year 800 the government paid
to the indigenous soldiery of Anatolia as their annual salary some 1 million gold solidi. The peasantry paid a portion
of its taxes in gold, and salaries and fines in the legal codes
were often reckoned in cash.[25]

To Latin and Muslim travelers, however, the most striking proof of the economic sinews of Byzantium was Constantinople itself.[26] Constantinople, like the solidus, was
the creation of a monarch of genius, and it remained the
largest and wealthiest city of Christendom for eight centuries. It was an international emporium governing the
carrying trade of east and west, north and south, and a
cosmopolis in the streets of which were to be heard not only
the Greek, but the Italian, Arabic, Persian, Turkish, and
Slavic tongues as well.[27] The harbor areas were full of
trading vessels, bickering merchants, and imperious customs officials. It has been customary to think of the Eastern Empire as a one-town affair, that town, of course,

[24] E. Winstedt, *The Christian Topography of Cosmas Indicopleustes*
(Cambridge, 1909), p. 323; S. Nai, "Zolotaia vizantiiskaia moneta,
naidennaia v mogile perioda dinastii Sui," *Vizantiiskii Vremennik*,
XXI (1962), 178–182.

[25] Vryonis, *op. cit.*, pp. 297–300.

[26] Among the most graphic descriptions are those from the hands of
the twelfth-century Jewish traveler Benjamin of Tudela and the
Latin Villehardouin.

[27] The Constantinopolitan poet John Tzetzes boasts that he can
address people in seven languages. For this and other literary references
to the cosmopolitan nature of the city, see S. Vryonis, "Byzantine
Demokratia and the Guilds in the Eleventh Century," *Dumbarton
Oaks Papers*, XVII (1963), 291–292.

being Constantinople. But its provincial urban centers
were also important: Thessalonica, Thebes, Corinth,
Ephesus, Nicaea, Caesarea, Trebizond, and others. These,
then, were some of the manifestations of the Empire's
economic strength.

The medieval resurgence of Hellas took both dynamic
and conservative form in the cultural life of the Byzantine
Empire. To Gibbon, this culture consisted of a rich base of
crass superstition among the masses overlaid with a thick
frosting of meaningless theology and lifeless literary com-
pilations at the level of the intellectuals. Let us listen to
Gibbon himself:

> In the revolution of ten centuries, not a single discovery
> was made to exalt the dignity or promote the happiness
> of mankind. Not a single idea has been added to the specu-
> lative systems of antiquity, and a succession of patient
> disciples became in their turn the dogmatic teachers of
> the next servile generation. Not a single composition of
> history, philosophy, or literature has been saved from ob-
> livion by the intrinsic beauties of style or sentiment, of
> original fancy, or even of successful imitation. . . . Their
> prose is soaring to the viscious affectation of poetry: their
> poetry is sinking below the flatness and insipidity of prose.
> The tragic, epic, and lyric muses were silent and in-
> glorious; the bards of Constantinople seldom rose above a
> riddle or epigram, a panegyric or tale; they forgot even the
> rules of prosody; and, with the melody of Homer yet
> sounding in their ears, they confound all measure of feet
> and syllables in the impotent strains which have received
> the name of political or city verses. The minds of the
> Greeks were bound in the fetters of a base and imperious
> superstition, which extends her dominion round the circle
> of profane science. Their understandings were bewildered
> in metaphysical controversy; in the belief of visions and
> miracles, they had lost all principles of moral evidence; and
> their taste was vitiated by the homelies of the monks, an
> absurd medley of declamation and scripture. Even these
> contemptible studies were no longer dignified by the abuse

of superior talents; the leaders of the Greek church were humbly content to admire and copy the oracles of antiquity, nor did the schools or pulpit produce any rivals of the fame of Athanasius and Chrysostom.[28]

As is so often the case, there is an element of truth in Gibbon's remarks on Byzantine culture, but again it is not the whole truth. Greek culture had experienced its greatest flowering in classical times and its greatest expansion in the Hellenistic era. But this Greek culture, for a variety of reasons which become more apparent in Miriam Lichtheim's chapter, remained a surface phenomenon in much of the Near East. In this latter area, it was strongest in the towns and weakest in the countryside of Syria, Egypt, and Armenia, where local traditions remained largely unchanged in the face of Greco-Roman political domination for the better part of a millennium. Greek culture proved to be most dynamic, or resurgent, in Anatolia. In this large peninsula the Greek language and eventually Greek Christianity presided over the extinction of both the local languages (Phrygian, Lydian, Lycian, Cappadocian, etc.) and the local religious cults. The process was long but was largely complete by the end of the sixth century of the Christian era.[29] Thus, the failure of Hellenization in Egypt, Syria, and Armenia was counterbalanced by its remarkable success in Anatolia. This phenomenon, along with the foundation of Constantinople, resulted in the displacement of the heartland of Greek culture northward and eastward from the original homeland of Hellas. At the same time, however, the linguistic tenacity of the older homeland is illustrated in the medieval Balkans. When the Slavic invasions of the early Middle Ages swept through

[28] *Decline and Fall,* ch. 53:VI, 107–108.
[29] K. Holl, "Das Fortleben der Volksprachen in Kleinasien in nachchristlicher Zeit," *Hermes,* XLIII (1908), 240–254; P. Charanis, "Ethnic Changes in the Byzantine Empire during the Seventh Century," *Dumbarton Oaks Papers,* XIII (1954), 26.

the Balkans, large numbers of Slavs settled not only in the northern half of the peninsula but in the southern half as well. In spite of the fact that these invaders largely Slavonized the Latin-speaking northern half of the area, they left very scant linguistic traces in the Greek language. In the Peloponnese they were Hellenized and left behind them as the only evidence of their existence the great numbers of Slavic placenames in the Peloponnesian countryside.[30]

The Christianization of the Russians, Serbs, and Bulgars was one of the more dramatic expressions of Hellas Resurgent. In this respect, the Byzantine church did for these peoples what the Latin church did for the Germanic barbarians. Byzantium thus indelibly colored a very important portion of future Europe. This Christianization included not only religion, but the elements of civilization itself—alphabet, literature, art, and so forth. The victory of Byzantine culture here is all the more indicative of strength in that the Greek East won these areas not merely by default but after rather stiff competition with the Papal West.[31]

In the intellectual realm, we saw that Gibbon condemned the thinkers of Byzantium because "not a single

[30] The question of the Slavic settlement in Greece is in many ways the "Homeric Question" of Byzantine studies. The controversy, centering on the descent of the modern Greeks, threatens to blossom once more with the announced republication of the work of J. Fallmereyer, *Geschichte der Halbinsel Morea während des Mittelalters* (Stuttgart, 1830–1836). That the Slavs came into Greece in large numbers during the sixth and seventh centuries is no longer doubted by serious scholars, a conclusion made abundantly obvious by the study of place names (M. Vasmer, *Die Slaven in Griechenland*, in *Abhandlungen der Preuss. Akademie der Wissenschaften, Philosophische-historische Klasse*, XII [1941]). The Slavs in Greece were largely absorbed through Christianization and Hellenization (Ostrogorsky, *History of the Byzantine State*, p. 85; F. Dvornik, *The Slavs: Their Early History and Civilization* [Boston, 1956], pp. 116–117).

[31] Dvornik, *op. cit.*, pp. 218 ff., and *Les Slaves Byzance et Rome au IXe siècle* (Paris, 1926).

idea has been added to the speculative systems of antiquity." It is true that Byzantium produced no Platos and
Aristotles; few societies have. Pagan society itself was not
able to do so for the six hundred years that separate the age
of Aristotle from that of Constantine. To this one may
perhaps retort that at least the late pagan world produced
certain lesser figures, such as Plotinus, who worked the
older body of philosophical material and gave it a new
twist. The vapid ideas of late Hellenistic and Roman philosophers, however, were already the products and instruments of the ossification of the ancient philosophical tradition.

What the Christians did was to create theology, or a
Christian philosophy. The love of metaphysical speculation
which is so characteristic of the pagan intellectual world
did not die with the victory of Christianity. Pagan philosophy had already come to a dead end before the triumph of
Christianity. The Christian intellectuals, the Church Fathers, and authors such as Origen and the Cappadocians
who were educated in the classics, opened new channels for
this Greek predisposition to indulge in metaphysical speculation.[32] Christianity was grafted onto Greek philosophy,
and, by a cultural metamorphosis, the pagan love of philosophical discussion was transformed into a passion for
theological speculation. The result was the philosophical or
theological definition of the Christian faith, one of the
great intellectual monuments of Western civilization. This
was, to a great extent, the work of the Greek East, where
the first seven ecumenical councils took place. It is true, at
the same time, that after this extraordinary manifestation
of theological energy, theology became conservative, and
the church henceforth considered it a sacred duty to preserve the results of these councils unaltered and unchanged. This philosophical definition of Christianity was

[32] This theme is incisively developed in Jaeger, *op cit*.

something Gibbon did not appreciate, mainly for the same reasons that modern society largely ignores it. Gibbon was a modern man and, as such, was the product of a series of evolutions and revolutions which finally caused interest in theology to dwindle. In the *Decline and Fall* he repeatedly justifies the discussion of any theological issue purely on the grounds that it affected the political history of the times, but he never bothers to explain why an etherial matter should so frequently and so violently affect political history. He does not conceive of theology as something which has an existence, importance, and interest of its own and as an intellectual discipline which in medieval times was considered to be the queen of the sciences.

Byzantine art likewise represents the sublimation of an expressive form of pagan Antiquity into something new. The art of the ancient world had run its own course and then began to decline in originality and vigor when the Byzantines took it, transformed it, and created a new art.[33] The examples of philosophy and theology, on the one hand, and of pagan and Byzantine art, on the other, are quite parallel in this respect. Because they were religious (that is to say, related to a hierarchically structured religion) and therefore quite different from classical art and philosophy, Gibbon despised both Byzantine theology and art. In our own day, however, the originality, the importance, and even the beauty of Byzantine art have finally been recognized.

Yet, because it does contain a part of the truth, once more one must consider Gibbon and his pejorative judgment of Byzantine culture. Its conservatism was so powerful and so pervasive that it successfully obscured the more creative aspects of this civilization. Byzantium was the

[33] For elements of continuity, see E. Kitzinger, "The Hellenistic Heritage in Byzantine Art," *Dumbarton Oaks Papers,* XVII (1963), 97–116.

child of Antiquity, a most obedient child that was never able to destroy completely the father image. Its literary and linguistic inheritance was particularly rich, for the parent was one of genius. If the Byzantines worshiped Homer, Aristotle, Polybius, and Thucydides, their taste has been vindicated by the taste of the modern world. The pagan world had already bestowed the canonization of perfection on these great figures and their works. Thus the late pagan world was as Byzantine as the Byzantines themselves in their faithful imitation of and enslavement to these works. This aspect of the Byzantine tradition certainly did not provide the optimum conditions for the freeing of new rivulets of literary experimentation and creation. It did result, however, in the preservation of many of the Greek classics until the West was ready to receive this priceless treasure and to reevaluate it under the powerful renaissance light of Humanism.[34] Byzantine monks toiled endlessly in copying the texts, Byzantine professors and bishops wrote copious commentaries on them, and the bureaucrats and men of letters all studied these writings as the basis of their education. But, as Gibbon remarks, they often studied the form rather than the content. At the same time, the preservation of this body of literature assured the Byzantines a higher level of civilization than that of the West in the earlier centuries of the Middle Ages. The barbarians, strangers to this tradition, were forced to resort to their imaginations, and the felicitous results of this fact would not become apparent until the West faced the East in the period of the Crusades. It is this circumstance that Gibbon underlines when he remarks that while Byzantium was absorbed with theology, the Latins developed something called technology. Byzantine

[34] The literary inheritance is traced by R. Jenkins, "The Hellenistic Origins of Byzantine Literature," *Dumbarton Oaks Papers.* XVII (1963), 37–52.

technology has not yet been investigated, but it is quite possible that Gibbon's view in this particular matter will be partially vindicated once such an investigation is carried out. One is struck by the comparative frequency with which the Byzantines copied and used the classical manuals on agriculture, warfare and tactics, hunting, fishing, and so forth. Their continued use would indicate that the methods and technics worked out in them satisfactorily fulfilled the needs of society in the eastern Mediterranean. So long as a particular arrangement in society fulfills its function, it is not likely to change easily. It is only when it is forced to compete or face a new challenge that the old arrangement or order must change. On the other hand, one must acknowledge that it was Byzantine conservatism that aided the Empire in the utilization of its energies in the most economical manner and thus enabled it to survive the storms of the early Middle Ages.

Lest it appear that I have fallen victim to the Gibbonian view on Byzantine culture, it should be added that Byzantine literature had a newer, more creative strain in addition to that which Gibbon ascribed to it. It developed a new religious poetry of great beauty, truly worthy of its classical predecessor. Hagiography, in spite of Gibbon, was a living genre, largely devoid of the artificiality of the atticizers. Vernacular poetry and literature also appeared and developed. Finally, one should note that those servile Byzantine historians, as Gibbon referred to them, at least maintained the standard of excellence of their ancient models, even though they did not create something new. Their historiographical production was superior to its contemporary counterparts in the West; they recorded for later ages the greatness of this millennial state in almost unbroken succession from Constantine to the fall in 1453. They are also far more objective than Gibbon would have us believe when he speaks of them as "servile": they do not hide the weakness or shortcomings of Byzantium, and they fully acknowledge the prowess of both Latins and Muslims. This is more than their Western and Muslim counterparts did.

It may seem that this chapter has been nothing more nor less than a running criticism of what is rightly considered to be one of the classics of modern historiography. But such has been the fate of many great histories. In spite of the fact that Gibbon distorted the picture of an entire civilization, and did so with considerable prejudice, biting malice, and obvious pleasure, his work will abide as an object of contemplation.

IV

AUTONOMY VERSUS UNITY
IN THE CHRISTIAN EAST

Miriam Lichtheim

I HAVE SOUGHT for records of events of earlier date amongst the established laws appertaining to religion, amongst the proceedings of the synods of the period . . . and in the epistles of kings and priests. Some of these documents are preserved in palaces and churches, and others are dispersed, and in the possession of the learned; I thought seriously, at one time, of transcribing the whole, but on further reflection I deemed it better, on account of the prolixity of the documents, to give merely a brief synopsis of their contents; yet whenever controverted topics are introduced, I will readily transcribe freely from any work that may tend to the elucidation of truth. If any one who is ignorant of past events should conclude my history to be false because he meets with conflicting statements in other writings, let him know that since the dogmas of Arius and other more recent hypotheses have been broached, the rulers of the churches, differing in opinion among themselves, have transmitted in writing their own peculiar views, for the benefit of their respective followers; and further, be it remembered, these rulers convened councils and issued what decrees they pleased, often condemning unheard those whose creed was dissimilar to their own . . . Still, as it is requisite, in order

to maintain historical accuracy, to pay the strictest attention to the means of eliciting truth, I felt myself bound to
examine all writings of this class with great diligence."
Thus Sozomen.[1] The modesty and naïveté underscore the
timeless rightness of this historian's approach to his craft.
He will search out the truth and tell it, even at the risk of
offending. Not so Theodoret, for whom discretion and
edification come before accuracy and candor: "I deem it
desirable to treat these revolting events [the banishment of
St. John Chrysostom] only briefly and to cover up the
faults of the persons involved, as they are of our faith."[2]

Gibbon chose candor at all times, and chose it the more
readily as his fighting humanitarianism wished to expose
man's inhumanity. His prejudices and exaggerations are an
easy target for criticism. Yet, the alliance of genius with
essential rightmindedness makes even his least adequate
chapters memorable.

With Oriental studies in their infancy, and Syriac and
Coptic sources largely beyond his reach,[3] Gibbon's account of the schismatic movements in Eastern Christendom (*Decline and Fall*, ch. 47) cannot but be wholly
inadequate for our time. Yet, there are enough insights in
his judgments to make his account of the major schismatic
churches, Nestorian and Monophysite, challenging:

> Under the rod of persecution, the Nestorians and Monoph-
> ysites degenerated into rebels and fugitives; and the most
> ancient and useful allies of Rome were taught to consider
> the emperor not as the chief, but as the enemy of the Chris-
> tians. Language, the leading principle which unites or sep-

[1] *The Ecclesiastical History of Sozomen*, trans. Edward Walford
(London, 1855), I.1, p. 11.

[2] Theodoret, *Ecclesiastical History*, V.36.

[3] Gibbon made use of the great Syriac text collection compiled by
Joseph Simon Assemanni, the *Bibliotheca Orientalis Clementino-Vati-
cana* (4 vols.; Rome, 1719–1728), and he paid eloquent tribute to the
learned Maronite.

arates the tribes of mankind, soon discriminated the sectaries of the East by a peculiar and perpetual badge which abolished the means of intercourse and the hope of reconciliation. The long dominion of the Greeks, their colonies, and above all, their eloquence, had propagated a language, doubtless the most perfect that has been contrived by the art of man. Yet the body of the people, both in Syria and Egypt, still persevered in the use of their national idioms; with this difference, however, that the Coptic was confined to the rude and illiterate peasants of the Nile, while the Syriac, from the mountains of Assyria to the Red Sea, was adapted to the higher topics of poetry and argument.[4]

In emphasizing the linguistic aspect of separatism, Gibbon raised a cardinal point. A few pages later, his ironic wit produced a memorable two-sentence portrait of Monophysitism's pivotal leader: "The rule of the Monophysite faith was defined with exquisite discretion by Severus, patriarch of Antioch: he condemned, in the style of the Henoticon, the adverse heresies of Nestorius and Eutyches, maintained against the latter the reality of the body of Christ, and constrained the Greeks to allow that he was a liar who spoke truth." [5]

Outlining the consolidation of the Monophysite churches, Gibbon, without losing sight of the primacy of theology, sounded the twin themes of national sentiment and resentment of Byzantine rule, themes which, along with the language factor, have been at the center of scholarly debate to this day. Quoting the Coptic patriarch Theodosius, whom Justinian was trying to bring into line by threats and promises: "The churches are in the hands of a prince who can kill the body; but my conscience is my own; and in exile poverty or chains, I will steadfastly adhere to the faith of my holy predecessors, Athanasius, Cyril, and Dioscorus. Anathema to the tome of Leo and

[4] *Decline and Fall*, ch. 47:V, 144.
[5] *Ibid.*, ch. 47:V, 153.

the synod of Chalcedon . . . ," [6] and having described
the patriarch's exile and death, Gibbon summed up dramatically and, by and large, justly:

> A perpetual succession of patriarchs arose from the ashes
> of Theodosius; and the Monophysite churches of Syria and
> Egypt were united by the name of Jacobites and the com-
> munion of the faith. But the same faith, which has been
> confined to a narrow sect of the Syrians, was diffused over
> the mass of the Egyptian or Coptic nation; who, almost
> unanimously, rejected the decrees of the synod of Chalce-
> don. A thousand years were now elapsed since Egypt had
> ceased to be a kingdom, since the conquerors of Asia
> and Europe had trampled on the ready necks of a people,
> whose ancient wisdom and power ascend beyond the rec-
> ords of history. The conflict of zeal and persecution re-
> kindled some sparks of their national spirit. They abjured,
> with a foreign heresy, the manners and language of the
> Greeks: every Melchite, in their eyes, was a stranger, every
> Jacobite a citizen; the alliance of marriage, the offices of
> humanity, were condemned as a deadly sin; the natives
> renounced all allegiance to the emperor; and his orders, at
> a distance from Alexandria, were obeyed only under the
> pressure of military force.[7]

Scholars of the late nineteenth and early twentieth centuries placed greater emphasis on the national spirit and
other secular forces in attempting to explain the dissident
movements.[8] At the present time, the concern with doctrinal rightness is once again seen as the central fact; but
there is no consensus on how to define and weigh the con-
comitant secular motives. Especially the language factor is
frequently misconstrued by classical scholars who persist

[6] *Ibid.*, ch. 47:V, 161.

[7] *Ibid.*, ch. 47:V, 162.

[8] E. L. Woodward, *Christianity and Nationalism in the Later
Roman Empire* (London, 1916), stated the case for nationalism, but
his broad generalizations rest on very slender evidence. Jean Mas-
pero, *Histoire des Patriarches d'Alexandrie* (Paris, 1923), is even
more emphatic but highly prejudiced. The theme is frequently sounded
but not substantiated.

in evaluating the Eastern cultures by the degree of their Hellenization.[9]

If we are to account for the separatist movements in the eastern provinces of the Byzantine Empire (confining our-selves to Egypt and the Syro-Mesopotamian region), it would seem that the contribution made by oriental studies, especially in the last hundred years, affords the right per-spective. The ever-growing number of Syriac and Coptic text editions, though representing only a tiny fraction of what once existed, are witnesses of the vital literary activ-ity that is the cardinal fact behind the viability of the schismatic churches.

From the beginning, the spread of Christianity in Egypt was accompanied by a linguistic dichotomy: the Church's leadership, concentrated at Alexandria, spoke and wrote Greek—predominantly, not exclusively [10]—while the

[9] The imperialism of classical scholarship reached its high point in the nineteenth century and still lingers. Cf. Th. Mommsen's char-acterization of the partly Hellenized peoples of Syria and Mesopotamia as the "verderbteste und verderbendste Element in dem römisch-hell-enischen Völkerconglomerat," *Römische Geschichte*, 5 (1885), 455, and Th. Nöldeke's critical review in *Zeitschrift der deutschen mor-genländischen Gesellschaft*, 39 (1885), 331–351. The new Roman history by A. H. M. Jones, *The Later Roman Empire, 284–602* (Ox-ford, 1964) II, 992, contains the amazing statement: "No educated Egyptian deigned to write in Coptic, and Coptic literature, apart from translations, was confined to popular lives of the saints." The searching study of P. Peeters, *Le tréfonds oriental de l'hagiographie byzantine* (Brussels, 1950), contributes much toward a more balanced assessment.

[10] Hieracas of Leontopolis is known to have written in Greek and in Bohairic. That St. Athanasius wrote some of his works in Coptic is now considered probable. See S. Morenz, "Die koptische Literatur," in *Handbuch der Orientalistik*, ed. B. Spuler (Leiden, 1952), I.2, pp. 212 f., with all relevant bibliography; especially G. Steindorff, "Bemerk-ungen über die Anfänge der Koptischen Sprache und Literatur," in *Coptic Studies in Honor of W. E. Crum* (Boston, 1950), pp. 189–214, with quotations from Epiphanius of Salamis (himself multilin-gual) on Hieracas.

country at large spoke the various dialects of Coptic. Such Hellenization as existed in the urban centers outside of Alexandria was dwindling with the decline of the middle class. The Christianization of the countryside thus depended from the start on the wholesale translation from Greek into Coptic of the Scriptures and of the instructions in the new faith that issued from the theologians of Alexandria. The oldest preserved Coptic versions of biblical texts date from the third century and are written in Sahidic, the leading dialect of Upper Egypt. If Christianity and Bible translations were the principal forces that transformed the Coptic dialects into literary languages, another impetus was provided by Christianity's great rival, Gnosticism. The rich library of Coptic Gnostic papyrus codices discovered in 1946 near the village of Nag Hammadi in Upper Egypt, most of them dating from the third century, has underscored the strength of Gnosticism, whose many sects are known to have flourished in Egypt, and the vital part it played in the birth of Coptic literature.[11] In the fourth century, Coptic literature reached maturity in the sense that, alongside translations, there began the production of Coptic original works. The force that created these works was Upper Egyptian cenobitic monasticism, founded early in the fourth century by St. Pachomius (d. 346). Except for fragments, the bulk of his Sahidic writings—letters and the monastic rule—are extant only in Latin translation. Their importance for the history of monasticism is too well known to require mention. Suffice it to say that Pachomius and his successors produced a body of writings which, in their Greek and

---

[11] For a preliminary survey of these texts, see Jean Doresse, *The Secret Books of the Egyptian Gnostics* (New York, 1960). The original French edition was published in Paris in 1958. See also H. Puech, "Les nouveaux écrits gnostiques découverts en Haute-Egypte," in *Coptic Studies in Honor of W. E. Crum*, pp. 91–154.

Latin translations, promoted the spread of monasticism throughout the Empire, while the Sahidic originals carried Sahidic into Akhmimic and Fayyumic linguistic territory and, at the expense of the latter dialects, established Sahidic as the literary language of all Upper and Middle Egypt. The decisive role that Shenute of Atripe, abbot of the White Monastery near Akhmim since 385, played in this development has been retold many times. His powerful personality and his voluminous writings produced a vast expansion of monasticism as well as a Christian homiletic literature that became normative for all of Coptic Egypt.[12]

In Lower Egypt, meanwhile, Christian asceticism had found its expression in the anchoritic dwellings of Nitria and Scete, whose Lower Egyptian dialect, Bohairic, was going through a parallel evolution. Beginning with Bible translations, it became the vehicle for original compositions. The Bohairic Bible translations originated in the fourth century, hence about a century later than the Sahidic ones; and the two groups are independent of each other. At this very time, the desert hermits of Nitria and Scete created the most important literary work of all Coptic Egypt, the *Apophthegmata Patrum* ("Sayings of the Fathers"). In Bohairic, Sahidic, Greek, Latin, Syriac, Armenian, Arabic, and Ethiopic, these "Sayings" were to radiate throughout the Christian world. They reflect with unequaled directness and simplicity the nature of ascetic piety and the way of life of the desert hermits of Lower Egypt in the fourth and fifth centuries.[13] The anchoritic ideal appears here in its purest form: ascetic practice is dis-

[12] See the basic work by J. Leipoldt, *Schenute von Atripe und die Entstehung des national-ägyptischen Christentums* (Leipzig, 1903).

[13] Fundamental and luminous is W. Bousset, *Apophthegmata: Studien zur Geschichte des ältesten Mönchtums* (Tübingen, 1923). The "Sayings" I quoted are taken from the fine work of Helen Waddell, *The Desert Fathers* (paperback ed., Ann Arbor, 1957), pp. 98, 103, 152, 129, 153, 84, respectively.

creet, not ostentatious; gentleness is the supreme virtue; the young and inexperienced are counseled moderation:

> The abbot Antony said, "There be some that wear out their bodies with abstinence: but because they have no discretion, they be a great way from God."
>
> A brother came to the abbot Pastor and said to him, "Many thoughts come into my mind, and I am in peril from them." And the old man pushed him out under the open sky, and said to him, "Expand thy chest and catch the wind." And he answered, "I cannot do it." And the old man said to him: "If thou canst not do this, neither canst thou prevent thoughts from entering in, but it is for thee to resist them."
>
> He said again, "If there be three in one place, and one of them lives the life of holy quiet, and another is ill and gives thanks, and the third tends them with an honest heart, these three are alike, as if their work was one."
>
> The brethren asked the abbot Poemen concerning a certain brother that did fast for six days out of the seven with perfect abstinence, but was extreme choleric, and for what reason did he suffer it? And the old man made answer, "He that hath taught himself to fast for six days and not to control his temper, it would become him better to bring greater zeal to a lesser toil."
>
> An old man was asked by a certain soldier if God received a penitent man. And after heartening him with many words, he said to him at the last, "Tell me, if thy cloak were torn, wouldst throw it away?" He said, "Nay, but I would patch it and wear it." The old man said to him, "If thou wouldst spare thy garment, shall not God have mercy on His own image?"

Absolute peacefulness, gentleness, moderation, and a common-sense approach to the rigors of asceticism are the principal virtues that the hermits teach one another in a language of pithy, forceful simplicity. This realization of the otherworldly life differs greatly from the demonstrative asceticism of the Syrian pillar saints, and from the inevitably coarser and worldlier communal monasticism that was to absorb them both.

Given the otherworldly character of the anchoritic ideal, the absence of theological speculation, indeed the refusal to engage in theological discussion, is not surprising: "At one time there came heretics to the abbot Poemen, and they began to speak ill of the archbishop of Alexandria: but the old man kept silence. But calling his disciple he said to him, 'Set the table, and give them to eat, and so send them away in peace.' " What is surprising is the small space that demonology, miracles, and visions occupy in the *Apophthegmata*. This sets them apart from the bulk of Coptic religious literature, especially the abundant hagiography. It has been pointed out that the large influx of demonology corrupted the monastic ideal, and that it was both the cause and the effect of the anti-intellectualism that came to play a considerable part in Eastern monasticism.[14] Yet radical otherworldliness itself, free of demonology, would seem to be the principal root of the anti-intellectual attitude:

> The abbot Theodore of Pherme had three fine codices. And he came to the abbot Macarius and said to him, "I have three codices, and I profit by the reading of them. And the brethren also come seeking to read them, and they themselves profit. Tell me, therefore, what I ought to do?" And the old man answering said, "These are good deeds: but better than all is to possess nothing." And hearing this he went away and sold the aforenamed codices, and gave the price of them to the needy.

The anchorites, then, were aware of the dilemma—saintliness or culture—a dilemma both false and real. Eventually coenobitic monasticism solved it, in the East no less than in

[14] A. J. Festugière, *Les moines d'Orient* (Paris, 1961———), pt. 1: "Culture ou sainteté."

the West. The popular misconception of the European monk who tended the light of learning while his Eastern brother sank into sloth results from projecting into the early Christian centuries, which were times of great vigor in the East, the image of the shrunken, decayed, and impoverished Eastern monasticism that travelers from the West had begun to encounter since the end of the Middle Ages.[15]

Along with composing original works, the "rude and illiterate peasants of the Nile" translated the writings of the Greek Church Fathers, Athanasius, Basil, Gregory of Nazianzus, Gregory of Nyssa, John Chrysostom, and others—translations in which Sahidic and Bohairic translators have an approximately equal share. To this early period also belong the beginnings of historiography, again in the dual form of translations—for example, the *Ecclesiastical History* of Eusebius—and original works dealing with the patriarchate, works that have not survived but became the sources for the extant *History of the Patriarchs* written in Arabic at the end of the tenth century.[16]

The two dynamic forces that had created Coptic literature, Gnosticism and Christianity, also account for the transformation of the East-Aramaic dialect of northern

[15] The introductions to the great manuscript catalogues contain a wealth of interesting detail on the monastic libraries of the East and on the formation of the rich collections in the West, e.g., W. Wright, *Catalogue of the Syriac Manuscripts in the British Museum Acquired since 1838* (London, 1872), and W. E. Crum, *Catalogue of the Coptic Manuscripts in the British Museum* (London, 1905). On the monasteries of Lower Egypt, see especially H. G. Evelyn-White, *The Monasteries in the Wadi'n Natrun* (3 vols.; New York, 1926–1933), and in particular vol. 2, *The History of the Monasteries of Nitria and of Scetis*.

[16] Sawirus ibn al-Muqaffa (or Severus, bishop of Eshmunein), *History of the Patriarchs of the Coptic Church of Alexandria*, ed. and trans. B. Evetts, Patrologia Orientalis, I.2 (Paris, 1948————).

Mesopotamia into literary Syriac. The parallel ends here, for in all other respects the character of the Syro-Mesopotamian region differs profoundly from that of Egypt. Where all factors in the Nile Valley tended to homogeneity, uniform culture, and unified rule, here all was diversity, regionalism, and turbulent change. Seleucid Hellenization, far from unifying, increased the diversity by superimposing Greco-Macedonian settlers and Greek city culture; Roman reorganization rebuilt the local autonomous structures. Moreover, with its central location and proximity to Byzantium, Syria was the nerve center of the eastern provinces and was the first to be affected by imperial policy. Thus, when Syriac literature was born in the verdant city of Edessa, "the Athens of the East," to quote the ever-felicitous Gibbon, its rapid spread throughout the Aramaic-speaking territories promoted not only the new faith but also the articulation of separatist tendencies.[17]

The migration of St. Ephraem and other Christians from Nisibis to Edessa, after Nisibis had been ceded to the Persians in 363, produced the first full flowering of Syriac literature as well as the rise to fame of Edessa's Christian school of higher learning, the "School of the Persians." In Ephraem's immense literary output, the hymns stand out as his most original and influential contribution, becoming the classic model for all subsequent Syriac poetry and affecting also the development of Byzantine hymnody, in

---

[17] Syriac literature is surveyed in a number of very good histories: W. Wright, *A Short History of Syriac Literature* (London, 1894), dated but still excellent and very readable; R. Duval, *La littérature syriaque* (3d ed.; Paris, 1907); C. Brockelmann, "Die syrische und die christlich-arabische Literatur," in *Geschichte der christlichen Literaturen des Orients* (Leipzig, 1907); A. Baumstark, *Geschichte der syrischen Literatur* (Bonn, 1922), the basic work, immensely learned and comprehensive; J.-B. Chabot, *Littérature syriaque* (Paris, 1934), addressed to a wider audience and eminently readable.

particular that of the Syrian-born Romanos.[18] Much of their repetitiveness can be accounted for by their sheer bulk and by the fact that all the hymns were meant to be sung in chorus. Yet his poetic inventiveness and the skill with which he handled a large variety of complex metrical forms justify his fame; and Sozomen's lavish praise underscores Ephraem's influence in the Greek world:

> His style of writing was so replete with splendid oratory and sublimity of thought that he surpassed all the writers of Greece. If the works of these writers were to be translated into Syriac, or any other language, and divested, as it were, of the beauties of the Greek language, they would retain little of their original elegance and value. The productions of Ephraim have not this disadvantage: they were translated into Greek during his life, and translations are even now being made, and yet they preserve much of their original force and power, so that his works are not less admired when read in Greek than when read in Syriac.[19]

The sample I have translated consists of the first five strophes of Ephraem's second "Hymn to Paradise." [20] The translation is literal and reproduces the exact metrical scheme, a line of ten syllables of which four are accented, with a caesura after the fifth syllable. The fourth line of each six-line strophe has only seven syllables of which three are accented. Occasionally, there is an extra unaccented syllable; but the number and position of the accented syllables does not vary.

[18] See W. Meyer, *Anfang und Ursprung der lateinischen und griechischen rhythmischen Dichtung* (Munich, 1885); H. Grimme, *Der Strophenbau in den Gedichten Ephraems des Syrers* (Freiburg i. d. Schweiz, 1893); and the new edition of Romanos, *Sancti Romani Melodi Cantica,* ed. P. Maas and C. A. Trypanis (Oxford, 1963).

[19] *Ecclesiastical History* III.16.

[20] New edition by E. Beck, *Des Heiligen Ephraem des Syrers Hymnen De Paradiso und Contra Julianum,* Corpus Scriptorum Christianorum Orientalium (CSCO), Scriptores Syri, vols. 78–79 (Louvain, 1957).

Bléssed the mán whom/ Páradise cóvets
Éden's gate ópens/ swállows the ríghteous
Préssed to its bósom/ crádles him sínging
Cléaving, ópening fór him.
Bút if it hátes a man/ spéws and rejécts him,
Gáte of discérnment/ grácious to mánkind.

Hásten to móuld thee/ Páradise's kéy
Gáte runs towárd thee/ rádiant and smíling
Gáte of discrétion it/ meásures the cáller
Shrínking, gŕowing, to fít him.
Gréatness and státure/ gáte will acknówledge
Fúll-size or wánting/ gáte's height will téll it.

Mánkind shall sée this:/ góne are their ríches
Wéalth it has vánished/ góods they are nóthing
Beáuty and pówer/ góne and forgótten
Fílled with móurning they wónder:
Whý did they cóvet/ why disbelíeve that
Dréam their posséssions/ dárkness their éarnings.

Lóst their belóngings/ fóund what was nóthing
Góne what they chérished/ cóme what they háted
Náught what they hóped for/ fóund what they dréaded
Chéated, fállen they griéve.
Lífe has betráyed them/ reál now their súffering,
Jóy it forsóok them/ páin now pursúes them.

Bút the right mínded/ sée their pains énded;
Súffering has vánished/ lábors are fínished,
Sórrows forgótten/ vóid, without súbstance,
Náught but a dréam their fásting;
Ás from sleep rísing/ Páradise greéts them
Spréad out befóre them/ feást of the kíngdom.

With Rabbula, bishop of Edessa (d. 435), who wrote in Syriac and in Greek and translated some of the works of Cyril, the preschismatic period comes to an end. In the tripartite structure of Syrian Christianity which resulted from the councils of Ephesus and Chalcedon—Nestorians,

Monophysites, and Melkites—the first two account for almost all subsequent Syrian literature, whether in Syriac or
in Greek.[21] Both schismatic communities are characterized by an ubiquitous bilingualism and a sheer inexhausti-
ble literary production. The Nestorian Ibas (d. 457), who
succeeded Rabbula as bishop of Edessa, bears the epithet
"the translator" for his vast translating activity, which
centered on the works of Diodore of Tarsus, Theodore of
Mopsuestia, and Aristotle. After his death, his followers
were expelled by Bishop Nonnus (d. 471), and they established themselves on Persian soil, where most of them became bishops of the nascent Nestorian church which, in
the following decades, absorbed all the Christian communities of Persia. This development was brought to its
formal conclusion when the general synod of the churches
in the Persian realm, held at Seleucia in 486, declared itself
Nestorian. Three years later the closing of the "School of
the Persians" at Edessa, by order of the Emperor Zeno,
completed the Nestorian migration to Persia and the transfer of its center of learning to Nisibis, where Narsai (d.
after 503), then Nestorianism's chief theologian, teacher,
and poet, had started a school in 457 which he continued to
lead for more than four decades. In the fifth and sixth centuries Nestorian intellectual activity branched out into the
various fields of learning which were to continue flowering
for several more centuries under Arab dominion. Narsai's
three outstanding pupils, the theologians Abraham and

[21] From the vast literature on the doctrinal disputes and the formation of the schismatic churches a few comprehensive works may
be singled out: A. Grillmeier and H. Bacht (eds.), *Das Konzil von
Chalkedon, Geschichte und Gegenwart* (3 vols.; Würzburg, 1951–
1953); B. Spuler, *Die morgenländischen Kirchen* in *Handbuch der
Orientalistik*, I. Abtlg., Bd. 8/2 (Leiden, 1964). On the Monophysite hierarchy, see E. Honigmann, *Evêques et évêchés monophysites d'Asie antérieure au VIᵉ siècle*, CSCO, Subsidia, vol. 2 (Louvain,
1951).

Yohanan, and Joseph Huzaya, the pioneer of grammatical studies, brought the school of Nisibis to its peak in diversified studies which also included the translation of the works of Nestorius. Mar Abha (d. 552), Persian convert to Christianity, after studying at Nisibis and Edessa, visited Palestine, Egypt, and Constantinople and subsequently, as catholicus of Seleucia, organized the capital's theological school and, vigorously leading the church in the face of Magian hostility, used his seven-year exile to translate the Greek liturgy into Syriac. The circle of his outstanding students includes Paul, bishop of Nisibis (d. 571), who participated in a theological disputation at Constantinople, and Theodore, bishop of Merv (fl. 550), who studied Aristotelian philosophy and maintained a philosopher's friendship with his opposite number in the other camp—Sergius of Reshaina, whose devotion to philosophic studies seems to have been coupled with an unstable faith. A new and troubling element was introduced into Nestorian higher learning when Henana (d. 610) expounded Origenist views at the school of Nisibis, thereby causing a prolonged crisis. Historiography, biography, a growing interest in science, especially medicine, and in secular belles lettres, for which translations from Pehlevi are symptomatic—all these branches of literature flourished abundantly. Monasticism, discouraged by the ecclesiastical hierarchy of the fifth century, but growing strong since the second half of the sixth, peopled the mountain regions of the Adiabene under the leadership of the "Great Monastery" founded by Abraham of Kashkar (d. 586). More autonomous, less integrated in the life of the church than Monophysite monasticism, the Nestorian monasteries ultimately became the last centers of resistance to Islam.

To recount these facts is to stress the physical and intellectual vigor of the Nestorian community; the bilingual, often trilingual, character of its higher education and its literature; its missionary zeal which carried the cross as far as China; and a dedication to learning which encompassed ever-larger portions of Greek philosophy and science, to the ultimate benefit of both the Arab East and the Latin West.

> Since you, Christ-loving Eupraxius, dwelling in the palace and laboring in the service of the king, desire to learn what befell the holy Church of God in the reign of Marcian, and who they were who successively became chief priests in Alexandria, Rome, Constantinople, Antioch and Jerusalem from the time of the Council of Chalcedon— that Council which, on account of Eutyches, introduced and increased the heresy of Nestorius, and shook all the world, and heaped evil upon evil, and set the two heresies against each other, and filled the world with divisions, and confused the perfect faith of the apostles and the good order of the Church, and tore into a thousand shreds the perfect, seamless, garment of Christ: therefore we, condemning those two heresies and every lying and corrupt teacher who rose against the Church of God and against the orthodox faith of the three holy Synods, which had skillfully preserved the true doctrine, shall now undertake the narration to which you encouraged us.

Thus Zacharias Rhetor, friend and biographer of Severus of Antioch, in the Syriac version of his lost Greek historical work.[22] The note of passionate protest runs through all Monophysite literature: Chalcedon had vindicated Nestorianism and thereby betrayed Ephesus (431) and misrepresented St. Cyril. There could be no peace until the two-nature heresy that corrupted the apostolic faith had been wiped out. Alexandria had led the fight against the Arian heresy; it would lead again against the Nestorian-

[22] *Historia Ecclesiastica*, ed. E. W. Brooks, III.1, CSCO, Scriptores Syri, vols. 38–39 (Louvain, 1953). English translation: *The Syriac Chronicle Known as That of Zachariah of Mitylene*, trans. F. J. Hamilton and E. W. Brooks (London, 1899).

Chalcedonian blasphemy. If the emperor could not be won over, he would be resisted.

The emperors strove for reconciliation. In 484 the deposition of the bishops who refused to sign Zeno's *Henoticon* restored Peter the Fuller to the patriarchate of Antioch, brought Philoxenus to the see of Mabbog, and everywhere consolidated the gains Monophysitism had made. Egypt had become impregnably Monophysite. In Syria, the Monophysite victory required imperial benevolence for its near-complete realization during the patriarchate of Severus of Antioch (512–518; d. 538). Only Palestine, after three decades of predominantly Monophysite sentiment, had turned to Chalcedonian orthodoxy and allied itself with Rome. The learned and ascetic Severus, subtle and moderate theologian as well as dynamic and uncompromising leader, is a compelling figure. And the almost total loss of his Greek writings (incompletely preserved in Syriac translations) is the more regrettable as it prevents a full assessment of the literary talent of Greek-oriented Monophysitism's leading exponent. Syriac Monophysitism found its most brilliant leader in Severus' close friend, the fiery Philoxenus (d. 523), like him a man of action as well as a studious and ascetic scholar. His Syriac prose is invariably defined as elegant, ever since Assemani, who reviled him as "scelestissimus haereticus," grudgingly praised it: "Scripsit Syriace, si quis alius, elegantissime. . . ." [23]

In these auspicious decades, Simeon of Beth Arsham (d. before 548) had wandered throughout Persian territory preaching the Monophysite faith to Nestorians and Manicheans, while the quietly studious Jacob of Serugh (d. 521), Monophysitism's principal poet, composed 763

[23] *Bibliotheca Orientalis*, ii.20. The passage is quoted by Wright, *A Short History of Syriac Literature*, p. 74. See also A. de Halleux, *Philoxène de Mabbog: Sa vie, ses écrits, sa théologie* (Louvain, 1963).

metrical homilies in dodecasyllabic lines, of which close to 300 have been preserved.[24]

When the brutal repression under Justin I (518–527) and in the early years of Justinian (527–565) turned Severus into a fugitive and exiled more than fifty Monophysite bishops, the leaders resisted with passionate determination. From his precarious refuge in Egypt (519–538), the hunted Severus continued to lead his flock through pastoral letters and polemical writings, which increasingly dealt with the threat from within the ranks posed by the Aphthartodocetist teachings of his onetime friend and fellow refugee, Julian of Halicarnassus:

> Against the last fatuous work of the wickedly impious Julian, which promulgates the same arguments upon the same subjects, I have not up to today begun to write, although it is refuted beforehand by what has been already written by me before, so that everyone who meets with it will know its feebleness and the futility of the erroneous phantasy which he confessed. During the whole time of the summer, and that though I have been hiding in corners, I have never ceased being worried by constant letters from men who in various ways ask different questions at different times, and beg to have now scriptural expressions, now doctrinal theories explained to them. Also the loneliness of solitude, and the fact that I have not men at hand to serve as scribes when I want it in addition to the other things hinder me from writing.[25]

Nor did Philoxenus' painful exile dim his prose.[26] And the lives of other banished bishops further bear out that, far

---

[24] Bar Hebraeus gives their number as 760, and says that 70 scribes were employed in copying his works. See Wright, *op. cit.*, p. 70; Baumstark, *op. cit.*, p. 149.

[25] *The Sixth Book of the Select Letters of Severus, Patriarch of Antioch,* ed. and trans. E. W. Brooks (London, 1904), Vol. II, Pt. II, 358.

[26] E. g., *Philoxène de Mabbog: Lettre aux moines de Senoun,* ed. A. de Halleux, CSCO, Scriptores Syri, vols. 98–99 (Louvain, 1963).

from "degenerating into rebels and fugitives," the Monophysite leaders pursued an increasingly abundant literary
activity that contributed much to the movement's subsequent resurgence. Paul of Callinicus found refuge at
Edessa and devoted himself to translating the works of
Severus. John bar Aphtonius (d. 537), abbot of the con-
vent of St. Thomas at Seleucia on the Orontes, renowned
as a center for Greek studies, upon being expelled (ca.
531), took his monks with him to Kenneshrin on the
Euphrates and founded a new monastery which soon out-
shone its parent. Mara of Amida (d. ca. 529) used his
Alexandrian exile to collect a large library which was
brought to Amida after his death and became the property
of the Church.[27] Egypt provided refuge for the expelled
bishops, for there the emperors contented themselves with
sporadic police action, while repression in Syria was violent
and on a large scale. Moreover, the Alexandrian patriarchs
now were moderates rather than dynamic fighters; active
leadership had passed to the Syrians and remained in their
hands even in the twilight period, 518–542.

John of Tella is the precursor, Jacob Baradaeus the
founder, and John of Ephesus the cofounder and historian
of the reconstructed Monophysite (Jacobite) church.
Driven out of his see in 521 and hunted to his death in 538,
John of Tella secretly ordained priests and bishops for the
leaderless communities. In 542, persecution having been relaxed, Jacob Baradaeus (d. 578) was made missionary
bishop for Syria and Asia Minor by the Coptic patriarch
Theodosius, who was in exile in Byzantium, and began his
ceaseless travels throughout his vast diocese, ordaining
priests, bishops, and, ultimately, two successive patriarchs
of Antioch. Since Chalcedonian bishops could no longer be
dislodged, the separate Jacobite church, with its own complete hierarchy, canon law, and liturgy, came into being.

[27] Zacharias Rhetor, *Ecclesiastical History*, VIII.5

The writings of John of Ephesus (d. *ca.* 586) missionary bishop to the heathens of Asia Minor (whose successful labors included the burning of 2,000 pagan works), chronicled its tribulations and its growth.[28] Written when renewed persecution under Justin II (565–578) made him once again a prisoner and a fugitive, only partly preserved and bearing the marks of its hasty composition under difficult circumstances, his *History* is an enduring monument owing to his striving for accuracy, truth, and impartiality.

Meanwhile, Egypt was plagued by internal schisms, lack of leadership (owing to the exile of Theodosius, 536–566), imposed Chalcedonian patriarchs, and quarrels with the Syrian sister church. In 616 communion between the two churches was at last restored. At the same time, the Persian sweep through the eastern provinces (610–622), in which Orthodox Palestine succumbed just as easily as Monophysite Egypt, revealed the military weakness of the Empire, and Heraclius' supreme effort in driving the Persians out (622–629) left both powers exhausted. This is to say that the disaffection of the peoples of Syria and Egypt played a minor part in the Persian victories and in the ease of conquest with which the Arab armies, between 634 and 642, overwhelmed Syro-Mesopotamia, Palestine, Egypt, and Persia as well. The weakness of the Byzantine Empire was the weakness of all empires: to rule from a narrow base over vast populations of different cultures who had known independence and were, if not actively hostile, at best docile and who were not expected to bear arms in the defense of their territories. The Achaemenid empire, the most successful of the pre-Roman power structures, had endured for two hundred years and disposed of large ar-

---

[28] *Iohannis Ephesini Historiae Ecclesiasticae Pars Tertia*, ed. and trans. E. W. Brooks, CSCO, Scriptores Syri, vols. 54–55 (Louvain, 1952); *Lives of the Eastern Saints*, ed. and trans. E. W. Brooks, Patrologia Orientalis, XVII.1, XVIII.4, XIX.2 (Paris, 1924–1925).

mies and considerable wealth when Alexander the Great overthrew it. Yet the Hellenization of the East, though immensely fruitful and beneficial, paved the way for the oppressive Roman Empire, which degraded the ancient Eastern cultures and nations to the status of "provinces" whose primary function was to feed Rome. Christianity had been a unifying, hence strengthening, force in the Empire. Yet separatism in all its forms—and religious autonomy affecting not only the Christian communities but also Jews, Samaritans, and pagans, was its principal form—counterbalanced Christian unity. The primacy of religious motivation appears beyond doubt. That Christianity's search for unity was ever foiled by schism is proof that autonomy of conscience overrode all other loyalties and was the nucleus around which national and other communal structures were formed. The followers of Nestorius did not attempt to convert the Empire to their doctrinal position. But rather than yield, they sacrificed Christian unity and formed a separate church on Persian soil which embraced Syrians and Persians. Monophysitism, more broadly based and more aggressive, did strive to convert the Empire to its view of the faith, and accepted a separate existence only when it failed to win imperial power. The Syrian Monophysite church had no national basis and it shared a common Christian culture and a common tongue with the hated Nestorians. It also shared with them a propensity for Greek studies and for bilingual literary production. That in the course of their communal development both churches depended increasingly on the native tongue is proof of cultural vigor rather than of an anti-Greek attitude.

Egypt alone (since we are not speaking of Armenia here) affords an example of the complete coalescence of a nation and a faith. It has often been argued that Severian Monophysitism is so close to Chalcedonian orthodoxy that

the many concessions the emperors made to the Monophysites (from the *Henoticon* of Zeno to the *Ecthesis* of
Heraclius) should have sufficed to reconcile them; hence
their refusal to be reconciled is proof of a nationalist hostility to Byzantium. The argument would carry more weight
if Monophysitism had been confined to Egypt. Moreover,
to stress the doctrinal closeness of Severian Monophysitism
to Chalcedonian orthodoxy is to underrate the passionate
character of Monophysite soteriology and the gulf of emotion which lay between "from two natures" and "in two
natures." Yet Egypt undoubtedly possessed a sense of national identity. To say this is not to endorse the many un-
substantiated remarks about Coptic nationalism which one
encounters in the scholarly literature. The sources from
which supporting evidence is drawn are few and mostly
late.[29] Only with caution and qualifications can passages
from the tenth-century *History of the Patriarchs* be used
as evidence of sixth-century nationalism. That the Pharaonic Egyptian possessed a sense of national identity is a

[29] The few "nationalist" passages culled from the histories of the
Patriarch Michael I and John of Nikiu which are invariably quoted
in support of the argument for nationalism are themselves proof of
the overriding concern with religion. The oft-quoted passage from the
Chronicle of Michael I reads: "The God of vengeance, seeing the
wickedness of the Romans, who, wherever they ruled, cruelly plun-
dered our churches and monasteries and condemned us without mercy,
brought from the South the Sons of Ishmael to deliver us from
them. . . . It was no mean gain for us to be delivered of the cruelty
of the Romans, their wickedness, violence, and jealousy, and to find
ourselves at peace" (*Chronique de Michel le Syrien,* ed. J.-B Chabot,
XI, 4). Similarly, John of Nikiu links Egypt's feeble defense against
the conquerors to the people's hostility against the Byzantine emperor:
"When the Moslems saw the weakness of the Romans and the hostility of the people to the emperor Heraclius, because of the persecution wherewith he had visited all the land of Egypt in regard to
the orthodox faith, at the instigation of Cyrus the Chalcedonian
patriarch, they became bolder and stronger in the war" (*The Chronicle
of John, Bishop of Nikiu, translated from Zotenberg's Ethiopic text* by
R. H. Charles [London, 1916], CXV. 7, p. 184).

well-documented fact. And a very close reading of the sources, Pharaonic, Greco-Roman, and Coptic, might produce *verbal* proof of the continuing sense of identity. But given the paucity of preserved (and published) source material, this is not the most promising approach. The existence of Coptic literature as such is primary proof of a sense of communal identity as in the parallel case of Syria. In Egypt this community happened to be coextensive with an ancient and homogeneous nation, which, under Greco-Roman rule, had lost its means of self-expression and regained them when Christianity destroyed Hellenic culture and gave new faith and dignity to an oppressed people. Hence the upsurge of creative energies; hence the willingness to be led by the powerful archbishop of Alexandria; hence the close cooperation between monks and clergy, a union that was largely the work of St. Athanasius, who gave the Coptic church its firm organization and its homoousian faith. It has often been said that the power politics of the patriarchs played a role in the evolution from homoousian to Monophysite doctrine. But to weigh the strength of this factor exactly is impossible; nor is it necessary, given the primacy of theological motivation. Gibbon understood this very well and aptly chose to quote the patriarch Theodosius to illustrate Egypt's tenacious adherence to Monophysitism in the face of imperial concessions and oppressions.

To sum up, schismatic behavior in Syria and Egypt, even in its fully developed form of Nestorian and Monophysite churches, did not entail a rejection of Greek language and culture; and at no time were orthodoxy and heterodoxy divided along linguistic lines. What the language factor truly means is that the creation of Coptic and Syriac literatures, antedating the schisms, made possible the growth of schismatic churches and their independent existence.

In the first three centuries of Muslim domination, the literary productivity of the two schismatic churches did not diminish. In these centuries Nestorian activity is characterized by its missionary expansion into the Far East and by the large-scale absorption of Greek philosophic and scientific works and their translation into Syriac and thence into Arabic. The name of Ḥunain ibn Isḥāq (d. 876) serves as a symbol for these scientific efforts in three languages. The same receptivity to Greek learning distinguishes the Jacobite community of the eighth and ninth centuries. Jacob of Edessa (d. 708), the "St. Jerome of the Syrians," [30] had studied Greek letters at Kenneshrin and Alexandria and soon exchanged his episcopal duties for monastic studies which encompassed a revised translation of the Old Testament, innumerable letters, exegetical and polemical works, and a chronicle, no longer extant in itself but incorporated in the great *History* of Michael I, the Syrian Monophysite Patriarch (d. 1199). And before Syriac literature, declining after the tenth century, flickered to an end, it found its summation in the many-faceted works of the polyhistor and polymath, Bar Hebraeus (d. 1286).

In the seventh and eighth centuries, the monasteries of Egypt underwent a certain amount of secularization. Hence the few surviving examples of secular storytelling belong to this time, such as the Alexander romance, which was translated from the Greek, and the Cambyses romance, which was composed in Coptic. There are also a few folktales in which secular and religious motifs are interwoven, such as the tale of Theodosius and Dionysius, two simple laborers who lived in Constantinople and who, from their humble state, rose to the highest, with Theodosius becoming emperor. What is notable about this tale is that it is written in verse and forms part of a versified pop-

[30] Cf. Baumstark, *op. cit.*, pp. 248–256.

ular literature written in Sahidic, which culminates in the tenth century in a final flowering of religious poetry. This poetry is of three kinds: (1) strictly liturgical, (2) church hymns not forming part of the liturgy, and (3) popular poetry of a reflective or narrative character. The chief characteristic of this popular poetry is that much of it is built on Old Testament themes, and it favors especially those parts of the Old Testament known as wisdom literature, for example, the Proverbs of Solomon, Ecclesiastes, and the Song of Songs (in the customary allegorical interpretation). Other favorite themes are Solomon and the Queen of Sheba and the stories from the Book of Genesis.

Ancient Egyptians, Israelites, and Mesopotamians had shared the love of wisdom literature. Indeed, wisdom literature, in poetry or prose, from the Old Kingdom to the New, is the finest flower of Pharaonic literary culture. Its reappearance here, in Christian garb, is a link with, or revival of, the pagan past. It is more than that. Ancient Egyptian and Israelite wisdom literature have so many close resemblances that an interdependence of the two, as part of the overall close relations between the two cultures is beyond dispute. By and large, it was the older culture that influenced the younger: the "Wisdom of Amenemope" found its way into the Book of Proverbs.[31] With the advent of Christianity the wheel had come full circle.

The following is a rough translation of a tenth-century Coptic poem.[32] The underlying metrical, or rather rhythmical, principle is the same as that of Syriac poetry: a fixed

[31] See P. Humbert, *Recherches sur les sources égyptiennes de la littérature sapientiale d'Israël* (Neuchâtel, 1929); T. E. Peet, *A Comparative Study of the Literatures of Egypt, Palestine, and Mesopotamia* (London, 1931); M. Noth (ed.), *Wisdom in Israel and in the Ancient Near East, presented to H. H. Rowley*, Vetus Testamentum, Supplement 3 (Leiden, 1955).

[32] From H. Junker, *Koptische Poesie des 10. Jahrhunderts* (2 vols.; Berlin, 1908–1911), II, 103–107.

number of syllables are stressed regardless of their length, and, as in Syriac, all these poems were sung. The number of unaccented syllables, however, is not rigidly fixed, and the overall structure is simpler as well as more flexible than the Syriac forms. I have not attempted to reproduce the precise number of accented and unaccented syllables, and their respective positions.

[Introduction]:
The world in which we live
Mocks us as a dream
Night endows us with treasures
Morning sees them gone.

Happy the man who finds grace
When he implores the judge
That he have mercy upon him
And forgive his sins.

[First recitative]:
The Preacher has instructed us
That all things mortal are in vain
There is nothing in the life of man
But that he care for his soul
Along with food and wine.
As these go down your throat
They are annihilated
As if they had never been.

[Solo]:
He who builds a fine mansion
His labors are in vain
Comes death and three cubits of soil
Suffice for his poor flesh.

[Chorus]:
Happy the man who finds grace
When he implores the judge
That he have mercy upon him
And forgive his sins.

[Second recitative]:
> There's a time to build up, said he
> And also a time to tear down
> A time to weep
> And a time to laugh.
>
> Man's youth is filled with turmoil
> And pityful is his age
> He who reaches manhood
> A load of care is upon him.
>
> He who takes a wife bears a burden
> And he who has none is lonely.

[Solo]
> He who begets children begets sorrow
> But he who lacks children lacks roots
> In short, no joy but grief only
> Is all of life in this world.

[Chorus]
> Happy the man who finds grace
> etc.

The theme of the vanity of all things is very prominent in this poetry. It need hardly be added that the resigned moral of the Preacher is replaced by the hope of resurrection. The central concern of the ancient Egyptian had been the quest for immortality. When the old gods began to fail, the new faith brought salvation:

> Awake o my soul from thy slumber and dreams
> For the night has passed and the sun has arisen
> Behold the Lord as He rules from His cross
> Firmly has He founded the world, it trembles not.[33]

Does this simple poem not suggest why it was that only the concrete, undivided Logos Incarnate could bring salvation to this much-oppressed ancient man?

[33] *Ibid.*, I, 76.

If it is still true that the Roman Empire declined and fell,[34] we may view the fall with equanimity. In the East, the first phase of the Empire's dissolution was the reemergence of ancient peoples and cultures to whom Christianity had given a new identity and a new intolerance. The easy tolerance of Greco-oriental polytheism gave way to the insistence on doctrinal rightness without which there could be no salvation. It was the surge of the new faith which revitalized the indigenous cultures of Egypt and Syria and made them newly capable of an autonomy demanded by their conscience and supported by their past.

[34] Cf. A. Momigliano (ed.), *The Conflict between Paganism and Christianity in the Fourth Century* (Oxford, 1963), p. 1.

V

ISLAM:
THE PROBLEM OF
CHANGING PERSPECTIVE

G. E. von Grunebaum

I N WORDS that now sound dated but which may
be left untransposed with their quaintly monumental
ring, Johann Gottlieb Fichte (1762–1814), discussing in
1805 *The Nature of the Scholar,* has this to say on the
stratified perception of the world and the function this
stratification assigns to the scholar:

> The whole material world, with all its adaptation and
> ends, and in particular the life of man in this world, are by
> no means, in themselves and in deed and truth, that which
> they seem to be to the uncultivated and natural sense of
> man; but there is something higher, which lies concealed
> behind all natural appearance. This concealed foundation
> of all appearance may, in its greatest universality, be aptly
> named *The Divine Idea. . . .*
>
> A certain part of the meaning of this Divine Idea of the
> world is accessible to, and conceivable by, the cultivated
> mind, and, by the free activity of man, under the guidance
> of this Idea, may be impressed upon the world of sense and
> represented in it. . . .
>
> In every age, that kind of education and spiritual cul-
> ture by means of which the age hopes to lead mankind to
> the knowledge of the ascertained part of the Divine Idea

is the Learned Culture of the age; and every man who partakes in this culture is a Scholar of the age.[1]

Consequently, the life of the perfect scholar is "the life of the divine idea within the world, continuing the creation and refashioning the world completely." [2]

The task of the historian, understood as a particular manifestation of the scholar as such, finds itself, by implication, clearly circumscribed by this concept. The terse formula of the scholastic logician completes location and limitation of the historian's function: *Quidquid recipitur ad modum recipientis recipitur* [3]—"Whatever is perceived, is perceived after the mode of the percipient."

The high-flown language of the Romantic philosopher and the skeletal phrase of the scholastic encircle the Janus-headed fact that reality must, time and again, be recaptured by the interpreting mediator and that the mediator is inevitably confined by his disposition, or, more pertinently, by his position in history which chains him doubly, to his experience and to the expectations of his public.

It would be wrong to deduce from these reflections a sense of arbitrariness as a directing factor of scholarly investigation; what would be valid is a realization of the dominance of the contexts (which include the aspirations), psychological and methodological, in which insights are gathered and expounded, and therewith the further realization of the necessity of a *retractatio* of the fundamentals of past phases of our history to make them live in terms of our own fundamental problems and intui-

[1] *On the Nature of the Scholar and Its Manifestations*, in *The Popular Works of J. G. Fichte*, trans. Wm. Smith (London, 1889), I, 207 ff., at pp. 201–211.

[2] *Ibid.*, p. 281. I have, however, preferred the translation given by W. H. Bruford, *Culture and Society in Classical Weimar, 1775–1806* (Cambridge, 1962), p. 269.

[3] Quoted by G.-C. Anawati, "Gnose et philosophie," *Cahiers de civilisation médiévale*, VI (1963), 159–173, at p. 164.

tions. The possibilities for knowledge and insight change, and in the two centuries since Gibbon they have changed for the better. The available sources, available approaches, and available experiences are infinitely richer than in his time; most importantly, our concerns and the concepts that the growth of historicism has put at our disposal are, perhaps only for a fleeting moment, more adequate than those commanded by the eighteenth century for repossessing the spirit of the declining Roman Empire, the story of Byzantium, and the rise of Islam.

When Gibbon wrote not too much was knowable about the religion of the Arabs which Islam was to supersede; but it is not the sources alone that will have to bear the blame for the scant insight Gibbon made them yield. For he approached them with an aprioristic sense of their irrelevancy. "I am ignorant, and I am careless, of the blind mythology of the barbarians; of the local deities, of the stars, the air, and the earth, of their sex or titles, their attributes or subordination." This *parti pris* against an unreasoned religion leads Gibbon as it must to a totally mistaken notion of what a religion is and can be and allows him to continue: "Each tribe, each family, each independent warrior, created and changed the rites and the object of his fantastic worship; but the nation, in every age, has bowed to the religion, as well as to the language, of Mecca." And thus the lemma ends on a factual as well as a conceptual error; for the pre-Islamic Arabs were certainly not a nation as Gibbon would have understood the term.[4]

Famed though he is for his portrayal of rulers, his negative attitude toward unenlightened religion and more particularly toward religion as a factor in statecraft induces Gibbon to sum up the complex figure of the Umayyad

[4] *Decline and Fall*, ch. 50:V, 327–328; cf. G. E. von Grunebaum, "The Nature of Arab Unity before Islam," *Arabica*, X (1963), 5–23.

caliph, ʿUmar II (717–720), by noting that on the death of Sulaimān, his brother and predecessor, "the throne of an active and able prince was degraded by the useless and pernicious virtues of a bigot." [5] Caught between the conflicting pressures of Islam's basic egalitarianism made politically acute by the rise of a large stratum of non-Arab converts, and the exigencies of fiscal and military realities emphasized by the desperate insistence of an overwhelming majority of Arab Muslims on their privileged status, this caliph, driven as much by his conscience as by administrative needs, found himself in a situation not too unlike that of the United States Government vis-à-vis the Southern segregationists of the 1960's. His early death, entailing a change of policy, makes an assessment of his measures difficult; his canonization by the nostalgia of the pious, as consummated by the late authors at Gibbon's disposal, gave him the profile of an obstinate *Betschwester*, a bigoted zealot, and gave Gibbon a welcome opportunity for a devious attack on the Church.

By contrast, his prejudices, or expectations, would on occasion allow him to see more clearly than we do, or at least to stand by his insights with fewer inhibitions and less embarrassment than we suffer by dint of a sense of political expediency and human postulates. The flamboyancy of the phrase with which Gibbon explains the initial success of Muslim expansion and which underscores rather than glosses over the oversimplification it expresses must not induce us to wink at its essential truth. "While the [Byzantine] state was exhausted by the Persian war, and the church was distracted by the Nestorian and Monophysite sects, Mahomet, with the sword in one hand and the Koran in the other, erected his throne on the ruins of Christianity and of Rome." [6]

[5] *Decline and Fall*, ch. 52:VI, 8.
[6] *Ibid.*, ch. 50:V, 311.

Gibbon himself well knew that he was using "Mahomet" metonymically for the Muslim state, and he also knew that ecclesiastical oppression and a sense of almost national alienation had come between the government at Constantinople and its Syrian and Egyptian subjects. He certainly was aware that neither Christianity nor Rome fell into ruins on the Muslim attack. We, on the other hand, know better than Gibbon could have known the actual process of conversion and the comparatively small concern the ruling Arabs felt at the outset for developing a homogeneously Muslim population. Yet, in denying rather than sharpening the accuracy of the formula, we are primarily motivated by an image of how Islam should have been, an image developed largely to chastise ourselves for the atrocities of religious warfare still plaguing our conscience, and supplementarily to accommodate the recently developed self-view of our politically leading Muslim contemporaries whose fight against Western domination has seemed to them to gain considerably in justification and to be notably assisted by contrasting the peaceable persuasiveness of early Islam with the more drastic methods at times applied by Christian rulers. And yet, what empire was ever won without the sword or its shadow? And what binding force was there aside from military might and Arab racialism, except the Koran? Subjection, not conversion, was the initial goal of the conquerors; but conquerors they were, and their sole spiritual bond and banner was indeed the Koran.

The more remote from our concerns the interest to which historical investigation is made subservient, the more readily will it be spotted. When in the travel literature of the eighteenth century, for example, the black Africans, their mode of living and their institutions, are set forth, the material is apt to be presented in a manner to corroborate the unity of mankind, as predicated by the

Old Testament, and the original unity of religious beliefs, again as read into Scripture.[7] Political and, on occasion, educational efforts of today are distinguished from those vagaries merely by being better masked—the appropriateness of the theme to the prejudgment that is to be substantiated, concealing at times the actual motivation, as in some investigations into the conditions of the proletariat during the incipient stage of industrialization. Yet there is no evading the fact that the selection from the infinite mass of events, of relatively few data considered as deserving of examination, is dictated by the cultural values of the researcher and his society. Without a keen sense for the significance of the data for the presentation of cultural factors important to the investigator, in other words, without a sense of their values and a previously adopted scale of valuation, no evocation of the past nor a manageable orientation in the present is as much as conceivable.[8] When coincidence of such valuation with the structure of the cultural, political, or other, universe is claimed not in connection with a specific object or phase but in absolute terms, the claimant has left history and science altogether to seek refuge, under the false pretense of scientific exploration, in archetypal intuition of man's eternal nature (traceable even among very distinguished contemporary scholars [9]), millenarianism, or extrahuman illumination of some other kind.

To understand historical knowledge as a necessarily ongoing process and thereby indirectly to situate and assess

---

[7] Cf. R. Mercier, *L'Afrique noire dans la littérature française. Les premières images (XVIIᵉ-XVIIIᵉ siècles)* (Dakar, 1962), *passim*, esp. pp. 68 ff.

[8] Cf., e.g., C. Hinrichs in his "Einleitung" to F. Meinecke, *Die Entstehung des Historismus* (Munich, 1959; first published in 1936), p. xxx.

[9] Cf., e.g., Anawati, *op. cit.*, and his analysis of H. Corbin's interpretation of Avicenna's (d. 1037) *Ḥayy b. Yaqẓān*, pp. 164–167.

the achievement of Gibbon as of the none too numerous historians of comparable scope, we must, therefore, take into account a threefold indeterminism. That is to say, as components of historical knowledge and comprehension at any given point, we must envisage three distinct factors that interlock constantly but variously like three connected cogwheels in one piece of machinery, with the striking difference, it is true, that the cogwheels of the machinery do not change once they are put in place, whereas the factors of historical knowledge are subject to ceaseless development (and occasional mutation). These factors are: (1) the available knowledge of the historical subject, in the present case, the knowledge of Islam and Islamic history optimally accessible to Gibbon; (2) the intellectual and emotional disposition of the observer— motivating the questions he would ask, the facets of the past that would evoke his response, and so forth; and, finally, (3) the objective role of the particular segment of history considered within the contemporary situation coupled with its objective role in the formation of the period's, or the researcher's, self-view.

Not only what Gibbon knew or could know but also how he would choose from available knowledge and why, and what the subject of his concern would mean in the total political and intellectual economy of his time—all three limiting elements need to be faced; and they must be faced with the realization that their ceaseless interaction subjects them to as ceaseless modification. This analysis may create the impression of disarray and uncertainty, but such suspicion is unwarranted. For the interplay of those factors tends toward increasing the precision of historical perception by (a) impelling a widening acquaintance with sources and a sharpening of methods to explore and exploit them, which in turn limits the potential arbitrariness of the observer. His subjectivity is (b) further limited by the constant regress to the contemporary situation, whereby (c) a double testing of the subjective factor against the sources and the present reality is imposed. Needless to say, this largely self-correcting progression— self-correcting as long as the scope of intellectual perception continues to widen—does not preserve the individual scholar or scholars from aberrancy; but in time such aberrancy creates a discrepancy of such dimensions between postulate and observation that a new outreach toward Fichte's Divine Idea, however heretical it may appear at the moment, will be dared.

Our problem thus is: in addition to his personal genius, what phases of the three formative factors does Gibbon's treatment of Islam reflect, and where, or rather, why, has this treatment become less acceptable or satisfying to us than it was to the overwhelming majority of eighteenth-century readers?

Throughout his discussion of the Islamic world, Gibbon had to contend with the limitations of his sources. One wonders whether he realized the narrowness of the historiographical segment at his disposal. It is clear, however, and it hardly could have been otherwise, that he failed to note the peculiar stylization in which personalities and events of the formative and classical periods appear in his authorities, all but one summarizing epigones—al-Makīn (d. 1273), Bar Hebraeus (d. 1286), Abū 'l-Fidāʾ (d. 1331)—with the earlier Eutychius (Saʿīd b. Biṭrīq; d. 939) as a Christian condemned to, rather than privileged by, an atypical perspective. In compensation, a certain blandness of the sources and their abstention from analytical (in contrast with moral) judgment came to his aid by leaving his path free to impose his own explanation, his own synthesis.

The fortuitous seizing by the earlier Western orientalists

on postclassical authors naturally determined much of what Gibbon's predecessors had to say. The religious and, at key points, decidedly hagiographic outlook of the Arab historians was in something like a preestablished harmony with that of the Christian writers whose approach, although for the most part decidedly critical of Islam and, in some instances, of religion as a historiogenic factor altogether, was well fitted to exploit those late medieval texts. Gibbon's Western contemporaries no longer needed to dissociate themselves unequivocally from what the great J. H. Hottinger in 1660 had called the *Muhammedica spurcities*,[10] or to use Muslim tenets to discredit seemingly similar doctrines of Christian sects. In fact, an inclination to give the civilizing influence of the Arabs on Europe its due, and more than its due, was making itself felt. Following Hume (*History of England*, 1754–1762) and Thomas Warton (*History of English Poetry*, 1774–1781), Joh. Gottfried Herder (*Ideen zur Philosophie der Geschichte der Menschheit*, 1784–1791, esp. in Part IV) had emphasized the role of the Arabs as the only carriers of enlightenment in the Middle Ages. What is more, to Herder, "The whole civilization of north-eastern and western Europe is a growth from Roman, Greek and Arabian seed." [11] But the development of a more sympathetic approach and the realization that the phenomenon of Islam could be put to potent and positive use in the battles of the present did not in themselves enrich the store of information on which the eighteenth-century scholar was able to draw. The detailed work of J. Gagnier, for example,[12] whose influence on Gibbon is considerable, relies heavily on

[10] *Historia orientalis* (Zurich, 1660), p. 230, quoted from G. Giarrizzo, *Edward Gibbon e la cultura europea del Settecento* (Naples, 1954), p. 488.

[11] Quoted by Bruford, *op. cit.*, p. 229; cf. also Voltaire, *Essai sur les moeurs* (begun in 1740, first published in 1753–54), ch. 6.

[12] *La vie de Mahomet* (Amsterdam, 1732).

Jannābī, who lived in Asia Minor under the Ottomans and died in 1590. It is hardly an exaggeration to state that, apart from the Koran, authentic material from the early periods reached Gibbon only through late quotations or by reflection in Byzantine authors. Thus his more balanced judgment on the flowering of "Arabian learning" as "coeval with the darkest and most slothful period of European annals," [13] but as impeded by the Muslims depriving themselves "of the principal benefits of a familiar intercourse with Greece and Rome, the knowledge of antiquity, the purity of taste, and the freedom of thought," [14] is, in a sense, as little justified by contact with primary information as the more dithyrambic or more vituperative statements with which the European public was regaled by others.

Despite his suspiciousness of organized religion and of religious leaders altogether, Gibbon was unable to sift and assess the traditional Muslim narratives of the time of the "blessed origins" of Islam for what they are, a blend of genuine recollections and of projections into the authoritative past of the human and political ideals of the pious condemned to live in an age of social and moral decay and anxious to locate precedents for their own desires, spiritual and mundane, in a setting that would not be doubted or gainsaid. The dismay felt by the godly at the luxury of the caliphs of their time expressed itself in overdrawn pictures of the asceticism of their predecessors. Abū Bakr (632–634), says Gibbon, "thought himself entitled to a stipend of three pieces of gold, with the sufficient maintenance of a single camel and a black slave; but on the Friday of each week he distributed the residue of his own and the public money, first to the most worthy, and then to the most indigent, of the Moslems. The remains of his wealth, a coarse

---

[13] *Decline and Fall*, ch. 52:VI, 28.
[14] *Ibid.*, ch. 52:VI, 32.

garment and five pieces of gold, were delivered to his successor, who lamented with a modest sigh his own inability to equal such an admirable model. Yet the abstinence and humility of Omar [634–644] were not inferior to the virtues of Abū Bakr: his food consisted of barley-bread or dates; his drink was water; he preached in a gown that was torn or tattered in twelve places; and a Persian satrap, who paid his homage to the conqueror, found him asleep among the beggars on the steps of the mosch of Medina." [15]

The conquests of the new faith were as startling as the self-abnegation of the rulers. "In the ten years of the administration of Omar, the Saracens reduced to his obedience thirty-six thousand cities or castles, destroyed four thousand churches or temples of the unbelievers, and edified fourteen hundred moschs for the exercise of the religion of Mahomet." [16] The armies to which such exploits fell would merit them by their behavior. "All profane or frivolous conversation, all dangerous recollection of ancient quarrels was severely prohibited among the Arabs; in the tumult of a camp, the exercises of religion were assiduously practised; and the intervals of action were employed in prayer, meditation, and the study of the Koran." [17] When the Prophet feels his end approaching —the episode has no root whatever in the earlier sources although they, too, are interspersed with edifying anecdote —he ascends the pulpit. "If there be any man . . .

[15] *Ibid.*, ch. 51:V, 400.

[16] *Ibid.*, ch. 51:V, 401; see also ch. 51:V, 431, 444, for Gibbon's peculiar relation to figures, and, by contrast, his critical remarks, ch. 51:V, 457–459. Preserved listings of Byzantine towns contain 73 names for Egypt before 535 and 53 for the end of the sixth century, and, for the Diocese of the Orient at the same time, 197 (exclusive of the towns founded or reestablished by Justinian I). Cf. F. Dölger, "Die frühbyzantinische und byzantinisch beeinflusste Stadt (V.–VIII. Jahrhundert)," *Atti del 3° Congresso internazionale di studi sull 'Alto Medioevo* (1956) (Spoleto, 1959), pp. 65–100, at p. 76.

[17] *Decline and Fall*, ch. 51:V, 416.

whom I have unjustly scourged, I submit my own back to the lash of retaliation. Have I aspersed the reputation of a Musulman? let him proclaim *my* faults in the face of the congregation. Has anyone been despoiled of his goods? the little that I possess shall compensate the principal and the interest [!] of the debt." "Yes," a voice from the crowd replied, "I am entitled to three drachms of silver." Mahomet heard the complaint, satisfied the demand, and thanked his creditor for accusing him in this world rather than at the day of judgment." Where the older reports are totally silent and, in fact, leave one with the impression that Muhammad did not realize that death was upon him, the more recent descriptions of his end fill in all conceivable gaps. "He beheld with temperate firmness the approach of death; enfranchised his slaves (seventeen men, as they are named, and eleven women); minutely directed the order of his funeral; and moderated the lamentations of his weeping friends, on whom he bestowed the benediction of peace." [18]

Admiration for the Prophet as a person is curtailed by aversion to the prophet as a type. In telling the defeat of the *ridda,* the revolt of the tribes after Muhammad's death, Gibbon observes that the "various rebels of Arabia, without a chief or a cause, were speedily suppressed by the power and discipline of the rising monarchy." [19] He was intensely aware of the political task the Prophet had set for himself, his single-mindedness and the value, to the Arabs, of the establishment he was endeavoring to create. Torn between the appreciation of his achievement and aliveness to the essential dishonesty of his means, a special instance of the distinction, typically maintained by writers of the Enlightenment, between a (socially) useful religion or prejudice and one that is useless or damaging,[20] the his-

[18] *Ibid.,* ch. 50:V, 373–374.
[19] *Ibid.,* ch. 51:V, 399.
[20] Cf. Giarrizzo, *op. cit.,* p. 320.

torian remains of a divided mind in the apportionment of praise and condemnation. Gibbon clearly sees the difference between the character of the Prophet in the several phases of his life, "the solitary of mount Hera, . . . the preacher of Mecca, . . . the conqueror of Arabia." [21] He feels impelled to "decide whether the title of enthusiast or impostor more properly belongs to that extraordinary man." [22] He but executed his duty as "a man and a citizen to impart the doctrine of salvation, to rescue his country from the dominion of sin and error." [23] But even as Socrates deceived himself into believing in his *daimon,* so Muhammad deceived himself into attributing his insights to an angel of God. His original motives may have been pure, but in establishing the political edifice of his religion he was constrained to the use of "fraud and perfidy," "cruelty and injustice," until gradually his character deteriorated. He must have perceived that "his interest and religion were inseparably connected," and if "he retained any vestige of his native innocence, the sins of Mahomet may be allowed as an evidence of his sincerity." [24]

The problems that history was intended to solve and, conversely, the questions that were to make history understandable and meaningful, insofar as Islam is concerned, in large measure were implied in these sketches and judgments of Muhammad and the early caliphs. In at least partial contrast to the thought of Islam, Western thinking had never been willing to acquiesce in the dissociation of idea and reality. Ideas as motive forces, reality as the locus of their imperfect materialization, the cleavage between *civitas Dei* and *civitas terrena,* sometimes dealt with on the level of theology and metaphysics and sometimes on that of historical, more or less empirical observation—this dual-

[21] *Decline and Fall,* ch. 50:V, 375.
[22] *Ibid.,* ch. 50:V, 375.
[23] *Ibid.,* ch. 50:V, 376.
[24] *Ibid.,* ch. 50:V, 377.

ism has been, to us, a permanent factor; its inherent tension makes itself felt in all constructing of history and all questioning addressed to it.

Gibbon's sense of security in progress as attained by his period at least in western Europe does not remove the dismaying problem of the retarding and, at worst, decomposing effect that must be attributed to some of the strongest forces that mold history, above all, organized religion, and the equally dismaying experience of the dialectics of success: the inability of a political structure when grown past a certain dimension to maintain its stability or even to survive as a unit. The eighteenth century, perhaps from an exaggerated appreciation of the logistic weaknesses of its technology, while witnessing the establishment of empires, was inclined toward the homogeneous state of moderate size. To mention but a few influential writers, in Germany, Justus Möser (1720–1794) and Goethe, and in England, Gibbon himself, distrusted size in a political structure. Next to the decline of martial virtue among the Arabs and the subsequent preponderance of Turkish praetorian guards, it is "the weight and magnitude of the [Muslim] empire itself" which is responsible for its decline.[25] The victories that led to the enlargement of England's colonial holdings in the 1760's "occasioned doubts in the minds of enlightened British politicians, whether or not such immense acquisitions of territory would contribute to the felicity of the Parent State." David Ramsay, the celebrated historian of the American Revolution (who published in 1789), continues, "Power, like all things human, has its limits, and there is a point beyond which the largest and sharpest sword fails of doing execution." [26]

It is remarkable that Gibbon, who is extremely sensitive

[25] *Ibid.*, ch. 52:VI, 51.
[26] David Ramsey, *The History of the American Revolution* (London, 1793), I, 41.

to the destructive effect on the Roman Empire of its gigantic extent, does not examine this aspect of the Muslim empire when relating its breakup. Does the docility of their subjects counteract the debilitation of the caliphs' power toward the fringes of their realm? "They reigned by right of conquest over the nations of the East, to whom the name of liberty was unknown, and who were accustomed to applaud in their tyrants the acts of violence and severity that were exercised at their own expense." The Empire stretched a journey of two hundred days from East to West, and "the solid and compact dominion from Fargana to Aden, from Tarsus to Surat" takes a caravan from four to five months to negotiate. "We should vainly seek the indissoluble union and easy obedience that pervaded the government of Augustus and the Antonines; but the progress of the Mahometan religion diffused over this ample space a general resemblance of manners and opinions. The language and laws of the Koran were studied with equal devotion at Samarcand and Seville; the Moor and the Indian embraced as countrymen and brothers in the pilgrimage of Mecca; and the Arabian language was adopted as the popular idiom in all the provinces to the westward of the Tigris." [27] No explanation, either in terms of overextension or of religious cleavage, is suggested, however, when Gibbon tells of the dissolution of the ties of obedience between Spain (and soon after "Mauretania" and Egypt) and the Abbasid ruler. "In the tenth century, the chair of Mahomet [!] was disputed by three caliphs or commanders of the faithful, who reigned at Bagdad, Cairoan and Cordova, excommunicated each other, and agreed only in a principle of discord, that a sectary is more odious and criminal than an unbeliever." [28]

Even were one to overlook the fact that relevancy has

[27] *Decline and Fall*, ch. 51:V, 493–494.
[28] *Ibid.*, ch. 52:VI, 22.

indeed been sacrificed to effect, for the caliphs of Spain and Baghdad were equally orthodox, the impression would remain that Gibbon's customary realism is somewhat weakened by the circumstance that the Arabo-Turkish world was only just emerging from the haze of myth which even keen-eyed observers had not been able to pierce, or to dispel when writing, despite firsthand experiences in Constantinople and the Levant.[29] The (partial) misdrawal of the profile of the Islamic political society allows one, however, to discern more clearly the points Gibbon wishes to make in describing it. As a matter of fact, the disillusionment with the Chinese previously used as ideal contrast to Europe had already set in when Gibbon wrote, so the need he shared with his century to be in touch, for and through his theories, with "original man" or, at any rate, with a "better," less gnarled and contorted society, could hardly be met except by using the Muslim world as the object of demonstration.

In Islam Gibbon found a society without a Middle Ages, that is to say, a society that never had lost contact with its origins, unlike our own which had to find its way back to its mainsprings in ancient Rome and Greece after an alienation of many a century. At the same time, this closeness to the origins made it a striking illustration for the relations of religion and state, religion and civilization, which, broadly speaking, were his (and his contemporaries') principal concern in the examination of history. That the supernaturalism of Islam was brought into the world by a "mere man" devoid of any supernatural claims for his person made the phenomenon both more attractive and more significant. Muhammad was born into an ideal setting which, I am afraid, existed only in Gibbon's and his times' dreaming, compensatory as it was for the age-old pressures of an elaborated, militant, and state-sustained re-

[29] Cf. Giarrizzo's observations, op. cit., pp. 479, 480.

ligion. Nor is there any realization of the genesis and nature of religious experience as such, which is seen as nothing but a calculated syncretism.

Exposed to many doctrines, the "liberty of choice was
presented to the tribes: each Arab was free to elect or to
compose his own private religion; and the rude superstition of his house was mingled with the sublime theology of
saints and philosophers." There was thus accessible to them
the basis of all religion, and certainly of religion as the
eighteenth century envisioned it. "A fundamental article
of faith was inculcated by the consent of the learned
strangers: the existence of one supreme God, who is ex-
alted above the powers of heaven and earth, but who has
often revealed himself to mankind by the ministry of his
angels and prophets, and whose grace or justice has interrupted, by seasonable miracles, the order of nature." [30]

Muhammad, sprung from a noble family and well endowed with a commanding presence, an impressive and
winsome deportment, great gifts of the mind, and persua-
sive speech, was yet "an illiterate barbarian; his youth had
never been instructed in the arts of reading and writing;
the common ignorance exempted him from shame or re-
proach, but he was reduced to a narrow circle of existence,
and deprived of those faithful mirrors which reflect to our
mind the minds of sages and heroes. Yet the book of nature
and of man was open to his view. . . . He compares the
nations and the religions of the earth; discovers the weakness of the Persian and Roman monarchies; beholds, with
pity and indignation, the degeneracy of the times; and re-
solves to unite, under one God and one king, the invincible
spirit and primitive virtues of the Arabs. . . . The faith
which, under the name of Islam, he preached to his family
and nation is compounded of an eternal truth, and a necessary fiction, THAT THERE IS ONLY ONE GOD, AND

[30] *Decline and Fall,* ch. 50:V, 332.

THAT MAHOMET IS THE APOSTLE OF GOD." [31]

The verdict on the Prophet is pragmatic: "His beneficial or pernicious influence on the public happiness is the last consideration in the character of Mahomet. The most bitter or most bigoted of his Christian or Jewish foes will surely allow that he assumed a false commission to inculcate a salutary doctrine, less perfect only than their own. He piously supposed, as the basis of his religion, the truth and sanctity of *their* prior revelations, the virtues and miracles of their founders. The idols of Arabia were broken before the throne of God; the blood of human victims was expiated by prayer and fasting and alms, the laudable or innocent arts of devotion; and his rewards and punishments of a future life were painted by the images most congenial to an ignorant and carnal generation. Mahomet was perhaps incapable of dictating a moral and political system for the use of his countrymen; but he breathed among the faithful a spirit of charity and friendship, recommended the practice of the social virtues, and checked, by his laws and precepts, the thirst of revenge and the oppression of widows and orphans. The hostile tribes were united in faith and obedience, and the valour which had been idly spent in domestic quarrels was vigorously directed against a foreign enemy." [32]

It was not her religion that lost Arabia her happiness. "Had the impulse been less powerful, Arabia, free at home and formidable abroad [it is as though, in these six words, Gibbon were depicting his England], might have flourished under a succession of her native monarchs. Her sovereignty was lost by the extent and rapidity of conquest." [33] By analogy, it is less Muhammad's success than the continuance of his faith that calls for admiration. "Are we

[31] *Ibid.,* ch. 50:V, 336–337.
[32] *Ibid.,* ch. 50:V, 395–396.
[33] *Ibid.,* ch. 50:V, 396.

surprised that a multitude of proselytes should embrace the doctrine and the passions of an eloquent fanatic? In the heresies of the church, the same seduction has been tried and repeated from the time of the apostles to that of the reformers. Does it seem incredible that a private citizen should grasp the sword and the sceptre, subdue his native country, and erect a monarchy by his victorious arms? In the moving picture of the dynasties of the East, an hundred fortunate usurpers have arisen from a baser origin, surmounted more formidable obstacles, and filled a larger scope of empire and conquest." [34]

The flow of the argument must here be broken to point out that Gibbon misconstrued to some extent the actual role and position of the Prophet whom, in another passage, he sees as assuming "the exercise of the regal and sacerdotal office" and whom he shows as using a "seal of gold, or silver," "inscribed with the apostolic title" [35]—projections of European ideas and adoption of later legend that are not merely verbally misleading.

The analysis of Muhammad's success continues perceptively but not without a measure of irony aimed at the workings of religious emotion in general. "Mahomet was alike instructed to preach and to fight . . . : The operation of force and persuasion, of enthusiasm and fear, continually acted on each other. . . . His voice invited the Arabs to freedom and victory, to arms and rapine, to the indulgence of their darling passions in this world and the other; the restraints which he imposed were requisite to establish the credit of the prophet and to exercise the obedience of the people; and the only objection to his success was his rational creed of the unity and perfections of God." From here on the characterization of Islam is styled to serve as anti-Christian polemics. The stability of the

[34] *Ibid.*, ch. 50:V, 394.
[35] *Ibid.*, ch. 50:V, 358.

Muslim faith, the detachment shown by its theologians, and most of all the absence of a clergy—all three, but especially the last which reflects, slightly distorted, the non-existence in Islam of a consecrated priesthood, are clichés of considerable usefulness in the anticlerical battles of Gibbon's day. "It is not the propagation but the permanency of his [Muhammad's] religion that deserves our wonder: the same pure and perfect impression which he engraved at Mecca and Medina is preserved, after the revolutions of twelve centuries, by the Indian, the African, and the Turkish proselytes of the Koran." [36] This, of course, in contrast to the unapostolic accretions with which the Christian churches overlaid the message of Jesus.

Protected by defective information and, more securely, by the absence of a feeling for the individuality of the historical phenomenon, Gibbon continues his generalizations. "The Mahometans have uniformly withstood the temptation of reducing the object of their faith and devotion to a level with the senses and imagination of man. . . . The intellectual image of the Deity has never been degraded by any visible idol; the honours of the prophet have never transgressed the measure of human virtue; and his living precepts have restrained the gratitude of his disciples within the bounds of reason and religion." Metaphysical questions did indeed disturb the Muslims as they had the Christians; "but among the former they have never engaged the passions of the people or disturbed the tranquillity of the state." Whether, at this point, unfamiliarity with the sources is shading into bad faith may be left undecided. The final explanation strikes inaccurately, if not inelegantly, a blow at *l'infâme*. "The cause of this important difference may be found in the separation of union of the regal and sacerdotal characters. It was in the interest of the caliphs . . . to repress and discourage all religious innova-

[36] *Ibid.*, ch. 50:V, 394.

tions: the order, the discipline, the temporal and spiritual ambition of the clergy are unknown to the Moslems; and the sages of the law are the guides of their conscience and the oracles of their faith." [37] This passage cannot be correctly appreciated unless it be placed in connection with Gibbon's verdict on the Christian clergy in promoting the disintegration of the Roman Empire but also in achieving a certain unity throughout (western) Europe.[38] Basically, Gibbon's interest in dogmatics is restricted to its influence on politics.[39]

Thus, the usefulness of Islam to Gibbon is in its exemplifying a religion (1) with a human founder, (2) developing without a priestly cast, (3) retaining essentially its primordial simplicity, (4) not weakening but rather activating society, (5) presenting a model of that judicious blend between rationally demonstrable verity and socially useful prejudice which is the best that can be hoped for in a religion, and hence, (6) apt to promote individual happiness. Culturally, (7) its loose organization has prevented it from obstructing human progress as effectively as the Christian church; but the spectacle of Muslim intellectual decline leaves Gibbon with ambivalent feelings. He realizes that it was not religion alone but taste, tradition, dissociation from antiquity which contributed to this decay. Yet theology has to bear its share of the responsibility. "In the libraries of the Arabians, as in those of Europe, the far greater part of the innumerable volumes were possessed only of local value or imaginary merit. The shelves were crowded with orators and poets, whose style was adapted to the taste and manners of their countrymen; with general

[37] *Ibid.*, ch. 50:V, 394–395.

[38] Cf. the observations at the end of ch. 38:IV, 160 ff., and Giarrizzo, *op. cit.*, pp. 304–306.

[39] Giarrizzo, *op. cit.*, p. 303 n. 4, appositely recalls Voltaire's dictum, *Essai*, ch. xi: "Le christianisme ouvroit le ciel, mais il perdoit l'empire."

and partial histories, . . . with codes and commentaries
of jurisprudence, . . . with the interpreters of the Koran
and orthodox tradition; and with the whole theological
tribe, polemics, mystics, scholastics, and moralists, the first
or the last of writers, according to the different estimate of
sceptics or believers." [40]

There can be little doubt regarding Gibbon's judgment.
One feels tempted to subsume the use the great historian
made of the phenomenon of Islam and the function he
essayed to assign to it in his narrative under the concept of
the *ragione di stato,* or an analogue to it, in other words,
the idea, somewhat aging and beginning to lose its luster in
his day, that to uphold and increase the strength of the
body politic any effective tool may and must be employed
regardless of its intrinsic excellence and objective truth.
Among such tools the Muslim faith is a rather apt one,
superior in some ways to Christianity at least in its later
phases, constituting an example of a religion in which the
admixture of inevitable falsehood is not too disadvanta-
geous nor too overwhelming to necessary rational truth.

The question needs still to be asked: what did Islam
mean in Gibbon's political universe? Differently put, how
free was he, how unencumbered by concrete political experiences and considerations involving Islam, to interpret,
stylize, even intellectually manipulate the Muslim world?
The answer can be simple. Since the early decades of his
century, the only Muslim power that had forced Europe
on the defensive and taught her to be apprehensive and
accommodating, was visibly declining. Obsolete administrative methods, fissures in the internal structure, a tacit
refusal to adjust to a new military technology had brought
the Ottomans to a state that allowed Gibbon to speak of
"the feeble and disorderly government of the Turks." [41]

[40] *Decline and Fall*, ch. 52:VI, 29.
[41] *Ibid.*, ch. 52:VI, 3.

The memories of their glories and the combination of terror and admiration with which they had filled Europe, was still fresh, though. This admiration was excited primarily by their soldierly discipline and perhaps still more by the shrewd purposefulness European observers discovered in their internal organization. These factors impressed even Luther and made the Ottomans, because of the "diabolical rationalism" of their system of government,[42] a model for an analyst of the "reason of state" like Traiano Boccalini (d. 1613). So Gibbon speaks appreciatively of their former "martial discipline, religious enthusiasm, and their energy of the national character" as having "ennobled" their "domestic slavery." [43]

The Turks, as well as the Moors of North Africa, dreaded for their efficiency as pirates, had entered literature and ascended the stage nearly two hundred years before Gibbon wrote. Travelers' reports, fairly frequent since the end of the Middle Ages, were becoming more numerous and on the whole less *romancé* and thus more accurate. Piracy, commerce, and diplomacy secured a steady flow of usable information and, what is perhaps more important, the possibility of personal acquaintance with people of various descriptions who had direct experience with Islam and the lands under its dominion. With all this, to the average and even to the educated West European, the Muslim world had little immediate significance. It no longer threatened, nor did it inspire philosophy or medicine; it provided an example and a warning of greatness fallen from high estate. From the thinker's point of view it had become a mere object—of contemplation, dis-

---

[42] The expression is F. Meinecke's in his discussion of the fascination exercised by the Turkish state on Tommaso Campanella (1568–1639) in *Die Idee der Staatsräson in der neueren Geschichte* (Munich, 1960; first published in 1929), p. 123.

[43] *Decline and Fall*, ch. 64:VII, 1.

section, valuation—but, in any event, as unconcerned and unable to react to criticism or alleged misrepresentation as the Ancients.

It is one of the great differences in the position of scholarship on the Middle East and the Muslim world in general between Gibbon's time and today that some two generations ago the historical object was slowly resurrected into a historical agent. Its newly won power, however limited, together with such Western support as made possible its recuperation, inevitably changed the outlook of researchers on the past, as well as on the present, of Islam. It subjected them to subtle and not so subtle pressures on the part of spokesmen for resurging nations motivated as they were and are by the wish to impose on the West a politically effective self-view, by a certain lag in analytical sophistication combined with incomplete comprehension of the nature and ends of Occidental cultural studies, and, in some instances, by a reaffirmation of the Muslim dislike to be viewed by the non-Muslim, by the desire to keep the study of Islam to the initiated and preserve the charismatic community from the indiscretion, not to say defilement, of unbelieving eyes, not to mention the irritation caused by having the outsider deal relativistically with an absolutist position, already under attack from within the Muslim community, the *umma,* itself.[44] Besides, in the Muslim public at large, the double realization that history must comprise the totality of human events, an insight essentially owing to the Enlightenment, and that those events

[44] Cf. the references brought together in G. E. von Grunebaum, *Modern Islam: The Search for Cultural Identity* (New York, 1964), p. 224 n. 57. Cf. also the remark of Jacques Berque, *Dépossession du monde* (Paris, 1964), p. 143 n. 27: "La dénégation de toute spécificité par les sociétés sous-développées constitue l'un des problèmes de l'ethnologue d'aujourd'hui. ... Le refus du regard d'autrui est lui-même spécifique d'un certain stade d'évolution."

must be traced as closely as possible to their unique and unrepeatable profile, in other words, that their meaning is approachable only by way of their individuality—an insight essentially owing to romanticism and historicism—has not as yet taken creative roots.

It was Herder who said, a history of opinions, *"eine Geschichte der Meinungen,"* would be the true key to the history of actions (*"Tatengeschichte"*).[45] This outlook does away with the premises rooted in the thought world of natural law and still ingrained in traditional Islam of the changelessness of human nature, the changlessness of human ideals, and the timeless character of Reason, replacing it with the realization of the unrepeatable individual and the conditioned or contingent nature of human aspirations and human reason itself. The individual, person or event, in its many-facetedness never to be exhausted but ever more deeply illuminable by the discovery of new contexts (new lines of questioning, newly conquered areas of sensibility) in which it may be captured, is the heart and goal of our historical consciousness with its peculiar double-directedness: to identify and isolate the phenomena in their individuality and to arrive from their shared characteristics at general, universally comprehensive typologies of human behavior and the structure (and sequence) of historical events. This endeavor is formally guided by a concept of development, a concept more flexible than that of the gradual unfolding of a given seed (which the En-

---

[45] *Briefe zu Beförderung der Humanität, Fünfte Sammlung* (1795), no. 58, *Sämmtliche Werke,* ed. B. Suphan (Berlin, 1877–1913), XVII (1881), 321. The full text of Herder's observation reads: "Eine Geschichte der Meinungen, der praktischen Grundsätze der Völker wie sie hie und da herrschten, sich vererbten und im Stillen die grössesten Folgen erzeugten, diese Geschichte mit hellem, moralischen Sinn, in gewissenhafter Prüfung der Thatsachen und Zeugen geschrieben; wäre eigentlich der Schüssel zur Thatengeschichte." Meinecke, *Staatsräson,* p. 24, refers to Herder's idea.

lightenment combined with a doctrine of gradual but necessary, almost automatic perfection), because it completes the latter with the apprehension of the spiritual spontaneity of the developing entity and of its adaptability under the impact of nonrecurring factors. The new concept of development is thus designed, as it were, to unite necessity and freedom.[46]

A concept of this order could be evolved only when, toward the end of the eighteenth century, the need was accepted to examine the depths of one's own soul, and when it was perceived that a deepened awareness of one's own individuality would open a new road of access to the individualities of the past.[47] Today, one feels tempted to add, we have come to see and to seek out a new road of access to ourselves through a deepened, and mechanically and analytically ever more comprehensive, awareness of the individualities of the past, thus at the same time following and reversing the novel mode of making use of history, irrevocably imposed, at least for the West, by the century that begins with Herder and Burke and ends with Ranke. To activate this approach, not only did the "generalizing consideration" of historical forces have to be replaced by an "individualizing consideration," there also had to be renounced that teleological approach, that endeavor to see order into the randomly scattered happenings by interpreting them as oriented toward an end brought to them from outside—the plans of providence, ultimate perfection, uncontrollable decline. The idea of the lawgiver, the king, the statesman planning social structure and even *histoire événementielle* to achieve definite and distinct purposes, still potent in Gibbon, dominated historical analysis and the philosophical approach to history until Vico's *Scienza nuova* (first edition, 1725) proclaimed that *homo non in-*

[46] Cf. Meinecke, *Historismus*, p. 159.
[47] *Ibid.*, p. 66.

telligendo fit omnia,[48] that is to say, not everywhere is the direction given by self-consciously adopted aims, nor are institutions necessarily the work of legislating individuals. Besides, man is not everywhere the same, but he is everywhere driven as much, if not more, by emotion and imagination as by reason.

For Gibbon and his time the center of gravity of history still lay "outside individual man and the individual epoch," and so it has remained for traditional Islam. We, children and grandchildren of historicism, on the other hand, have located this center of gravity inside the individual, inside each epoch. To conclude this reflection with another saying by Herder, who, incidentally, adopts a terminology familiar from the Declaration of Independence (inspired though this document is by presuppositions of natural law): "Every nation, like every age of life, has in itself the central point of happiness [*Glückseligkeit*]."[49] Or, as Ranke was to say in 1854, "Every epoch is immediate to God; its value does not depend on what develops from it, but on its existence as such, on its own self." But once again I must remark that while we have come to accept this approach as axiomatic, we are going beyond it in demanding of the sum total of definable or separable experiences of historical (and this, to us, is primarily cultural) achievement and failure, to enlighten us, by analogy and contrast, mirror and caricature, kinship and alienation, about ourselves, our potential, and about legitimacy and limitation of our claim to absoluteness at this fleeting moment, to temporary universality, as it were, but most of all, to piercing through to, and perhaps to control, the

[48] *Ibid.,* p. 60.

[49] *Auch eine Philosophie der Geschichte zur Bildung der Menschheit* (1774), in *Werke,* V, 512; R. T. Clark, Jr. (trans.), *Herder: His Life and Thought* (Berkeley and Los Angeles, 1955), p. 191. I am beholden to Clark for the material offered in some of the preceding sentences.

deepest depths of ourselves by which we are fascinated and at which we shudder.

Leibniz (d. 1716) saw in the "infinite diversity of the individuals" the "infinite God" revealing himself [50] whence the individual derived its importance, a remote echo of the *concors diversitas* that Pope Gregory the Great (590–604) perceived in the Church.[51] To Gibbon's contemporary, the Scottish historian and philosopher, William Robertson (1721–1793), such periods as did not directly contribute to present perfection were of scant value— "they deserve not to be remembered." [52] We are going back beyond the Enlightenment in our conviction that the infinite diversity which Leibniz cherished will reveal to us, not God perhaps, but the real essence, the full potentialities

[50] *Historismus*, p. 31.

[51] Cf. J. Leclercq in J. Leclercq, F. Vandenbroucke, and L. Bouyer, *La Spiritualité du moyen âge* (Paris, 1961), p. 19.

[52] Said with reference to the early history of nations; quoted by M. Joyce, *Edward Gibbon* (London, New York, Toronto, 1953), p. 124. The same attitude is found in David Hume, *The History of England from the Invasion of Julius Caesar to the Accession of Henry VII* (1762). The present dictates the value of any given segment of the past. Only such events as exhibit significant analogies or connections with the present to which the historian strives to be useful deserves notice. By contrast, the historian of the nineteenth century and after proposes to view the phenomena of the past in the context of the past. History is not to judge the past nor to assist the future by advising the present (cf. L. Ranke's introduction to his *Geschichten der romanischen und germanischen Völker von 1494 bis 1514* [1824]). F. Châtelet, "Le Temps de l'histoire et l'évolution de la fonction historienne," *Journal de Psychologie normale et pathologique,* LIII (1956), 355–378, observes at p. 357 (with reference to the study of Eric Weil, "De l'Intérêt qu'on prend à l'histoire," *Recherches philosophiques,* 4 [1934–35], 105–126) that our concern for history is motivated by man's desire to know who he is. Conversely, a history of historiography could be made to show that our ways to deal with, or to neglect, the past are tied to our idea of the nature of action, and that they aim at illuminating this idea or its utility in the given context.

of man which, to our mode of feeling, is "the only true enigma." [53] Consistent with this outlook we have, in our studies, aimed at *extension humaine* rather than (as did the Middle Ages and the Enlightenment) at *approfondissement moral;* [54] besides, we seek in the data the structures in preference to the underlying principles, elements, or values. [55] Structure is our obsession as origin was in Darwin's time and creation had been before; [56] that is to say, the stability of the essentially completed and done has been yielding to development and growth and now to the search for the spiritual-technical laws and threads that control "becoming" of which "being" is, after all, but a *cas limite.* [57] Withal, there is at least one significant point of contact between Gibbon's purposeful historiography and certain segments of contemporary writing of history traceable, it is true, above all, in the new nations anxious to create a formative picture of their past and in the dogmatist atmosphere of Marxist or post-Marxist millenarianism. The spirit of this latter-day *Geschichtsklitterung* has been described in admirable succinctness by Jacques Berque. The aim of this kind of history, "like that of the exact sciences, is definitely to affect the life of the collective, that had equally been its point of departure, its subject matter, and which remains its objective. But it arrives at this goal in its own way, most often by proposing to those societies models of themselves in which they rediscover what they have still to do [*leur inaccomplissement*]." But Berque

[53] The phrase is F. Châtelet's in *La Naissance de l'histoire* (Paris, 1962), p. 10.

[54] Expression of R. Albérès, *L'Aventure intellectuelle du XXᵉ siècle* (3d ed.; Paris, 1959), p. 393.

[55] *Ibid.,* p. 396.

[56] Cf. Berque, *op. cit.,* p. 27.

[57] Already Hegel demonstrated that *being* can be conceived of only as *becoming*.

immediately breaks away from Gibbon in his description (or defense) of an *histoire engagée* by noting: "Thereby, history resembles tragedy." [58]

With different and richer and better sources, and surer methods to exploit them; different and more evocative questions to be asked of the historical object; and a different, and no doubt more important but also more problematical, more ambivalent role assumed by the historical object in the "economy" of our existence, as yet only in regard to the political, tomorrow perhaps also the intellectual, life—how could our picture of Islam and the Islamic world fail to differ decisively from that drawn by Gibbon? And further, in our epoch of diversified concepts of the nature of history, of diversified aspirations in every sector of life, how could a uniformly acceptable, let alone accepted, historical image be looked to? Nonetheless, our several modes of viewing and placing Islam have certain features in common, or are gravitating toward such similarities of portrayal.

Foregone shall be the analysis of certain studies, however meritorious in substance, which are inspired principally by an endeavor to conciliate the aggressive self-defense of certain Muslim apologists. Noncomprehension of the nature of power and the mistaking of sentimental monologue for genuine converse are apt to create a type of pseudoscholarship, footnoted pamphlets, in support of what one might call unilateral disarmament in intellectual attitudes and creative tensions, yielding the (often misplaced arrogance of) specificity of the Occidental to an all-enveloping egalitarianism not shared by its intended beneficiaries in their own approach to those groups that lag behind and fail to integrate with them. The replacement, by way of new clichés, of misplaced exclusivism by misplaced humility may have short-range political uses, but has so far con-

[58] Berque, *op. cit.*, pp. 187–188.

tributed little to that sharpening of distinctions by which scholarship progresses.

A more adequate and therefore, it may be predicted, more lasting reflection of our changed position vis-à-vis ourselves and the non-Western world is our strengthened sense for cultural units, autonomous and interacting, distinct yet shading into one another, and, more particularly, the active realization of the oneness of the cultural bases of those types of civilization that have grown out of the eastern Mediterranean. It may even be that the urge to elaborate this insight has tended to isolate the Islamic world, in our view, from the cultural resources of pre-Muslim and post-Muslim India and the "Farther" East. It certainly has both posed the problem and so far prevented any serious attempt at its solution, to present the internal history of the "Islamic complex" in terms of the interaction of the power structures among which it has been divided at a given period, for example, that among the Ottomans, the Safawids, and the Moghuls between the establishment of Babur in Delhi (1526) and the Battle of Plassey (1757).

The gift of our existential position to our historical scholarship and hence to our view of what we are not and thus of Islam is not a blurring of distinctions. I strongly feel with the old presbyter Salvianus of Marseilles (*ca.* 440) that "any wicked man would rather execrate the law than amend his character." [59] This gift rather is the compulsion, in the service of self-understanding, to capture our world, past and present, in terms of independent yet interacting, distinct yet kindred, interpretable yet irreducible culture units; these units, in turn, we are driven to understand, compare, contrast for their dominant organizational structure, the measure in which they aim to possess the inner and outer universe as well as for the aspi-

[59] *Ad ecclesiam contra avaritiam* iv. 9; quoted by E. M. Sanford, *Salvianus: On the Government of God* (New York, 1930), p. 18.

rations that flickeringly manifest themselves in their stated thoughts and visible deeds, and for their attitudes, to being and man as such, to community, to the nature and accessibility of truth, to time and space, to death and change, and not least, to the "other"—such as ourselves. For never must we allow ourselves to forget, under the seductive impact of that deterministic realism which lends to every dying moment the same absoluteness, authority, and irrelevance that the true order of things is imposed by thought and that "the profound rhythm of the world is that of the mind." [60]

[60] Ch. Morazé, *La France bourgeoise* (Paris, 1946), pp. 215, 216. It is perhaps not unnecessary to insist on the difference of the self-cognition *hic et nunc*, to be achieved by confrontation with other cultures, past and present, which animates our concern with history; and that self-knowledge enjoined by the Pythagoreans and the Delphian oracle which consists in the recognition of unity and continuity of our soul through its incarnations in different periods of history. For this view, which has been influential in ancient Greece far beyond its original locus, cf. the perceptive analysis of J.-P. Vernant, "Aspects mythiques de la mémoire en Grèce," *Journal de Psychologie normale et pathologique*, LVI (1959), 1–29, esp. pp. 14–16, 22–23.

VI

TWILIGHT IN THE WEST

C. Warren Hollister

*T*HE TITLE of this chapter may perhaps seem both uninformative and embarrassingly poetic, yet within it there lurks a thesis. The word "twilight" contains some exceedingly useful ambiguities. Most of us think of twilight as occurring in the evening, but there is another twilight—well known to farmers, milkmen, and roués— which precedes the dawn. Western Europe between the deposition of Emperor Romulus Augustulus in 476 and the coronation of Emperor Charlemagne in 800 was a twilight age in both these senses. It was a period in which an old ethos was fading and a new one was evolving. It was neither an age of high civilization nor a dark age, but rather a period of dusk, like the long twilight of a summer's night in the far North wherein the fading light of the past day mingles with the growing light of the next.

Although never utterly dark, the post-Roman West was unquestionably dim. By whatever standards one might wish to use, it was culturally far inferior to Periclean Athens or Augustan Rome, economically retarded by comparison with the thriving commerce of the Hellenistic Age or the Roman Principate, and politically backward when measured against the Age of the Antonines. Owing to the widespread loss of literacy in this twilight age and the general failure of its states to keep and preserve public records, it is also dim to modern historians. What records

179

we do possess from the period have been subjected to rigorous scrutiny, and their testimony has been augmented by archaeological investigations, place-name studies, analyses of agricultural field patterns, and other indirect techniques. These investigations have been pursued with remarkable ingenuity. Still, compared with other historical eras, the post-Roman West is a period about which we know relatively little. Indeed, one is inclined to the uncharitable suspicion that some scholars have been attracted to this period for the very reason that it yields a minimum of hard data to inhibit their soaring hypotheses. In this age, above all, it is the historian's task not only to cherish the fact and denounce the myth but to respect the uncertain.

All good historians have a fondness for basic trends and inexorable forces. Gibbon himself and nearly all his successors have sought to identify the fundamental elements involved in the decline and fall of the Western Roman Empire. By the mid-fourth century, Rome's sickness was far advanced, and scholars have devoted endless discussion to the various contributory germs: the breakdown of the imperial succession system in the third century, the flight from the towns, the freezing of productive men in their professions and the consequent immobilization of society, the spiritual metamorphosis, the rising expenses of government, the population decline, the loss of hope. There can be little doubt that these factors and others weakened traditional Roman society and made the mid-fourth century Empire radically different from its Augustan or Antonine predecessor. Nevertheless, one distinguished historian, J. B. Bury, has suggested that, even in the transformed and debilitated condition that it had reached by the mid-fourth century, the Western Empire might well have survived indefinitely were it not for a sequence of fortuitous catastrophes that occurred during the half-century or so following

A.D. 375.[1] In these years the ferocious Asiatic Huns burst unexpectedly into Europe, swallowing into their own military empire a number of Germanic tribes and pushing others against the Roman frontiers. The Visigoths, converted to Christianity in its heretical Arian form, sought and received sanctuary on the Roman side of the Danube. Mistreated by the local Roman authorities, they went on a rampage, administered a stunning defeat to an ill-prepared Roman army at Adrianople, and, after a period of quiescence, sacked Rome itself in 410. A few years earlier several barbarian tribes had poured into Gaul across the Rhine frontier, whose defending troops had been ordered south to meet the Visigothic menace. By the mid-fifth century the Western Empire was a shambles. The Vandals had seized North Africa and were ruining Mediterranean commerce with their piracy, the Visigoths and other Germanic tribes were established in Southern Gaul and Spain, and the Huns themselves, led by the ruthless Attila, were about to enter the Empire. The collapse of the Western imperial line a quarter-century later was an almost inevitable aftermath of these calamities.

Bury maintained that if the Huns had remained in their Asiatic homeland, if the fifth-century Western Empire had been better ruled, if Roman arms had been victorious at Adrianople, or if any number of other disasters had not occurred, the Empire might well have held on in the West as it did in the East—transformed, regimented, but enduring.

Bury may or may not have been right. We can never know, for his theory is one of those uncertain things that must be recognized as such. Because it stresses the fortuitous, which makes most historians uncomfortable, it has

[1] J. B. Bury, *History of the Later Roman Empire* (rev. ed.; London, 1923), I.

been widely and loudly ignored. For our purposes it serves
to dramatize a possible alternative. The late Empire, tax-
ridden, inflexibly stratified, authoritarian, yet providing its
subjects with a degree of peace and social coherence, might
possibly have lasted. We now know that Roman cities were
flourishing in Britain down to the end of the fourth century and even beyond; and, as Alfons Dopsch has pointed
out, allusions by Roman historians to the destruction of
urban centers on the Continent are often badly exaggerated. Ammianus Marcellinus reports that Cologne was destroyed by barbarians in 355; yet he describes it absent-
mindedly as a "well-fortified town" which the Emperor
Julian entered in 356! [2] By the later fourth century the
Western cities had suffered much, but they still existed
and, in many instances, were still vigorous. One might
conclude, tentatively, that although Rome's sickness was
self-induced, her death was directly attributable to the
barbarian invasions.

Bearing in mind the Roman Europe that might have
been and the barbarian Europe that was, one is strongly
tempted to ask whether the destruction of the Western
Empire was a disaster or a blessing. For Gibbon, there could
be only one answer to this question. Although fully alive
to the vices of late-imperial autocracy, he found in the
Germanic successor states no virtues whatever. The collapse of Rome, he well understood, was an exceedingly
complex and gradual phenomenon, but in the end he could
encompass everything in one contemptuous generalization:
". . . the Roman world was overwhelmed by a deluge of
barbarians." [3] This, to Gibbon, was the supreme historical
tragedy.

Subsequent historians have challenged Gibbon's verdict
repeatedly on a variety of grounds. Certain German and

[2] Ammianus Marcellinus XV. 8, 19; XVI. 2, 3.
[3] *Decline and Fall* ch. 38:IV, 162.

English scholars of the nineteenth century, whose burning patriotism embraced even their remote tribal forebears, argued, in essence, that modern democracy had its roots in the soil of primitive Germany. The bulwark of early Germanic society, so they said, was the free peasant who held his land in common with other peasants and shared in the governance of the tribe. The fall of Rome, therefore, resulted in the substitution of Germanic pluralism for Roman tyranny, Germanic virtue for Roman corruption. But subsequent research has demonstrated that early Germanic society was based on slavery and private property rather than proto-communism, that it was deeply aristocratic, and that the politically aware communal farmer was a product of the nineteenth-century imagination. Historians are quite willing to concede that the authority of early Germanic chieftains or kings was limited by immemorial custom and by the functioning of tribal assemblies, but they are skeptical of any attempt to read into the situation later concepts of limited constitutional monarchy or government under the law. The sanctity of custom and the existence of tribal assemblies are common to many primitive peoples. The remarkable thing is not that such institutions existed among the early Germans but that they persisted, to a degree, into the later Middle Ages. It might even be said that the primitive Germans were simply too ignorant to build sophisticated despotic regimes.

But despite the discrediting of proto-democracy in the Germanic forests, there remain some historians who see virtue in the barbarian and who rejoice at Rome's fall. Indeed, this position has been argued recently with considerable force. To be sure, scholars no longer put much faith in Tacitus' glorification of the early Germans.[4] One fairly recent champion of the barbarian West, C. Delisle Burns, conceded that they were, on the whole, "drunken, lecher-

[4] See Tacitus, *Germania*.

ous, cowardly, and quite untrustworthy." [5] Their stand-ards of hygiene can be judged from the fastidious comment of the fifth-century Roman gentleman, Sidonius Apollinaris: "Happy the nose which cannot smell a barbarian." [6] Still, Burns could conclude by speaking of "those men and women of the First Europe, who kept a light shining in dark ages, who built a home for the spirit out of the ruins among which they lived." [7] With such accomplishments as those to their credit, it ill behooves us to make an issue of their aroma.

The Austrian historian Alfons Dopsch, writing in the early 1920's, devoted his impressive erudition to the task of rehabilitating the primitive Germans, arguing that they preserved much of what was valuable in Roman civilization and added creative contributions of their own: "The Germans did not behave as enemies of culture, destroying or abolishing it; on the contrary they preserved and developed it." [8] Dopsch was interested in showing, above all, that a vigorous economic life persisted throughout the twilight period: ". . . the so-called migrations were not only no hindrance to the earlier trade, but indeed made new connections which must have stimulated it." [9] Even from the political standpoint, the Germanic invasions were, in Dopsch's eyes, a boon to humanity, tempering late-Roman autocracy with a degree of compassion and an instinct for social welfare. "The heavy social and economic oppression of late-Roman times," he concludes, "was done away with, and a political solicitude for the welfare of the mass of the

[5] C. Delisle Burns, *The First Europe* (London, 1948), p. 31.
[6] *Carmina* XXIII, 13.
[7] Burns, *op. cit.*, p. 667.
[8] Alfons Dopsch, *The Economic and Social Foundations of European Civilization*, trans. M. G. Beard and N. Marshall (London, 1937), p. 386.
[9] *Ibid.*, p. 348.

free population was substituted." [10] To Dopsch, so it would seem, the Germanic conquests brought about not only a new orientation but also a New Deal.

Dopsch surely carries his challenging thesis too far; yet there remains much value in what he says. In the years that followed, the continuity hypothesis was set forth in a still stronger form by the great Belgian historian, Henri Pirenne.[11] In Pirenne's works, the persistence of Roman civilization through the twilight age becomes one important element in a bold reinterpretation of early medieval history. The Roman economy and the Roman ethos, Pirenne maintained, survived and flourished in the West until the eighth century when the Islamic conquests shattered the unity of the Mediterranean world and isolated Europe from its traditional commercial contacts in the Near East. As a consequence of the catastrophic Arab expansion, the European economy became primarily agrarian, self-sufficient, and commercially stagnant. Forced to abandon the Mediterranean, eighth-century Europe turned northward. The first political manifestation of this new and darker age was the empire of Charlemagne which emerges from the pages of Pirenne, stripped of its former glamor, as an epoch of economic stagnation.

Thus, the Germanic tribes preserved the past rather than killed it. "What the Germans destroyed," Pirenne argues, "was not the Empire but the imperial government in the West. . . . Far from seeking to replace the Empire by anything new, they established themselves within it, and although their settlement was accompanied by a process of serious disintegration, they did not introduce a new scheme of government; the ancient *palazzo*, so to speak,

[10] *Ibid.*, p. 387.
[11] The strongest statement of Henri Pirenne's thesis is to be found in his *Mahomet et Charlemagne* (2d ed.; Paris, 1937).

was divided up into apartments, but it still survived as a building. In short, the essential character of 'Romania' still remained Mediterranean." [12]

Pirenne's barbarians are distinctly less stalwart than those of Dopsch. They contributed practically nothing of their own and seem to have preserved "Romania" simply because they had no real alternative. What we have called a twilight period Pirenne would prefer to regard as an Indian summer, civilized but fundamentally uncreative. Nevertheless, Dopsch and Pirenne would agree that the Roman sun still shone in the barbarian West.

Pirenne, like Dopsch, went too far, and his thesis has been under heavy attack for the past generation. Scholars have pointed out that the Germanic invaders did, indeed, interrupt the Roman Mediterranean commerce, that although the Germanic kings sometimes tried to be Roman, they usually failed, that there was less commerce in the sixth and seventh century West and more in the age of Charlemagne than Pirenne had thought. Most of the anti-Pirenne arguments were brought together and forcefully stated by William C. Bark in his recent book *Origins of the Medieval World*. Bark, perhaps more than any previous writer, has urged that the twilight age was intensely creative and that Rome's collapse must be regarded as a blessing for mankind. Released from the immobilizing grip of the late-Roman state, which enslaved its own people in an effort to preserve itself and enrich its wealthiest landowners, the men of the early Middle Ages "began to find the way toward liberty, dignity, and decency by striking off the shackles of ignorance, fear, poverty, disease, and despotism. . . ." This they accomplished, so Bark believes, through the agencies of a new agrarian technology, a revitalized Christian faith, and, above all, a series of calami-

[12] Henri Pirenne, *Mohammed and Charlemagne*, trans. B. Miall (New York, 1957), p. 140.

tous invasions that again and again broke the established patterns of conformity: "Constant change proved to be the enemy of closed-mindedness and the unwitting friend of liberty." [13]

It is, of course, less than fair to epitomize the conclusions of serious scholars in a few bare quotations. As when one tunes in on the coda of a Beethoven symphony, the result is apt to seem extreme, unwarranted, and even a little ridiculous. A Beethoven coda is the logical consummation of an extended work of art, and, similarly, the conclusions of historians such as Gibbon, Burns, Dopsch, Pirenne, and Bark rest, to a greater or lesser degree, on a rigorous analysis of the evidence. The limitations of space necessitate our severing the conclusions of these scholars from the supporting evidence, but we can, at least, sample some of the evidence ourselves. Let us turn, therefore, from these historians of the twilight age to the age itself, so that we may explore directly some of the questions that have been raised: was it creative or derivative, coherent or anarchic, "good or bad"?

To most articulate people of the late Empire, the preservation of Rome seemed essential to the maintenance of human civilization. On this point Christians and pagans saw eye to eye. The great fourth-century Church Father St. Jerome expressed the view succinctly: "If Rome be lost, where shall we look for help?" [14] And, on the surface of things, the course of western Europe after the collapse of the Western Empire in the fifth century would seem to justify St. Jerome's fears.

By the early sixth century, western Europe, once united

[13] William C. Bark, *Origins of the Medieval World* (Anchor ed.; New York, 1960), pp. 156–157.
[14] Trans. by W. H. Fremantle, in *Library of Nicene and Post-Nicene Fathers*, VI (New York, 1893), 237.

under Rome, had disintegrated into a cluster of political fragments ruled by Germanic monarchies. A Vandal dynasty ruled North Africa, a Visigothic dynasty dominated Spain, an able Ostrogothic dynasty was established in Italy, a Frankish dynasty known as the Merovingians was in the process of subduing most of Gaul, and Britain had been subdivided into a number of small kingdoms ruled by Angles, Saxons, and Jutes. Pirenne and others have stressed that, at least outside Britain, the rulers of these Germanic successor states perpetuated in its essentials the old Roman administration. The Roman edifice endured, and was merely subdivided into apartments. Bark used a similar metaphor to illustrate a radically different conclusion: "The old buildings had fallen, and could not be rebuilt as they had been. The old architects were dead, and the new architects had new ideas." [15]

From the standpoint of political administration, it is difficult to avoid the conclusion that the new ideas were distinctly inferior to the old ones. Our test case must be Merovingian Gaul, for it was the only continental successor state to survive the Byzantine reconquest of the sixth century and the Islamic incursions of the seventh and eighth. The rather limited historical evidence relating to Merovingian Gaul has been examined minutely and interpreted endlessly, yet even today historians disagree as to its meaning. Few would join Pirenne in maintaining that the Merovingian political institutions were mere extensions of late Roman ones. Mr. Wallace-Hadrill, who describes the Merovingian period as "sub-Roman," sees it as an age in which Roman administrative traditions persisted but in progressively decadent form. The Merovingians possessed no heritage of Germanic political institutions capable of adaptation to the governance of a large, sedentary state. Although they misunderstood and failed to use much of the

[15] Bark, *op. cit.*, pp. 138–139.

Roman administrative machinery that they inherited, "they certainly brought no alternative with them. Their rule was Roman-derivative." [16]

So much is clear. The Merovingian kings were uncreative. More than that, they were clumsy and ignorant in their effort to keep the old Roman system going. They allowed the minting of money to slip from their grasp into the hands of independent and often untrustworthy private minters. They indulged in reckless grants of public rights and revenues, giving to private individuals the very power to tax. They demonstrated equal prodigality and irresponsibility in alienating their judicial prerogatives and their administrative functions. Their own royal officers were greedy and ill-disciplined, to be sure, but more and more the essential functions of the state passed from the royal administration altogether into the control of men entirely unconnected with the central government. In time the central government existed in name only, and the Merovingian kings found their power and their chief source of income limited to their own estates.

One must search in vain in the Merovingian age for any real evidence of what Dopsch describes as "a political solicitude for the welfare of the mass of the free population." Merovingian government does not seem ever to have risen above the predatory level. To the typical Merovingian king, the state was simply a source of income and power which he exploited as a leech exploits its host. Indeed, in their promiscuous alienations, the Merovingians demonstrated their incapacity even as predators.

The economic conditions of the twilight period seem almost as dismal as the political. Pirenne and Dopsch both postulated a vigorous commercial life in Merovingian Gaul, but more recent and dispassionate investigations

[16] J. M. Wallace-Hadrill, *The Long-Haired Kings* (London, 1962), p. 9.

have made it clear that this bustling Merovingian economy was a mirage. As Robert Latouche has recently observed, "The now fashionable, if unpleasant, word 'rot' describes it to perfection." [17]

Two closely related phenomena shaped the economy of Merovingian Gaul: the disintegration of urban life and the decline of commerce. The Merovingian monarchs contributed to the economic decline by following a strict policy of laissez-faire, which arose not out of any physiocratic philosophy but out of sheer ignorance. By abandoning their control over minting, they were indirectly responsible for the progressively debased and wildly insecure gold coinage which, in itself, rendered a sound economy impossible. We know of only one instance of a Merovingian king establishing a fair.[18] In general, the economic picture was bleak indeed, and the Merovingians did nothing whatever to improve it. This statement should not be construed as a denunciation of the Merovingian kings, but a recognition of the more fundamental fact that the political leadership of primitive Germanic monarchs and aristocrats fell radically short of the desperate economic needs of the twilight age. We should not condemn the Germanic leaders themselves; they knew no better.

Our sources make it clear, however, that although trade declined sharply in Merovingian Gaul, it did not cease altogether. Historians such as Pierenne have seized upon occasional contemporary allusions to merchants in order to make their case for a vigorous Merovingian commerce. But nearly all these merchants were foreigners, Syrians for the most part, and although some of them doubtless transcended the level of common peddlers, they were in no

[17] Robert Latouche, *The Birth of Western Economy*, trans. E. M. Wilkinson (London, 1961), p. 139.

[18] L. Levillain, "Etudes sur l'abbaye de Saint-Denis à l'epoque merovingienne," *Bibliothèque de l'Ecole des Chartes*, XCI (1930), 14.

sense great entrepreneurs. The chief commodity in their trade was slaves, and, with a few rare exceptions, they seem to have carried out their activities on an exceedingly modest scale. The fact that so few Franks or Gallo-Romans were involved in commerce is itself damning testimony to the degeneracy of the Merovingian economy.

Towns, like commerce, survived after a fashion, but only on a profoundly reduced scale. The vigorous municipal administrations of old Roman times faded steadily and, in time, vanished altogether. But, in many instances, the centers of settlement survived, although with exceedingly modest populations, a few thousand inhabitants at the very most. One reason for the survival of towns was the fact that in certain situations the Merovingian kings valued them as fortified strongholds against their enemies. More important, they survived as ecclesiastical centers. They were often the sites of cathedrals, the centers of episcopal administration. Some cathedrals were the repositories of famous relics—wonder-working bones of noted saints— and, consequently, the towns in which these cathedrals were located became important pilgrimage centers. Moreover, there was a tendency for monastic foundations to establish themselves near the cathedrals on the peripheries of towns. Thus, the Church made a significant, perhaps indispensable, contribution to urban survival. But the towns had virtually no commercial life apart from supplying necessities to religious establishments. Christopher Dawson was not far from the mark when he described the urban center of the twilight age as "a sacred city rather than a political or commercial organism." [19]

Perhaps it is unfair to expect the Merovingian towns to be vigorous and self-sustaining commercial centers, for the commercial functions of towns in Roman Gaul itself were

[19] Christopher Dawson, *The Making of Europe* (Meridian ed.; New York, 1957), p. 228.

highly artificial. By and large, the cities of the Western
Roman Empire were not independent commercial entities.
Rather, they were administrative and military centers
which drew their sustenance from the surrounding countryside and which, from the economic standpoint, failed to
pay their own way. These towns were foci of Roman culture and Roman political and military administration, but,
in the commercial sense, they were parasites on the agrarian economy. Ferdinand Lot aptly describes them as "ten-
tacular." Often beautiful and impressive with their luxu-
rious baths and amphitheaters, their imposing aqueducts
and public buildings, they depended ultimately on the
ceaseless flow of Roman tax revenues and the protection of
Roman arms. With the steady decline of the late-Roman
economy, the wealthier town dwellers abandoned their
cities for their country villas, and, with the breakdown of
the Roman political regime in the West and the rupturing
of the frontiers, the cities were doomed. Survive they
might, but in nothing like their former state.

Some contemporary writers, as we have seen, exaggerated the destruction of towns. They were seldom annihilated altogether, but they nevertheless suffered grievously.
More important, their powers of recuperation were paralyzed by the collapse of the Roman regime. The devastation of the fifth century was followed by generations of
economic lethargy and political disintegration. There
could be no phenomenon akin to the impressive rise of
German towns out of the rubble of World War II.

The fate of the Western towns in the fifth century can
perhaps best be appreciated by quoting from two contemporary texts. Salvian, writing in the fifth century, employs
all the old pious clichés about towns being pits of evil and
temptation, their inhabitants reveling in the profane pleasures of theater and circus. But when Salvian turns his attention to three towns with which he is well acquainted—

Mainz, Cologne, and Trier—he is obliged to admit that the circus and theater had ceased to exist, not because of an upsurge of sanctity but because the towns had been severely afflicted by the invasions. In two of these towns, the buildings in which entertainments had been held were destroyed, and the third town had become a barbarian encampment.[20]

Sidonius Apollinaris presents an even more vivid picture in his apostrophe to the town of Narbonne: "Proud amidst half-ruined ramparts you display the noble scars of long ago battles and bear witness to the devastation caused by the blows that have been rained on you; these splendid ruins render you all the more precious to us." [21]

Such was the condition of a great Roman city at the onset of the twilight age. Conditions in the countryside were not a great deal better. As late as 791 a terrible famine drove the peasantry in parts of France to cannibalism, and a contemporary source assures us that some were in such desperate straits that they ate members of their own families.[22]

It should not be surprising that the fall of the Western Empire resulted in a profound political and economic decline, but the survival of the Church might well suggest a compensatory rise in the civilizing influence of Christianity and the life of the spirit. It is quite true that the Church was a significant force in the twilight age, but, in many respects, its efficiency was radically compromised by the general barbarization of society. The Church made a genuine effort to ameliorate the insecurity and impoverishment of the period by carrying on charitable activities. It helped believers to endure the grinding hardships of their

[20] Salvian *De gubernatione Dei* VI. 8, 15.
[21] Sidonius Apollinaris *Carmina* XXIII.
[22] *Monumenta Germaniae Historica, Leges,* Sec. II: *Capitularia Regum Francorum,* I. 76, no. 31.

present life by assuring them of a better life to come. But the personnel of the ecclesiastical hierarchy tended to be drawn more and more from the very classes that dominated lay society. By no means insulated from the world around it, the Church fell victim to the same process of barbarization which was afflicting other contemporary institutions.

Moreover, ecclesiastical organization was slow in adapting to the new rural orientation of the twilight age. The bishops remained in the crumbling towns; the monks gravitated to the suburbs and endeavored to escape from the world rather than reform it. Rural parishes were exceedingly slow in developing; it was not until the age of Charlemagne that they began to make a real impact on the countryside. Until then a peasant was fortunate if he saw a priest once a year. The Church was becoming a great landholder, and, to many of the tenants on its far-flung estates, it assumed the role of the acquisitive landlord rather than the shepherd of souls. By and large, the European countryside in the twilight age was spiritually adrift, and even as late as the eighth century one encounters reports of Christian priests who sacrificed to the pagan gods and filled their homes with concubines.

If political, economic, and religious life reached such depths, what can one say of the survival of Roman culture? Here again, two contemporary texts will suffice to give an impression of the general decline. The first is a passage from a letter of St. Gregory the Great (d. 603), the ablest pope of the early Middle Ages and one of the leading intellects of his epoch. In this letter, Pope Gregory admonishes Bishop Desiderius of Gaul in these words: "It later came to our attention, and we cannot mention it without shame, that your fraternity is accustomed to expound grammar to certain persons. This we took so much amiss and disapproved so strongly that we [were driven to]

. . . groaning and sadness; for there is not room in a single mouth for the praises of Christ and the praises of Jupiter." [23]

Pope Gregory, in this one passage at least, seems to be suggesting that classical learning is incompatible with Christianity. He did not always follow this precept himself, nor did his contemporaries. A noted ecclesiastical scholar of the next generation, Bishop Isidore of Seville, was reputed to have an encyclopedic grasp of ancient wisdom, and in his best-known work, the *Etymologies*, he attempted an exhaustive catalogue of all knowledge. He drew heavily from Roman authorities and was often badly misled by them. The chief characteristics of his work, a profound naïveté and a remarkably suppressed critical sense, are illustrated vividly in his discussion of monsters:

> The Cynocephali are so named because they have dogs' heads, and their very barking betrays them as beasts rather than men. They are born in India. The Cyclopses, too, come from India, and are so named because they have a single eye in the midst of the forehead. . . . The Blemmyes, born in Lybia, are believed to be headless trunks, having mouth and eyes in the breast. Others are born without necks, with eyes in their shoulders. . . . They say that the Panotii in Sythia have ears of so large a size that they cover the whole body with them. . . . The race of the Sciopodes is said to live in Ethiopia. They have one leg apiece and are of a marvelous swiftness, and . . . in summertime they lie on the ground on their backs and are shaded by the greatness of their feet.

Isidore discloses no sign of skepticism until the end, when he concludes: "Other fabulous monstrosities of the human race are said to exist, but they do not; they are imaginary." [24]

[23] Trans. by J. Barmby, in *Library of Nicene and Post-Nicene Fathers*, XIII, 69.
[24] *Etymologiae* XI. 3.

In discussing the subject of numbers, Isidore attaches particular significance to the numeral 22: "God in the beginning made twenty-two works." It follows that there are twenty-two sextarii in the bushel, twenty-two letters in the Hebrew alphabet, twenty-two generations from Adam to Jacob, and twenty-two books in the Old Testament—as far as Esther.[25]

Isidore did not invent this nonsense; he drew it from the past, chiefly the Roman past. On other subjects he shows to much better advantage. It is not intended here merely to ridicule him—very probably he was a person of immense intellectual potential—but rather to show the limitations of a man who is widely regarded as one of the best minds of the twilight age. A comparison of his writings with those of the better authors of the Roman Empire—Cicero, Virgil, Ptolemy, Plotinus, Jerome, Augustine, or others of their caliber—would disclose Isidore's limitations all the more dramatically.

Twilight, as we know, is an intermingling of darkness and light. In stressing the darker side of the twilight age, we have conveyed an impression that, although accurate as far as it goes, is one-sided and misleading. Now, having accustomed our eyes to the darkness, we are in a position to seek traces of light.

The intelligentsia of the twilight age would doubtless have agreed with Pirenne that Roman civilization still endured in the West. The articulate people of this epoch were keenly aware of their Roman heritage, and although some, like Pope Gregory, were apprehensive of the dangers of pagan writings on the Christian soul, almost everyone was anxious to preserve Roman culture at least in Christianized form. And, in the writings of great late-Roman

[25] *Ibid.*, XVI, 10.

Church Fathers such as Ambrose, Jerome, and Augustine, they had a powerful Roman-Christian synthesis to draw upon. These three Christian scholars, and others like them, were as sensitive as Pope Gregory to the danger of pagan contamination, but they had the will and the courage to employ the classical heritage for their own Christian purposes. St. Augustine expressed the point in these words: "If those who are called philosophers, particularly the Platonists, have said anything that is true and harmonious to our Faith, we should not avoid it but claim it for our own use from those who possess it unlawfully." [26]

Thus, the Christian could, with caution, take possession of the intellectual tradition of the pagan past and enrich it with the spirit of Christ. It was precisely this combination —this Christianization of the classical heritage—that the eighth-century monk Alcuin of York had in mind when he spoke to Charlemagne of the immense possibilities inherent in the Carolingian intellectual revival: "If your intentions are carried out, it may be that a new Athens will arise in Frankland, and an Athens fairer than of old, for our Athens, ennobled by the teachings of Christ, will surpass the wisdom of the Academy." [27] Alcuin was both indulging in flattery and yielding to illusion when he wrote these words, for Charlemagne's empire had not risen far from its barbaric past, and his intellectual renaissance seldom transcended the level of the grammar school. Nevertheless, the illusion itself is significant. Alcuin, like his contemporaries, looked for inspiration from two sources: the Christian religion and the classical past.

"Early medieval men," writes Wallace-Hadrill, "could

[26] *On Christian Doctrine*, trans. J. F. Shaw (3d ed.; Edinburgh, 1892), p. 75.

[27] *Monumenta Germaniae Historica, Poetae Latini Medii Aevi: Poetae Latini Aevi Carolini*, II. 279, no. 170.

live like barbarians; but they could think that they were Romans." [28] Their attitude is exemplified in a statement attributed to the fifth-century Gothic chieftain, Ataulfus, a statement that was related by Gibbon himself and has been repeated frequently by subsequent historians. Ataulfus is reported to have said that his first thought, when he entered upon the career of conquest, was to claim for the Goths the world leadership that had once belonged to the Romans, and to make himself a Gothic Augustus. But gradually his goal changed. He learned that Rome dominated the world not by the sword alone but by law, and that his own savage tribesmen had not learned the lesson of obedience to law which alone could fit them to rule. Now he desired only to restore and reinvigorate the Roman commonwealth, transforming and strengthening that which he had once hoped to destroy. [29]

Ataulfus' statement is exceedingly instructive. It illustrates at the secular level what we have already observed among Christian intellectuals: the early medieval world was haunted by the memory of Rome. Jerome, writing before the fall of the Western Empire, had mourned, "If Rome be lost, where shall we look for help?" One encounters the same sentiment in the great Northumbrian scholar, Bede, writing in the early eighth century: "When Rome falls, the world will fall." [30] Bede wrote at a time when the Western Empire had been defunct for a number of generations; yet he could speak as though Rome still endured. Indeed, it did endure—as a city, and, above all, as an idea. The intellectuals of the twilight age preserved their Roman legacy in profoundly debased form, to be sure; yet preserve it they did. Without the Roman heritage

[28] J. M. Wallace-Hadrill, *The Barbarian West* (New York, 1962), p. 146.

[29] Orosius *Historiarum adversum paganos* VII, 43.

[30] ". . . quando cadet Roma, cadet et mundus." See *Decline and Fall,* VII, 330.

there could have been no Bede, no Isidore, no Pope Gregory. And although Isidore was a far cry from Augustine, he was certainly no barbarian. Rome lived on in the twilight age, side by side with the rude institutions of the primitive Germanic peoples. Indeed, this intensely fluid, formative epoch witnessed a deeply significant synthesis of classical, Christian, and Germanic cultures. Only when this synthesis had taken form could a new civilization emerge, and it was in the twilight age that the essential process of fusion began.

If the people of the sixth and seventh centuries were preserving a past, they were also creating a future. The combination of old institutions and cultural ingredients into a new synthesis is itself a creative act of high importance. And to the three traditions they inherited—Roman, Christian, and Germanic—they added much that was new. Their creativity is most clearly demonstrated in the area of agriculture: they reclaimed lands from forest and marsh, placed the peasant on his plot, and organized his labor through a complex but workable series of institutions. Above all, they made the land more bountiful by developing a new agrarian technology.

Throughout the ancient world, agriculture had been man's fundamental economic enterprise, and any significant innovations in agrarian technology were bound to have a profound effect upon human life. In Roman times, agriculture had been of primary economic importance; now, in the twilight age, it was all important. The fact that the early medieval husbandman was able to improve significantly upon traditional Roman agrarian techniques testifies to his remarkable ingenuity. This generalization should perhaps be qualified by the fact that most of the important technological innovations of early medieval Europe were borrowed from elsewhere, but it is nevertheless notable that the West could adapt these techniques creatively to its own purposes. Underlying the relative brightness of Charlemagne's era and the far greater brightness of the twelfth-century renaissance was a steady rise in the productivity of western European agriculture.[31]

The generations between Romulus Augustulus and Charlemagne saw the introduction of two fundamental improvements in the husbandry of northwestern Europe: the heavy compound plow and the three-field system. Roman agriculture had depended, by and large, on a relatively ineffective scratch plow that had changed very little over the centuries and millennia of antiquity. By the seventh or eighth century, the fields of the northern districts of Western Christendom were being attacked by a heavy wheeled plow with colter, plowshare, and moldboard, a machine that cut deep furrows into the ground, pulverizing the soil and turning it aside into ridges. Certain elements of this heavy compound plow may have been employed occasionally by the late Romans, but it seems clear that they did not bring it into widespread use nor did they know it in anything like its fully developed form. The development of the new plow was complex and gradual; from the standpoint of the modern historian, it is exceedingly difficult to trace. There is some reason to believe that the basic idea was carried into western Europe by the Slavs in the sixth or seventh century. Once it had come into general use in the West, large areas of rich, heavy soil, which had defied the older scratch plow, could be opened to cultivation. The heavy plow, which required large teams of oxen to draw it, contributed to the shift from square or irregular fields to strip fields, for by plowing in long strips a peasant could minimize the difficult task of reversing the team. Moreover, the necessity of large teams of oxen re-

<hr>

[31] See Lynn White, jr., *Medieval Technology and Social Change* (Oxford, 1962), pp. 39–78, on which the following paragraphs are based.

quired the peasants to pool their animals and their labor, and out of this necessity arose the cooperative village communities that became so characteristic a feature of medieval husbandry.

The heavy compound plow brought vast new areas under cultivation. More than that, it made possible a significant change in the rotation of fields. Roman agriculture had been dominated by a two-field system: one field was planted each year while the other was allowed to lie fallow. But the rich new lands that the heavy plow opened to cultivation did not require a full year's rest between crops. Hence, by the time of Charlemagne considerable areas of northern Europe had shifted to a three-field system of rotation: each of the fields followed a three-year cycle of autumn planting, spring planting, and fallow. The shift from two to three fields, by increasing appreciably the total yield of a given quantity of land, resulted in a significant rise in productivity and, concomitantly, in the standard of living of the peasantry. Disasters such as the terrible famine of 791 could still occur, but, in the larger view, peasant prosperity was steadily increasing. Lynn White has suggested that the new plow and the three-field system, which were unsuited to the light soil and dry climate of the Mediterranean Basin, contributed much to the northward shift in the orientation of Carolingian Europe which Pirenne had earlier attributed to the Islamic conquests.[32]

The three-field revolution was accompanied by a concurrent trend toward mechanization. By the end of the twilight age the water mill had come into general use on northern European farms. Rome had known the water mill, but had used it only rarely. By Charlemagne's time it was employed on a large scale for the grinding of grain, and, in later centuries, Western Christendom applied it to

[32] *Ibid.*, pp. 76–78.

other tasks such as driving trip-hammers in forges and powering the textile industry that rose to prominence in the eleventh century.[33]

Thus, the technological progress of the twilight age was only a beginning. Subsequent centuries saw new improvements in the exploitation of the soil and its products. By 1000, the ox was gradually giving way to the more efficient draft horse whose use as a beast of burden was made possible by a radically improved horse collar and the introduction of the horseshoe, both of which seem to have originated in Siberia or Central Asia. And the twelfth century witnessed the advent of the windmill in the western European countryside. Taken altogether, these innovations resulted not only in a notable increase in productivity but also in a profoundly significant shift from human labor to the energy of animals and machines. Slavery, which had been a fundamental ingredient of the Roman economy, was declining rapidly in the age of Charlemagne and had faded to insignificance by the twelfth and thirteenth centuries. Western Civilization is humanity's first nonslave civilization. Except for the early phases of colonial exploitation, and an exotic and relatively brief episode in the antebellum South, chattel slavery has never been important in the West, and it is no exaggeration to suggest that the decline of the slave owes much to the achievement of the twilight age. For here are to be found the roots of that almost demoniac technological inventiveness that has brought our civilization such remarkable success and such fearful difficulties.

How was it that the savage and turbulent post-Roman centuries could contribute so much to the exploitation of the soil and the clearing of new lands? William Bark has found the explanation for its creativity in the turmoil of successive invasions which repeatedly shattered the estab-

[33] On medieval mechanical innovations, see *ibid.*, pp. 79–134.

lished forces of conformity.[34] Another explanation has
been suggested by Lynn White: The conversion of western
Europe to Christianity, although accompanied by the survival of much that was pagan, wrought a profound change
in human attitudes toward nature. Ancient peoples, Roman and Germanic alike, had been deeply affected by animism: the notion that natural objects—trees, stones,
mountains, and the like—possessed divine souls. A peasant
affected with such ideas might cut down a tree out of necessity, but he would do so with considerable fear and mis-
giving. We know that this attitude was particularly common among the heathen Germans, who venerated trees and
were loath to destroy them. But Christianity, by banishing
divinity from the natural world, enabled its adherents to
approach nature in a new light as something that might be
fearlessly manipulated and exploited for the good of man.
Here we encounter the germ of an idea that has been fundamental to our civilization: nature need not rule humanity but can be made to serve it.

Agrarian technology was merely one area of creativity
in the twilight age. The Church, for all its weakness, retained its potential to lead and inspire. Through the two
supreme ecclesiastical institutions of the era—the papacy
and Benedictine monasticism—it gradually brought coherence to its organization, deepened the life of the spirit, and
significantly expanded the frontiers of Christendom by
bringing its gospel and its civilization to the heathen peoples
of England and Germany. Pope Gregory the Great, although suspicious of Roman literature, was an important
popularizer of Augustinian theology and a living example
of wise and compassionate ecclesiastical leadership. His
handbook on the duties of a bishop, the *Pastoral Care*, with
its sensitive understanding of human nature, served as an

[34] Bark, *op. cit.*, p. 157 and *passim*.

inspiration to subsequent generations of churchmen. It was Pope Gregory who sent a mission of Benedictine monks to convert Anglo-Saxon England in 597, and there the Benedictines came into contact with the rich tradition of Celtic Christianity which had developed almost in isolation in Wales, Ireland, and western Scotland. How these two traditions—the Celtic and the Roman-Benedictine— joined to produce a remarkable cultural flowering in seventh- and eighth-century Northumbria, and how St. Boniface, Alcuin, and other monks from Christian England brought the fruits of this vibrant culture back to the Continent in the eighth century, are explained and discussed in another chapter. These developments are therefore not elaborated here, but they must at least be noted, for Celtic Christianity, Benedictine monasticism, and the papacy all made heroic and significant contributions to the building of a new civilization out of the richly promising but disorganized materials of the twilight age.

If the fall of the Western Roman Empire was in some respects a disaster for western Europe, in other respects it was a priceless opportunity. The disintegration of political organization and commercial life, the barbarization of the Church, and the decline of culture must be weighed against the fact that the late Roman Empire was a mummified autocracy, a police state teeming with spies and informers, with a predatory and stultified economy based on a caste system. Its demise brought disorganization and savagery, but it also gave Europe the chance for a new beginning, an escape from old customs and lifeless conventions, a release from the stifling prison that the Roman Empire, for most of its inhabitants, had come to be. Yet early medieval Europe was by no means obliged to start from scratch. Without being trammeled by Roman conventions, it could still draw inspiration from the Greco-Roman past. Life in the post-Roman West was hazardous, ignorant, foul, and deeply insecure, but such was the price of the new beginning. Periods of momentous change are seldom comfortable. In the East, where the Roman Empire survived for another millennium, there was no such relapse into savagery, nor, when all is said, was there any such buoyant creativity as characterized the later medieval and modern West. The twilight age, wherein some of the most fundamental elements of our civilization achieved coherent form, was the essential prelude to the new dawn.

VII

THE CONTINUITY AND PRESERVATION
OF THE LATIN TRADITION

Philip Levine

*T*HE LONG and notorious struggle of early Christianity for official recognition and ultimate ascendancy over traditional Roman paganism culminated during the fourth century in a series of momentous events. Historians of the period have carefully traced the course of this movement from the proclamation of the so-called Edict of Milan by Constantine in 312 or 313 on behalf of the Christians through the sequence of repressive measures instituted against the old religion by Constans and Constantius to the fatal thrust against the ancient state cult by Gratian in 382. It was in that year that the emperor, probably at the instigation of Pope Damasus, symbolically and financially obstructed the performance and maintenance of the public rites of worship in Rome. By his action, the altar that had stood in the Curia before the statue of Victory and received an offering of incense from the senators before each meeting was removed; at the same time, the Vestals and the Roman priests were deprived of their time-honored immunities and revenues.

The ramifications of these steps were far-reaching, for they struck at the very heart of what Romans had been traditionally indoctrinated from their most impressionable years to regard as a vital and essential part of their venerable heritage. The specific details of their polytheistic worship and the nature of their divinities need not be examined here, nor is it necessary to elaborate at length upon the curious, yet real, dichotomy that often existed between an enlightened Roman's public observance of ancestral divine rites and his private mental reservations or doubts regarding the very being or activity of their gods. This theological ambivalence or compartmentalization of thought and deed not infrequently gave rise to rather striking paradoxes. It allowed Cicero, for example, in his *De Natura Deorum* to represent a Roman high priest as inquiring skeptically into the very bases of religious belief and in his *De Divinatione* to portray himself, a member of the state augural college, as condemning the superstitious practices of divination, including augury. Their official priestly positions were apparently sufficient safeguards against charges of heresy. Hardly more than lip service seemed to be expected, and hence Romans like Pliny the Younger and Trajan at the beginning of the second century must have been puzzled as to why some early Christians would risk persecution or even death rather than pay formal tribute to their pagan rites.[1]

The official attitude of the Romans was that they were a people whose successes were attributable to their gods and whose fortunes were dependent on their favor, which was to be secured through the proper worship of them. This tenet, frequently echoed in Latin literature, was hallowed by Virgil in his *Aeneid* and enshrined by Livy in his *History of Rome* in the Augustan Age.[2] Thus Rome's manifest destiny became intimately associated with and appeared inextricably bound to her ancestral religion, so that

[1] Cf. Pliny the Younger *Epistulae* 10.96, 97.
[2] For references to this belief in literature, see A. S. Pease's notes on Cicero *De Natura Deorum* 2.8 (*superiores*); 3.5 (*fundamenta iecisse*).

Gratian's restrictions, like those earlier of Constans and Constantius and later of Theodosius, constituted for the pagan aristocrats of that time a dire threat to the very foundations of their entire national heritage. This conflict of ideologies provoked the guardians of the old order to vindicate their position and labor to protect the continuity of their sacred tradition.

Gratian's ears were effectively stopped by Pope Damasus and Ambrose against the entreaties of the pagan senators; he would not even grant their delegation a hearing. But after his death in 383, Faustina, who exercised the regency on behalf of her young son, Valentinian II, found it advantageous to court the support of the pagan aristocracy, and she did so by appointing two of its leaders to high public office, naming Praetextatus pretorian prefect of Italy and Symmachus prefect of Rome. Thus, since the situation now seemed favorable for further action on the religious issue, Symmachus, seizing the opportunity, proceeded to Milan in 384 with a senatorial petition in his hands, and, in a famous address, which is preserved, made an impassioned plea for the revocation of Gratian's decrees of 382.[3] He based his arguments on considerations of justice, tolerance, and present expediency, and eloquently reinforced them with touching appeals to ancestral tradition and poignant clichés of the past: Rome's success, prosperity, and safety, he held, were owing to and dependent on the observance of her ancient rites of worship. But Ambrose, like Augustine

---

[3] Symmachus *Relatio* 3, ed. O. Seeck, *Monumenta Germaniae Historica, Auct. Antiquiss.* 6.1 (1883), 280–283. For a convenient collection of the relevant texts of Symmachus and Ambrose, with a German translation and commentary, see J. Wytzes, *Der Streit um den Altar der Viktoria* (Amsterdam, 1936). On this entire subject cf. the excellent article by H. Bloch, "The Pagan Revival in the West at the End of the Fourth Century," in *The Conflict between Paganism and Christianity in the Fourth Century*, ed. A. Momigliano (Oxford, 1963), pp. 193–218.

later, demolished these claims by hard logic and the evidence of historical realities.[4] The petition was denied, as were similar ones brought later to Theodosius and Valentinian II. The revival of official paganism in Rome, fostered by the temporizing benefactions of Eugenius in 393, was short-lived, being decisively terminated by Theodosius' victory over the usurper on the river Frigidus on September 6, 394.

This familiar background of threat, challenge, and final defeat in the cause of their ancestral religion is essential to an understanding of the urgency attending the concern and efforts of the pagan aristocrats also to preserve other important aspects of their cultural heritage. Much of earlier Latin literature seems to have survived at least until the archaizing period of the Antonines, though it is by no means certain to what extent citations and allusions in Aulus Gellius' *Noctes Atticae* actually come from firsthand knowledge. The conservative curriculum of the Roman schools, with its emphasis on literature and rhetoric, contributed, as always, to the continuity of the Latin intellectual tradition, while the industry of legal scholars like Gaius under the Antonines and like Papinian, Ulpian, and Paulus under the Severi helped notably in the transmission of Rome's rich legacy in jurisprudence to posterity. But it was undeniably the religious crisis of the fourth century which kindled a keener consciousness of the country's glorious past and a deeper reverence for her sacred traditions in the hearts and minds of the pagan nobility.

Such, in fact, is the situation revealingly portrayed in Macrobius' literary dialogue *Saturnalia,* composed during this period. The *terminus ante quem* of its dramatic date is fixed by the death of Praetextatus, one of its chief participants, in 384. Following a fashion long ago established by

[4] Cf. Ambrose *Epistulae* 17; 18; 57.

Cicero in this genre, the author had the event take place on a Roman festival, as indicated by the very title, a significant detail designed to point up the fact that the learned discussions were held at a time of enforced leisure, when the interlocutors could not have been engaged in the performance of their state responsibilities or other serious business. Moreover, in casting the dramatis personae, Macrobius, like his predecessor Cicero, selected men of the highest distinction for the key roles, for their *auctoritas* would lend considerable weight and dignity to the occasion. His principal speakers included Vettius Agorius Praetextatus, Nicomachus Flavianus, and Aurelius Symmachus, all outstanding public figures and vigorous defenders of the old religion. Among others, young Servius, later renowned as a Virgilian critic and commentator, was also a member of the group. The work itself is replete with historical, philological, religious, and other antiquarian lore. The author's avowed purpose was educational, for his aim was to incorporate this mass of information in a convenient form for his son's instruction, even as Cato the Elder had put together a sort of encyclopedia for the edification of his boy centuries earlier. In the wholly pagan milieu of the dialogue, which vividly recalls the golden days of the Roman Republic, the contemporary Christian menace to the survival of the old Latin tradition can only be inferred from the profound sympathy and nostalgia expressed for things of the past.

Particularly striking and symptomatic of the pagan crisis is the elaborate treatment accorded to Virgil in the *Saturnalia*. As the poet par excellence of Rome's traditions, achievements, ideals, and aspirations in the Augustan Age, he occupied soon after his death a very privileged position among the writers of his country. Indeed, along with Horace, he suffered the fate of becoming a school textbook as early as the first century.[5] But in Macrobius an aura of

[5] Cf. Juvenal 7.225–227.

holiness and inviolability attaches to his memory, while his *Aeneid* is regarded almost as divinely inspired pagan scripture. Thus in Book 1 of the *Saturnalia,* when the brash Euangelus, a carping critic who serves as a foil to the others, comments unfavorably on the epic poem, Symmachus replies, in the shocked presence of the others, "Virgil's fame is such that it can be neither augmented by anyone's praise nor diminished by anyone's censure." [6] And a little later, when Symmachus disparages the myopic view of most teachers who confine their interpretation of the *Aeneid* to the elementary level of verbal exegesis, and indicates that a detailed study of Virgil's work will be a principal aim of the dialogue, he speaks of the poem in terms quite appropriate to Holy Writ. "Let us not," he says, "allow the sanctuary of the sacred poem to lie concealed. Rather let us search out the entrance to its secret thoughts, unlock the inner shrine of its temple and make it accessible to the educated so that they may honor it with their worship." [7]

Thus the aristocratic circle of Symmachus and his friends, in its efforts to maintain the ancient Roman heritage, did not restrict its activity to the religious front, where pagan catholicity and tolerance, as epitomized in the plea presented at Milan in 384, proved no match against a Catholicism completely intolerant of all other beliefs (see pp. 208–209, above). The *Saturnalia* shows the great importance attached at this time also to earlier Latin literature and to Virgil in particular. Herein, perhaps, lies the key to a palaeographical enigma that has long baffled scholars of the history of calligraphy in the West. The normal capital hand used in Latin manuscripts through the fourth and fifth centuries was the so-called rustic, an uppercase lettering whose thicker strokes were executed on a slanted axis (fig. 1). But in two fragmentary parchment codices of

[6] Macrobius *Saturnalia* 1.24.8.
[7] *Ibid.,* 1.24.13.

Virgil (figs. 2, 3), known as the Augusteus and the Sangallensis, the capital writing is extremely formal in aspect,
with the thicker strokes drawn on an axis that tends,
though not consistently, to be more vertical.[8] This script
seems strikingly epigraphical in character and is generally
designated as square capital. Palaeographers, chiefly on in-
tuitive grounds, have long been inclined to regard this elegant book hand, which appears to have been reserved exclusively for Virgil, as a peculiar phenomenon of the
fourth or fifth century. They have not, however, been able
to explain satisfactorily its appearance at such a date and
the complete lack of evidence for its use prior to the
fourth century on either papyrus or parchment. But in
view of the intense desire of the pagan society depicted in
Macrobius' *Saturnalia* to glorify Virgil and to exalt him to
an almost saintly status, the idea of honoring the poet with
a monumental script of his own may quite possibly have
emanated from the circle of Symmachus. The square capital in the two manuscripts [9] is an obvious tour de force,
but the exquisitely beautiful lettering on contemporary inscriptions engraved for the Christian pontiff Damasus by
his famed calligrapher Furius Dionysius Filocalus (fig. 4)
could readily have furnished a model and provided the impulse for pagan scribes to imitate it as a special tribute to
Virgil, whose profound knowledge of pontifical lore, according to Praetextatus in the *Saturnalia,* would, in fact,
have fully qualified him as a *pontifex maximus*.[10]

However that may be, Symmachus and his group
showed a remarkable interest in the condition and transmission of Livy's text. Like Virgil's *Aeneid,* Livy's prose

[8] Regarding these manuscripts, see E. A. Lowe, *Cod. Lat. Ant.*
1.13 and 8.**13 for the Augusteus, and 7.977 for the Sangallensis.

[9] A parchment scrap of another Virgil manuscript in this rare capital was found at Oxyrhynchus (Pap. Oxy. 1098) (see Lowe, *op. cit.,*
10.1569).

[10] Macrobius *Saturnalia* 1.24.16.

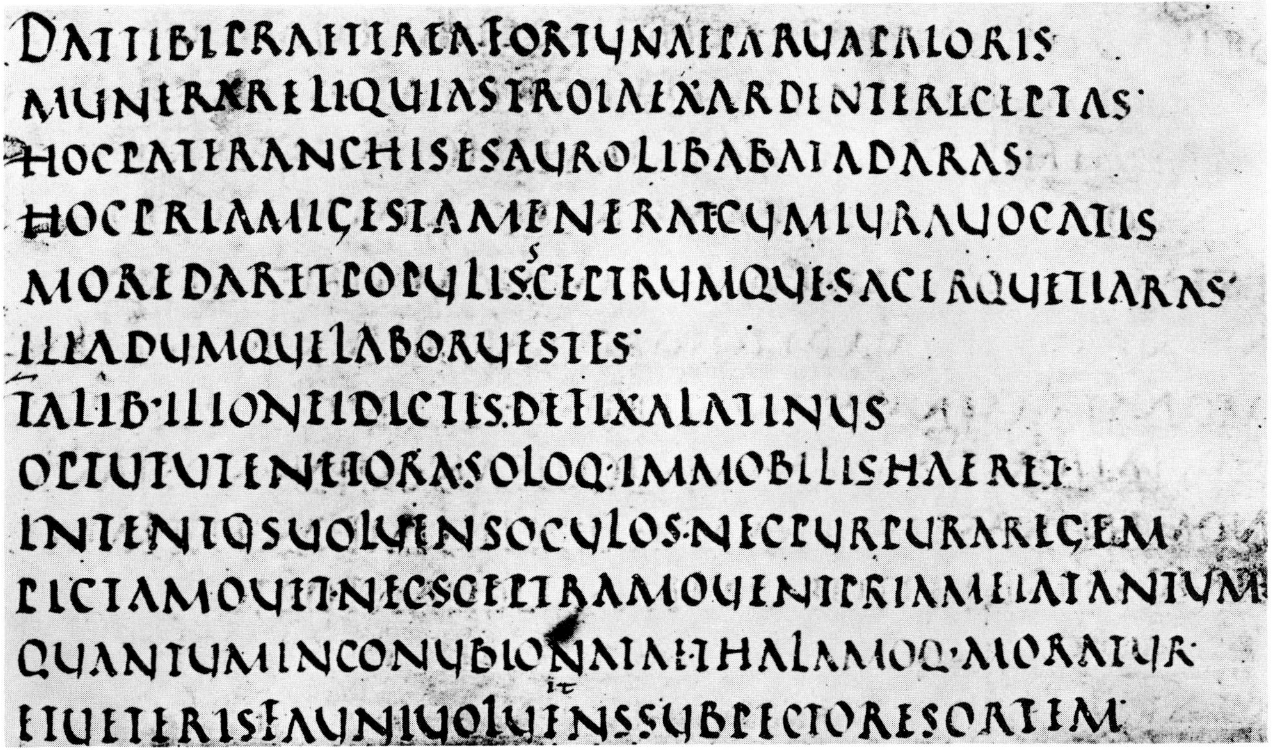

Fig. 1. Folio 62 recto of Cod. Vat. lat. 3225, a fourth-century rustic capital manuscript of Virgil.

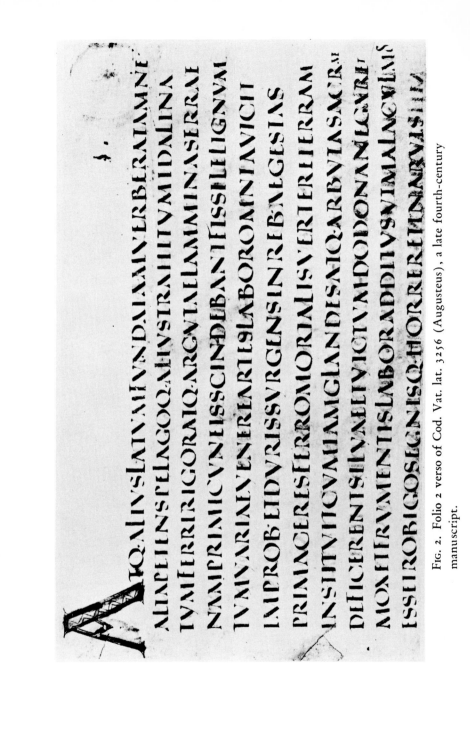

FIG. 2. Folio 2 verso of Cod. Vat. lat. 3256 (Augusteus), a late fourth-century manuscript.

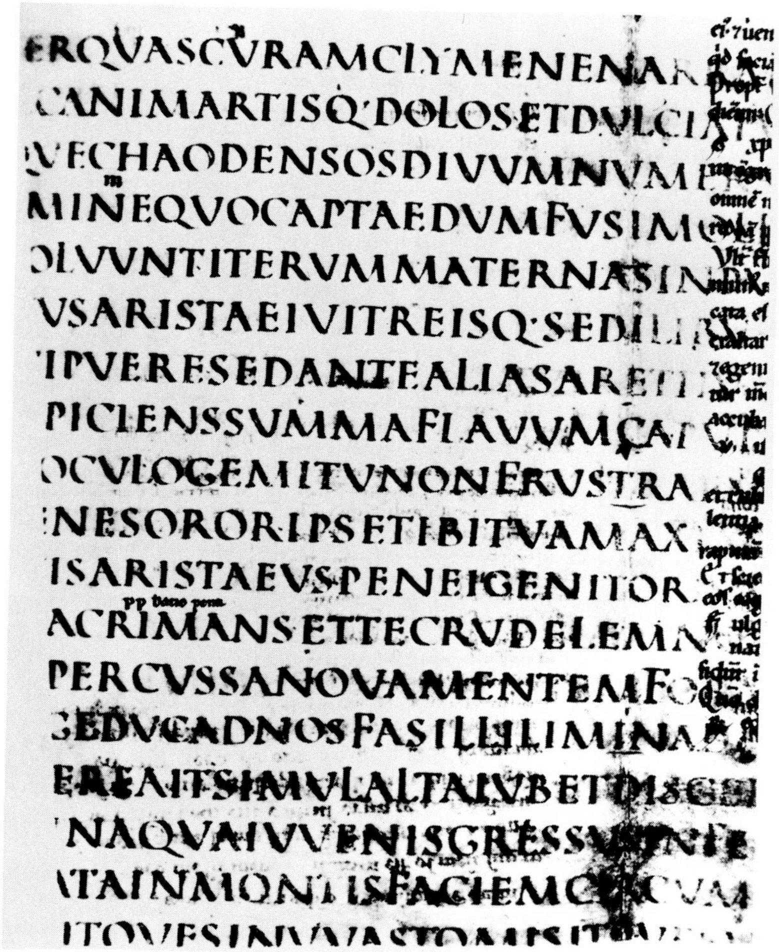

FIG. 3. Page 39 of St. Gall, Stiftsbibliothek, Cod. 1394 (Sangallensis), a late fourth-century manuscript.

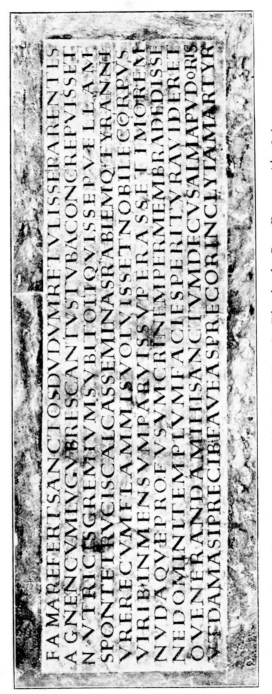

FIG. 4. Inscription executed by Furius Dionysius Filocalus for Pope Damasus (d. 384). From the Basilica of St. Agnes in Rome.

epic of Rome's history served to ennoble his country's grand traditions, and for that reason must have appealed strongly to the patriotic sentiments of those pagans who were so intent on conserving their ancestral heritage. Indeed, Symmachus seems to have projected an edition of Livy's entire corpus, for in a letter to Valerianus in 401 he speaks of a gift of the historian's complete works that he had promised but was as yet unable to provide because of the delay occasioned by the task of emendation.[11] The magnitude of this undertaking is best appreciated when it is recalled that Livy's history comprised 142 books. How far Symmachus succeeded in accomplishing his purpose cannot now be ascertained, but the manner of procedure is discernible in three subscriptions preserved in later manuscripts of Livy's first decade. The evidence points clearly to a cooperative enterprise. One subscription, occurring at the end of each of the ten books, indicates that a certain Victorianus emended the text for the Symmachi. A second subscription, found at the end of Books 6, 7, and 8, shows that Nicomachus Flavianus, the son-in-law of Symmachus, also helped to improve the text, while a third, recorded in Books 3, 4, and 5, reveals that Nicomachus Dexter, the son of Nicomachus Flavianus, also participated in Symmachus' grandiose scheme.[12]

Other early subscriptions of this sort, transmitted in medieval copies of older exemplars, give concrete proof that more Latin authors had benefited from similar editorial activity around the time of the pagan religious crisis. Among those whose works are known to have been emended during that period are Juvenal, Apuleius, Persius, Martial,

[11] Cf. Symmachus *Epistulae* 9.13, ed. Seeck, p. 239.

[12] For the text of the subscriptions, see O. Jahn, "Über die Subscriptionen in den Handschriften römischer Classiker," *Ber. Sächs. Ges. Wiss.* (1851), p. 335; K. Büchner, "Überlieferungsgeschichte der lateinischen Literatur des Altertums," in *Geschichte der Textüberlieferung*, I (Zurich, 1961), 355–356.

Quintilian, and Nonius.[13] In almost every instance, some connection between the editor and the senatorial aristocracy can be established. Moreover, this work of text recension must have been much more extensive than surviving subscriptions indicate, for their preservation in later manuscripts was more a matter of chance than of policy. Thus present knowledge of the editorial efforts of Vettius Praetextatus, the distinguished pagan aristocrat who vigorously supported the cause of the old religion and played a major role in Macrobius' *Saturnalia,* comes only from a poem addressed to him by his wife Paulina, in which she specifically alludes to his emendation of both Greek and Latin texts in poetry and prose.[14]

There is no reason to assume that the scholarship done in the improvement of an author's text was necessarily very sophisticated in those days. Generally it involved no more than the collation of one manuscript, perhaps a recent copy, with one or more others presumed or hoped to be better. Errors in transcription, whether of commission or omission, could thus be discovered and rectified; brief exegetical notes and simple punctuation might at times be supplied. On occasion, as in the case of Persius, emendation was attempted without recourse to another manuscript,[15] but in such instances probably only the most obvious verbal errors were corrected.

The importance, however, of such recension for posterity extends far beyond the elementary level of textual criticism on which it operated. This work assured the survival

[13] See Jahn, *op. cit.,* pp. 330–335, 360; Büchner, *loc. cit.* Cf. also E. Lommatzsch, "Litterarische Bewegungen in Rom im vierten und fünften Jahrhundert n. Chr.," *Zeitschr. für vergl. Litteraturgesch.* n. F. XV (1904), 186.

[14] For poem, see *Anthologia Latina.* pars post.: *Carmina Epigraphica* (1895), ed. F. Buecheler, no. 111, vv. 8–12; Jahn, *op. cit.,* p. 341.

[15] Cf. Jahn, *op. cit.,* pp. 332–333, 369.

of earlier Latin writers at a very crucial point in history, for the general chaos and intellectual sterility of the third century doubtless imperiled the continuity of their transmission from the preceding period of the Antonines. Moreover, although the distinct advantages of the parchment codex over the papyrus roll were known and celebrated by the poet Martial as early as the last quarter of the first century,[16] still the Romans were not at all inclined at first to adopt this convenient format for their literary texts. This reluctance may be attributed in great part to a common conservatism which naturally favors the retention of conventional practices regardless of the merits of an innovation. The humble origins of the parchment codex, which developed from the waxed tablet through the intermediate stage of the parchment notebook, probably militated against its acceptance for belles lettres. Existing evidence indicates that while the new format was employed for Christian theological writing from at least the middle of the second century and for juridical material from the middle of the third century, large-scale transference of pagan literature from the roll to the codex did not take place until the fourth century.[17] It cannot be determined what part, if any, the religious crisis played in expediting the changeover, but the fact is that the codex form was available and became generally used for literature about the time when circumstances were already requiring the pagan aristocracy to inventory its ancestral heritage and concern itself with the problem of recovering, salvaging, and preserving all that it could of its sacred tradition. The written Latin word was no less an integral part of that tradition than the ancient Latin worship, and the testimony

---

[16] For relevant details, see C. H. Roberts, "The Codex," *Proceedings of the British Academy*, XL (1954), 176–180.

[17] Cf. Büchner, *op. cit.*, p. 348.

of subscriptions in the manuscripts proves that literary texts were also treated with an appropriate reverence.

The striking paradox is, of course, that the defeat of Roman paganism in religion, where, in fact, it had the least of enduring worth to offer to posterity, facilitated and confirmed the success of its struggle for survival in other areas. Roman schooling, with its strong emphasis on grammar, including literature, and rhetoric, provided the basic framework and vehicle for the continuity of the Latin intellectual tradition. In this connection, mention should be made of Martianus Capella's curious allegorical handbook, which was probably composed early in the fifth century. This work, called *Liber De Nuptiis Mercurii et Philologiae* by Fulgentius in 520, enjoyed an enormous vogue for some eight centuries, and, since it was essentially a compendium of previous instruction in the seven liberal arts and provided the bases for the later *Trivium* (grammar, dialectic, rhetoric) and *Quadrivium* (geometry, arithmetic, astronomy, music), it well illustrates the enduring quality of the traditional classical education.

The Christian Latin apologists, who were pagan men of letters before their conversion, derived some of their most powerful weapons from their classical training to defend their adopted faith and attack their foes. Thus, in the middle of the second century or perhaps in the first part of the third, Minucius Felix, a lawyer by profession, wrote an engaging dialogue entitled *Octavius*, perhaps the earliest monument of Christian Latin literature. In this work, the author deftly used Cicero's literary art and much of his language to dramatize a discussion that culminated in the conversion of a pagan intellectual to the new religion. Probably at about the same time as Minucius Felix, Tertullian, also a lawyer, fulminated against pagans and all other dissidents from his views with a bombastic violence that was the *reductio ad absurdum* of Latin rhetorical instruction. Again, early in the fourth century, Arnobius, a rhetorician of note, made an assault on ancient paganism in a colorful style laced with constant reminiscences of the Epicurean poet Lucretius, while his distinguished pupil Lactantius, a professor of rhetoric under Diocletian and later tutor to Constantine's son Crispus, upheld Christianity and interpreted it to the educated Roman society with a wide array of classical learning and in an impressive Ciceronian manner. Neither Arnobius nor Lactantius hesitated to apply to Christ Lucretius' eulogistic utterances on Epicurus.[18] In these instances, as in many others, the best energies of intellectuals who were early nurtured on and thoroughly imbued with the Latin tradition were directed not only away from paganism but against it and to the support of Christianity.

Nevertheless, despite the official recognition of Christianity by Constantine and its formal victory over the old religion during the course of the fourth century, the Roman pagan and the Roman Christian still continued to receive the same traditional schooling in grammar, literature, and rhetoric. The fact is that the Latin Church had no suitable works with which to replace the pagan school texts, and a secular education remained a precondition for religious instruction. This situation, which persisted also through the fifth century and even later, has an important bearing on the apparent contradictions of attitude on the part of the Christian fathers toward pagan culture. The dilemma that confronted them can already be discerned in the ambivalence of Tertullian, who savagely attacked pagan literature on the one hand and recognized the necessity of its study on the other. Thus, in his *De Idololatria* he inveighs against schoolteachers and professors of litera-

[18] Cf. Arnobius 1.38 and Lucretius 5.1–54; also Lactantius *Divinae Institutiones* 7.27.6 and Lucretius 6.24–28.

ture for their traffic with manifold idolatry. He would
forbid the Christian from teaching literature, since this
would imply a personal commitment to its pagan substance, but allows a believer in Christ to be exposed to it,
since "without secular studies divine studies cannot be
pursued." [19] The religious indoctrination that the learner
presumably received at home would help him to reject
whatever conflicted with his faith. Tertullian's assault on
pagan philosophy is well known. In a characteristic out-
burst he rhetorically asks, "What is there in common between Athens and Jerusalem, the Academy and the
Church, heretics and Christians?" [20] The implications of
this question were destined to haunt the conscience and occupy the attention of the Church fathers for a long time
to come.

In the latter half of the fourth century, Ambrose, the
reluctant bishop of Milan and prominent antagonist in the
dramatic episode of the pagan religious revival, demonstrated how, in the best humanistic tradition, secular learning could be constructively employed to serve Christian
ends. Compelled, as he says, by his sudden elevation to the
episcopal seat in 374 to begin teaching before learning,[21]
he conscientiously and energetically went about the fulfil-
ment of his administrative and spiritual responsibilities,
and it was in this connection that he wrote for the guidance of young clerics a treatise called *De Officiis Ministrorum*, the first systematic presentation of Christian ethics.
This title, however, recalls a similar composition by Cicero, on which, in fact, it was modeled and which was itself
derived in good part from the ethical teaching of the
Greek Stoic philosopher Panaetius. Ambrose's procedure
here plainly evinces how the Latin tradition could con-

[19] Tertullian *De Idololatria* 10.
[20] Tertullian *De Praescriptione Haereticorum* 7.9.
[21] Ambrose *De Officiis Ministrorum* 1.1.4.

tinue to operate effectively in a Christian environment. From Cicero he borrowed not only the conception and the general arrangement of the work but also much of its language and content. Their motivation was similar, as Ambrose pointed out when he said, "Just as Tullius wrote to educate his son, so do I to instruct you who are my sons." [22] Though the illustrative examples drawn from pagan history by Cicero were supplemented or substituted with others from Scripture, the result was not a hybrid product, but a thoroughly Christian creation that was both a tribute and a challenge to the classical tradition. For not only did Ambrose pay Cicero the compliment of imitation, but he also showed that the best aspects of Stoic ethics were compatible with Christian doctrine and, in fact, were already present in the Christian tradition.

So powerful was the force of the Latin tradition in Ambrose's learned contemporary Jerome that it precipitated in him a memorable traumatic experience since it seemed to come into conflict with the Christian faith he had inherited by birth. Like many others of his age, he had been expertly initiated into Latin literature and thought during the period of his formal schooling. At Rome the famed pagan teacher Aelius Donatus, whose work on Latin grammar remained standard for more than a thousand years, counted him, as well as the Virgilian commentator Servius, among his pupils. On his first visit to the East, around 374, Jerome fell seriously ill with a fever, and, as he lay close to death, he had his wondrous vision of being arraigned before the tribunal of God. When, on being asked his status, he replied that he was a Christian, the judge who presided rebuked him, saying, "You are lying; you are a Ciceronian, not a Christian." [23] In the letter in which Jerome relates this episode to the nun Eustochium about a decade after

[22] Ibid., 1.7.24.
[23] Jerome Epistulae 22.30.1.

the event, that is, at the time of the pagan crisis occasioned by the removal of the altar of Victory, he discloses that on that trip to the East to fight the good fight, he brought along with him the personal library that he had put to-gether at Rome. His attachment to his books was so strong that he could not bring himself to part with them. Thus, as he writes in the letter, after piously fasting, he would turn to his Cicero, and, after long nocturnal vigils of tearful penance for sins, he would take up his Plautus. These acts, of course, were representative of the reasons for his pun-ishment in the dream, according to which he had solemnly vowed never again to own or read secular books on pain of being guilty of denying God. The recurrence of allusions to pagan authors in Jerome's subsequent writings has long puzzled scholars, but however the matter is explained, the fact itself demonstrates how profoundly he had remained addicted to the old tradition, which, in his conscience, he had not yet fully reconciled with his Christian commit-ment at the time of the vision.

Moreover, about 387, when the religious crisis in Rome was not yet completely settled, Jerome informs Paula and Eustochium that for more than fifteen years he had not taken up a book of Cicero, Virgil, or any other secular au-thor and that any mention of them in his citations comes from a misty reminiscence out of a distant past.[24] The truth or falsity of this claim is not an issue here. More sig-nificant is the positive stand that he takes in defense of his propensity for the ancient culture after the decisive defeat of Roman paganism in 394, when the forces of Theodosius crushed Eugenius' army near Aquileia on the bank of the Frigidus. In a letter of 397 or 398 to a certain Magnus, who inquired into the reason for the classical citations in his writings, Jerome replied that there was ample prece-

[24] Jerome *In Epistolam ad Galatas* 3, ed. Vallarsi, pp. 485–486 (*Patrologia Latina* [hereafter cited as *PL*], XXVI, 427–428).

dent for this practice in the Bible as well as in many Greek and Latin ecclesiastical authors. He pointed out, moreover, that by pruning offensive elements from secular learning he was creating a homebred literature that could serve the Lord, that a knowledge of pagan writing was desirable to meet the foe on his own ground, and that, except for the unlettered Epicureans, pagan authors offered much learning and information in their books.[25] No less indicative of Jerome's shift in position is his response in 401 or 402 to the charges of his bitter enemy Rufinus, who, referring to the vow made in the remarkable vision of 374, accused him of perjury and sacrilege. Rufinus reproached him not only because he continued to quote his favorite pagan writers, but because in Bethlehem he had monks copy Ciceronian dialogues for him and taught classics to children who had been entrusted to him to learn the fear of God.[26] Jerome now is much more cavalier in defending himself: he had promised, he argues, to refrain in the future, not to forget what he had retained from the past; besides, he had a strong suspicion that Rufinus himself was reading Cicero covertly; moreover, it was only in a dream that he had taken the vow, and even his foe could not claim to have lived up to all the promises that he had made at the time of his baptism.[27] The charges relating to the Ciceronian dialogues and the teaching of classics are wholly ignored. So obviously feeble and incomplete a rebuttal can only suggest that Jerome felt at this time that circumstances had sufficiently changed to make a fuller apology for his chronic classicism unnecessary.

With Augustine, a younger contemporary of Jerome, the reconciliation or fusion on the old pagan Latin tradi-

[25] Jerome *Epistulae* 70.

[26] Rufinus *Apologia contra Hieronymum* 2.6–8, 11, ed. M. Simonetti, pp. 87–90, 91–92 (*PL*, XXI, 588–590, 591–592).

[27] Jerome *Apologia adversus Libros Rufini* 1.30–31 (*PL*, XXIII, 421–424).

tion with the nascent Christian Latin tradition is further advanced. Like Jerome, he was by education and training deeply immersed in Latin literature and lore. Indeed, it was his youthful study of Cicero's dialogue *Hortensius* that had opened his mind to philosophy, especially Neoplatonism. In 384, on the recommendation of Symmachus, spokesman for the pagan party and then prefect of Rome, he was appointed to the chair of rhetoric in Milan,[28] where, under the influence of Ambrose, he underwent his conversion to orthodox Christianity.

The pagan backlash resulting from Alaric's sack of Rome in 410 provided the immediate motive for Augustine's monumental *City of God.* In this work he sought to lay once and for all the ghost of Roman pagan worship, of which vestiges inevitably long continued to persist, but his approach to the old tradition was far from being wholly negative or destructive. The *fatum Romanum,* canonized in Virgil's *Aeneid* as the manifest destiny of imperial pagan Rome, was reinterpreted as an essential and integral preliminary of the *fatum Christianum,* whose realization lay, not, as even the Spanish Christian poet Prudentius thought, in the Christianization of temporal Rome, but in the eternal *City of God.* This enlarged Augustinian view of the ancient past and its legacy provided a firm philosophic basis for the continuity of the Latin tradition in the now predominantly Christian context.

Such a perspective, in fact, underlies Augustine's enlightened attitude in the *De Doctrina Christiana,* where he says, "There is no reason why we should not have studied literature just because pagans say that Mercury is its god, nor need we avoid justice and virtue because they have dedicated temples to justice and virtue and preferred to worship in stone what should be borne in one's heart. Rather, every good and true Christian should understand

---

[28] Cf. Augustine *Confessions* 5.13.23.

that truth, wherever found, comes from his God." [29] Thus Augustine, no less than the pagan interlocutors in Macrobius' *Saturnalia,* could appeal to Virgil for a truth beyond the literal meaning of his words. His language needed only to be allegorized, Christianized, or regarded as prophecy. For example, though Jerome had ridiculed the notion,[30] Augustine himself was willing to believe that the coming of the Messiah was foretold in Virgil's fourth *Bucolic,* where the message is given on the authority of the Cumaean Sibyl.[31] In his interpretation, pagan Rome had not lived up to the high ideals prophetically set forth by Anchises in Book 6 of the *Aeneid,* where the future nation is enjoined "to spare the humbled and beat down the proud." [32] When Augustine exhorts noble Romans to abandon their gods, he alludes to the supreme sacrifice of Christian martyrs with words that Aeneas used to describe his men who had died in the fight against Mezentius: "With their blood they gained this fatherland for us." [33] But the fatherland is now, of course, the heavenly one, and in the same passage, Augustine, recalling the promise made by Jupiter to Venus regarding the future Romans, speaks of the one true God who, in the heavenly fatherland, "sets limits neither in space nor in time, / but will grant sovereignty without end." [34]

This transmutation of the Latin tradition is also observed in Augustine's adaptations of the literary form of the philosophic dialogue and rhetorical treatise. During the

[29] Augustine *De Doctrina Christiana* 2.72. Of this work, Books 1, 2, and part of 3 were composed in 397, the rest of Book 3 and all of Book 4 were completed in 426–427; cf. M. Schanz, C. Hosius, and G. Krüger, *Gesch. der Röm. Lit.,* 4.2 (Munich, 1920), 444.

[30] Jerome *Epistulae* 53.7.

[31] Augustine *Epistulae ad Romanos Inchoata Expositio* 3 (PL, XXXV, 2089).

[32] Virgil *Aeneid* 6.847–853.

[33] Augustine *City of God* 2.29, citing Virgil *Aeneid* 11.24–25.

[34] Cf. Virgil *Aeneid* 1.278–279.

critical period of his conversion and baptism in 386–387, he devoted himself to the composition of such works as *Contra Academicos, De Beata Vita,* and *De Ordine,* in which he sought, in artistic fashion, to organize and present his thoughts philosophically on fundamental questions that concerned him in the light of his recent espousal of the orthodox faith. Put long ago on the path of such speculation by his reading of Cicero's *Hortensius,* he followed his predecessor in style and method but transcended him and created something new by infusing into the old inherited mold the Christian essence of his original thinking. Similarly, in writing Book 4 of the *De Doctrina Christiana,* in which he addressed himself to the task of instructing the Christian preacher, Augustine resorted to Cicero's *Orator* for the broad outline of the work and for his general oratorical theory, but was alone responsible for its Christian orientation and the choice of apposite illustrations drawn from the writings of St. Paul, Cyprian, and Ambrose.

The pagan religious crisis of the fourth century and its aftermath thus contributed considerably to the preservation and revitalization of the Latin tradition. The pagan intellectuals attempted to salvage from it what they could, while the early Church fathers, who were bred on it in their schooling, made efforts to adapt it to the needs of triumphant Christianity. Moreover, during this period of transition at the end of the fourth century and the beginning of the fifth, the force of the old culture was still sufficiently dynamic to produce an excellent historian like Ammianus Marcellinus, who, though a Greek by birth from Syria, was the true follower and continuator of Tacitus, and poets like Ausonius, Claudian, and Rutilius Namatianus, who, though differing in their relative merits, alike cultivated the pagan Muse and justly claim a place in any literary account of Rome. Pagan religion as such, however, had been effectively administered its coup de grâce by Augustine in his *City of God*.

Despite the unsettling political, social, and economic conditions induced and aggravated by the vast Germanic inroads into the various sections of the Western Empire during the course of the fifth century, the Latin cultural tradition still remained firmly entrenched among the Roman aristocracy, which by now had been mostly Christianized, and in the classical schools, which, however restricted in some areas, continued to operate in others, particularly in Africa and Italy.[35] Though the deposition of the last Western Roman emperor, Romulus Augustulus, and the elevation of the Goth Odoacer in 476 marked only the formalization of a long-standing de facto situation, nevertheless the new rulers of western Europe regarded themselves as heirs to the Roman civilization, which, of course, by their conquests they had, in fact, helped to undermine. Many of the existing political, legal, and administrative institutions and practices were simply taken over by these barbarian invaders, but their attitude toward the more intellectual phases of classical culture varied: some were tolerant or sympathetic, others were indifferent or hostile.[36] In Italy, the long reign of the Ostrogothic king Theodoric from 493 to 526 provided an environment that was especially favorable to the preservation and continuity of these other aspects, now unencumbered by the religious conflict that raged a century earlier between paganism and Christianity. This king, perhaps more literate than tradition would have it, had his daughter Amalasuntha educated in both Greek and Latin; she, as regent, entrusted the in-

[35] Cf. H. I. Marrou, *A History of Education in Antiquity*, English trans. of the French 3d ed. by G. Lamb (London and New York, 1956), pp. 345–347; P. Riché, *Education et Culture dans l'Occident Barbare*, VIᵉ–VIIIᵉ Siècles (Paris, 1962), pp. 62–69, 76–78.

[36] For details see Riché, *op. cit.*, pp. 91 ff.

struction of her youthful son Athalaric to a Roman tutor. Moreover, Theodoric's nephew Theodat, who joined Amalasuntha on the throne in 534, was extolled by Cassiodorus for his knowledge of literature and characterized by Procopius as better versed in Plato's philosophy than in the art of war.[37]

Amid this stir of intellectual interests in the ruling family, despite the seething political intrigue in the background, the activity of conserving and transmitting Rome's literary heritage seems again to have been intensified. As before, subscriptions surviving in later manuscripts provide direct evidence. In some instances they reveal that third-generation descendants continued or resumed the editorial efforts of their renowned forbears, this time not as a hedge against Christianity, but for a culture menaced by the inevitable consequences of an encroaching tide of barbarization with which it was fundamentally incompatible. A subscription occurring at the end of Book 1 of Macrobius' *Commentary* on Cicero's *Dream of Scipio* indicates a remarkable perpetuation of ancestral connections and traditions, for, according to the note, this Neoplatonic work was emended and punctuated by Aurelius Memmius Symmachus with the assistance of Macrobius Plotinus Eudoxius.[38] Here a great-grandson of the Symmachus who played so important a role in the religious crisis of a century before is joined in editing a text by a relative, if not a direct descendant, of its author Macrobius, who, it will be recalled, also wrote the literary dialogue *Saturnalia*, where the elder Symmachus appears as a major figure and proponent of pagan Latin culture. The later Symmachus, however, who was the father-in-law of Boe-

[37] Cf. Cassiodorus *Variae* 10.3, ed. T. Mommsen, *Monumenta Germaniae Historica, Auct. Antiquiss.* 12 (1894), 299; Procopius *De Bellis* 5.3.1.
[38] See Jahn, *op. cit.*, p. 347; Büchner, *op. cit.*, p. 365.

thius and, like him, was eventually condemned to death by Theodoric, proved himself a ready defender of orthodoxy when he supported the position of his namesake Pope Symmachus in the Laurentian schism.[39] Consequently, while the religious loyalties of the old Roman nobility had changed, the inherited literary and intellectual tradition transcended them.

This sort of situation is strikingly reflected in other subscriptions going back to the same period. Thus, from the testimony of such evidence, Turcius Rufius Apronianus Asterius, *consul ordinarius* in 494, is known to have edited both the pagan Latin poet Virgil and the Christian Latin poet Sedulius.[40] Again, at the end of Horace's book of *Epodes,* there is appended in some eight manuscripts a note stating that the text was read and corrected by Vettius Agorius Basilius Mavortius, who was consul in 527.[41] This same name is also found in a rustic capital manuscript of Prudentius.[42] From such data as these the final resolution of the religious dispute of the last part of the fourth century can readily be inferred. The editor was doubtless a kinsman of the Vettius Agorius Praetextatus who, like the elder Symmachus, appears in the *Saturnalia* as a staunch partisan of the old tradition and was celebrated in his day for his expert knowledge of pagan worship (see p. 210, above). But now this Christian descendant of Praetextatus' family concerned himself both with the text of Hor-

[39] Cf. J. Sundwall, *Abhandlungen zur Geschichte des Ausgehenden Römertums* (Helsinki, 1919), pp. 159–160; E. Stein, *Histoire du Bas-Empire,* trans. from German, with additions, by J.-R. Palanque (Paris, 1949), II, 137.

[40] Jahn, *op cit.,* pp. 348–351; Büchner, *op. cit.,* p. 356; Sundwall, *op. cit.,* pp. 94–95.

[41] Jahn, *op. cit.,* pp. 353–354; Büchner, *loc. cit.*

[42] Paris, Bibl. Nat. lat. 8084, on which see Lowe, *op. cit.,* 5.571a; S. Jannaccone, "Le Par. 8084 de Prudence et la Recensio de Mavortius," *REL,* XXVI (1948), 228–234; M. P. Cunningham, "Some Facts about the Puteanus of Prudentius," *TAPA,* LXXXIX (1958), 32–37.

ace, who in many ways was the most pagan of Latin poets, and with that of the Christian Latin poet Prudentius. Yet the most remarkable aspect of this significant juxtaposition of textual and literary interests emerges only when it is recalled that in 402–403 Prudentius had written two books of hexameters entitled *Contra Symmachum,* in which he, like Ambrose earlier, attacks paganism and Symmachus' noble plea for tolerance and the ancient religion (see p. 208, above), turning the episode of the pagan revival into an epic of Christian victory over heathenism. Moreover, since the rustic capital script, in which this oldest extant Prudentius codex is executed, had almost exclusively been reserved for pagan Latin authors,[43] its extraordinary use at the end of the fifth century or at the beginning of the sixth for a Christian poet was probably owing to some special purpose or intention. The explanation for this phenomenon perhaps lies in the recognition accorded at that time to Prudentius' high literary achievement, for which he might well have been deemed worthy of the same calligraphy as the earlier Roman writers whose works were being transcribed contemporaneously in that majuscule book hand. He was, in fact, the Christian Virgil, and this venerable manuscript of his poetry constitutes a graphic symbol of the confluence of Latin and Christian currents uniting to form the swelling stream of a Christian Latin tradition that coursed through the Middle Ages.

The Latin literary and intellectual tradition, which is reflected in the above-mentioned manuscript notations, reached its zenith in the sixth century with Boethius, whose manifold genius harmoniously combined Christian

[43] Cf. G. Battelli, *Lezioni di Paleografia* (3d ed.; Vatican City, 1949), p. 60. Later use of the rustic capital for Christian writings reflects an artificial revival of this script; cf., e.g., fols. 2 verso–8 verso of Turin, Cod. Bibl. Naz. E. IV. 42, a Sedulius manuscript assigned to the seventh century, about which see Lowe, *op. cit.,* 4.447.

devotion with a profound sympathy for ancient culture and an earnest passion for pagan philosophy. Had his life not been cut short in 524 by execution on orders from Theodoric for political reasons, he might well have completed his ambitious plan to translate all Plato and Aristotle into Latin. Not even Cicero had ventured anything so grandiose. Boethius, however, was probably the last Roman sufficiently equipped to undertake and carry out such a project.

With Boethius and his long-lived contemporary Cassiodorus, a definite watershed is reached. The old classical schools, to be sure, were still functioning during the sixth century in places like Rome, Milan, Ravenna, and Carthage,[44] but the responsibility for the continuity or, at least, the preservation of the Latin tradition devolved more and more upon the Church and its monastic institutions. The protracted wars between the East Goths and Byzantium in 535–555 and the subsequent devastations of the Lombardic invasion commencing in 568 exacted a heavy toll in the economic resources and intellectual vigor of Italy during the latter half of the sixth century. Cassiodorus, frustrated in his cherished hope to establish at Rome a university of Christian studies by the death of Pope Agapetus in 536 and the generally troublous times, subsequently retired from his distinguished public career of many years in the service of the Ostrogothic kings Theodoric, Athalaric, and Vitiges. Around 540, or perhaps a decade or so later, he established at his ancestral Squillace in Bruttium a monastery aptly called Vivarium after the fishponds (*vivaria*) that adorned the picturesque site.[45] The precise relationship of the organization of Vivarium to the Rule of St. Benedict and the anonymous *Regula Magistri* is a much tormented question that need not be ex-

[44] See n. 35, above.
[45] For a description, see Cassiodorus *Institutiones* 1.29.

amined here. What is important is the program of work and learning instituted by Cassiodorus for his monks. He made specific provision for the mentally less gifted brethren to be occupied with manual labor in the fields and orchards, but for those who were better endowed intellectually he prescribed a course of theological instruction based not only upon a study of the Bible but also upon supplementary religious and profane readings that would aid in the interpretation of Scripture. The syllabus of this educational scheme is contained in the two books of his *Institutiones Divinarum et Secularium Litterarum,* a very significant formative work of the Middle Ages and an excellent bibliographical guide for the development of monastic libraries. In devising such a curriculum at Vivarium he was, of course, following the path of the Church fathers before him who had recognized that a properly designed secular indoctrination comprising the *artes liberales* could serve as a means to a better understanding of the Bible and Christianity.[46]

To implement his program and assure its success, Cassiodorus took pains to build up a library of both Christian and pagan literature in his monastery and made the copying of manuscripts an integral part of the rule under which his monks lived. The importance that he attributed to the occupation of transcribing books is manifest in the glowing praise that he bestows upon the copyist of Scripture: "Blessed is his effort, laudable his industry, to preach to men with the hand, to reveal tongues with the fingers, to give salvation to men in silence and to fight against the illicit deceits of the devil with pen and ink. Every word of the Lord written down by the scribe is a wound dealt to Satan." [47] Such enthusiasm for scribal activity inevitably

[46] Cf. *ibid.,* 1.27–28. See also Cassiodorus *Variae* 9.21, ed. Mommsen, pp. 286–287.

[47] Cassiodorus *Institutiones* 1.30. Cf. also his *Variae* 12.21, ed. Mommsen, pp. 377–378.

carried over to the copying of secular texts as well, for they provided the requisite classical foundation for the development and expansion of a Christian culture as envisaged by Cassiodorus. The ultimate fate of the books of Vivarium after the death of its founder in the last quarter of the sixth century is shrouded in uncertainty.[48] The once popular theory that some of them at least reached the monastery of Bobbio, which was settled in 612 by the Irish missionary St. Columban, appears untenable. More likely, parts of the library made their way into the Lateran collection in Rome. But wherever they came to reside, they probably served in many instances as archetypal sources of later editions of the Latin authors whose cultural legacy to posterity survived the ravages and attrition of time and events.

Hence, like the pagan aristocrats at the end of the fourth century and their Christianized descendants a century later, Cassiodorus, the last Italian representative of that illustrious intellectual line, made an enduring contribution to the preservation of the literature and learning of pagan Rome and thus sustained and assured the continuity of the Latin tradition at the very twilight of late antiquity. With the advent of the Dark Ages, this noble heritage of the past, now inextricably synthesized with Christian culture, yet retaining also its own integrity, discovered its refuge and haven in the Church and especially in monasteries created or revitalized by Irish monks in the late sixth and seventh centuries and by their English brethren in the eighth. From such centers, where it was sheltered and fostered under the Benedictine Rule, the ancient legacy emerged to be rediscovered in the Carolingian Renaissance and eventually to be transmitted to modern times.

[48] For bibliography, see A. Momigliano, "Cassiodorus and Italian Culture of His Time," in *Secondo Contributo alla Storia degli Studi Classici* (Rome, 1960), p. 194 n. 8.

VIII

CELT AND TEUTON

Jeffrey B. Russell

*I*T WAS the "triumph of barbarism and religion" that, for Edward Gibbon, doomed the Roman Empire. The victory of Christ over Olympus and the impact of the barbarian invasions did indeed work a profound transformation of occidental civilization. Though Gibbon was too subtle a historian to judge any event a pure catastrophe, it was the essence of his conception that the period of transformation was one of decline and fall. It was therefore with regret, tempered by stoic calm, that he contemplated the irruption of the Teutonic peoples into the Empire. Though he admitted that "the most civilized nations of modern Europe issued from the woods of Germany," [1] he had no great opinion of the virtues of these ancestors of ours. Skeptical of Tacitus' catalog of their merits and untouched by the romantic vision of the noble savage, Gibbon saw little to commend them to the civilized temperament. With the benefit of two hundred years of contemplation of the problem posed by Gibbon's genius, we may now view the period of transition with even more equanimity than he. Though the five centuries from the third to the eighth brought about the demise of much that was Roman culture, they also fostered the growth of much that was to be Western. The role of the Teutonic and

---

[1] *Decline and Fall*, ch. 9:I, 213.

Celtic barbarians was at least as creative as it was destructive.

Western civilization, comprising those elements of Christendom that followed the Roman church in the gradual schism between East and West, derives from a number of diverse traditions. Of these, the dominant are the Greco-Roman and the Jewish, Christianity itself being heir to both; of less importance, yet still influential, are the Teutonic and the Celtic. Civilization is the product both of assimilation and of synthesis. Assimilation of one culture by another is, in effect, conquest by the dominant culture; this process worked to cause elements of the barbarian cultures, such as their religion and many of their art forms, to vanish. Synthesis, on the other hand, is a creative union of two cultures that partakes of both; this process worked most effectively in literature, law, and political theory. The history of the third to the eighth century is a history of the formation of a culture by both processes. This unification of Romanic with Teutonic and Celtic may be sketched first by examining the barbarian elements of the union, second by studying the effects of assimilation and synthesis, third by establishing the chronology of the process of union, and finally by evaluating the new creativity it engendered.

Arnold Toynbee classified Western civilization as one of the children of the Hellenic, or Greco-Roman, civilization, and the dominance of the Hellenic in our culture must always be kept in mind. Whatever the part of Celtic or Teutonic elements in the formation of our civilization, early medieval thought was dominated by Plato and the Fathers of the Church, particularly Augustine, rather than by druids or the writers of sagas. The ideas of the early Middle Ages were expressed for the most part in Latin rather than in a Germanic or Celtic tongue. The mainstream of our civilization has flowed more from the forum of Virgil than from the hall of Hrothgar.

Yet Grendel, as well as Polyphemus, stalks our imagination, and it is the Celtic-Teutonic influence that is largely responsible for making Western civilization distinctive.

The Teutons were united by tenuous linguistic and ethnic ties and probably by a common origin now lost in the obscurity of prehistory. The southern and western Teutons long dwelt in the area of central Europe known to the Romans as *Germania;* it was these, the Alamanni, Suevi, Marcomanni, and their cousins, whom the classical writers of Rome described. The northern and eastern Teutons, whose origins are possibly to be sought in Scandinavia, were the Franks, Vandals, Burgundians, and Goths. It was the northern and eastern Teutons who invaded the Empire. In this respect, their influence was profound in a purely negative fashion: they administered the coup de grâce to the failing political structure of Rome and made a new cultural synthesis possible.

The invaders, especially the Goths, by the fifth century already had been affected by Roman civilization, and many had adopted Arian, though few had received Catholic, Christianity. The Austrian historian Alfons Dopsch argued that the Germans merely took up the mantle that clothed the now moribund Roman body politic. Nearly all historians would now agree that Dopsch exaggerated the importance of this Romanization and that the Teutonic invaders, at best semibarbaric, were for the most part wholly so. In even this capacity, however, the Teutons were influential. Without yielding to romanticism any more than did Gibbon, we may accept the notion that they imparted vigor, if not virtue, to a tired society. Certainly they restored to the consciousness of Europe the immediate sense of an heroic age, for the fourth and fifth centuries were, like the age that Homer sang and Virgil echoed, a

time of troubles producing epic warriors. Arthur and Attila were the Aeneas and the Achilles of the medieval
world; their wars, like the Trojan siege of Antiquity,
marked the "decline and fall" of one civilization, the creation of a new, and an age future generations would call
golden. Western civilization, like all societies, had its
Founding Fathers.

On a less elevated level, the persistence of magic, a pre-
scientific technology of controlling natural forces, was
abetted by the ingestion of Teutonic and Celtic barbarism.

The Teutons aided in the formation of our civilization
in the capacity of wreckers of the old order and in that of
rejuvenating barbarians, but they also contributed their
own peculiar genius as Teutons. Modern historians, fortified with twenty decades of monographs unavailable to
Gibbon, are now better able to assess this contribution.

In linguistics it is more realistic to speak of a battle between, rather than the mutual influence of, the Latin and
Germanic tongues. In areas where the invaders were relatively numerous, like Britain and the Rhineland, they imposed their language. In by far the greater part of the
European area once occupied by the western portion of
the Roman Empire, however, the romance languages won
the war, and they were little influenced along the way by
Germanic vocabularies. The linguistic line of demarcation
set in this process is still sharply defined, as anyone travel-
ing from the French to the Flemish part of Belgium today
will observe. In this respect, and in philosophy and art as
well, the less sophisticated Teutons made, for the most
part, only a very limited contribution. In these areas, assimilation of the Teutonic to the Latin was more common
than synthesis between the two.

The Teutons succeeded, however, in creating a vernacular literature, notably in Anglo-Saxon, long before the

continental vernaculars freed themselves from the sway of Latin. This literature finds its purest expression in Anglo-Saxon poetry, particularly in *Beowulf* and in *Widsith*. Continental vernacular literature, even in Germany, is less purely Germanic and represents more of a synthesis. This is true not only of the later romances, but also of epics like the French *Song of Roland* and the German *Song of the Nibelungs,* and even of many Icelandic sagas.

The Teutonic influence was particularly great upon the institutions of society. The impact of these peoples upon agricultural technology was less than was thought when historians ascribed to their ingenuity the invention of the heavy wheeled plough and with it the open-field system and communal agriculture. Still, as Lynn White has shown, the system of three-field rotation, which greatly increased yield and quality, was the product of an eighth-century synthesis between the autumn planting common in the Mediterranean region and the spring planting in use among the Teutonic peoples of the Baltic–North Sea area.

With the advance of historical studies in the last half-century, we now know less than we did before about the influence of Teutonic institutions in the development of feudalism. Nineteenth-century French and German historians, embittered by the political animosities of their day, made firm but mutually contradictory pronouncements upon the relative contributions of Roman and Teutonic customs to the feudal and manorial systems. Today cooler and more ecumenical spirits have declared a cease-fire and accepted F. L. Ganshof's declaration that the problem defies resolution. Institutions similar in both cultures blended in a union so indissoluble as to defy the historian's divorcing them. Feudalism and manorialism are the children of both the Latin and the Teutonic past and bear in their features the traits of both.

The Teutonic contribution was most significant in the fields of law and political theory. Teutonic law differs considerably from Roman law, both in general principles and in particulars. It is an unwritten customary law, judge-made and strongly traditional. It shuns codification. This Teutonic law wholly prevailed in England, where it formed the basis of English common law and, through English law, of our own. It dominated Germany and northern France until the "Reception" of Roman law in the later Middle Ages, and it was of great importance in the syntheses of law created when Roman and barbarian custom merged in Spain, Italy, and southern France. Germanic legal customs shaped much of the procedure of early medieval justice. Compurgation, wherein a defendant called friends to stand by him in court and as "oath-takers" swear to his innocence, is Teutonic in origin. So is the ordeal by fire or water, and so is trial by combat, or "wager by battle," which persisted in England until 1819. Also Teutonic is the joint responsibility of kin-groups before the law, an institution whereby a man's kin warrant his good behavior and are liable to punishment if he should breach the peace. Later, this responsibility was transferred to the local territorial unit, the English hundred or the German *Gau*. The peculiar system of wergeld, which classified all men according to rank and fixed the penalty for a crime according to the rank of the individual injured, is purely Teutonic. The jury system itself grew in part out of the Teutonic conception of local responsibility. Most of these customs have lapsed, but they left their mark upon our law and were of great importance in the early Middle Ages.

The Teutons and Romans shared an attitude toward law and government common to most cultures prior to the eighteenth century: they believed that true law, as distinct from the particular enactments of men, was unchangea-

ble. Law was not *made*, but *discovered*, and the model of
justice was in the mind of God and in a theoretical golden
age in the past. The Teutonic conception of the office of
the ruler was also similar to the Roman in that before the
advent of Christianity both Teutonic kings and Roman
emperors claimed divinity or divine descent, and after the
victory of the cross they continued to affect semisacerdotal
powers and authority over church affairs. In these matters,
as in feudalism, a wedding of similar elements occurred.
Teutonic theory also made other, more distinctive, contributions to the synthesis. By the sixth century, the theory
of Roman jurists like Ulpian held that the source of law,
under God, was the emperor, while the Germans, believing
that the source of law, under God, was the people, preferred to view the ruler as the servant of his subjects. Teutonic theory therefore insisted that a claimant to the
throne should not merely have "kin-right" but that he
should also prove himself capable of occupying that station
worthily. Even after the king was crowned, the people had
the right to resist and even depose him if he was derelict in
his duty. These German ideas merged both with the ecclesiastical notion that the ruler must act in accordance with
the eternal divine law and with the feudal notion of a con-
tract between lord and vassal. The result was the appearance in the later Middle Ages of theories, influential down
to the present, of the responsibility of the ruler to his people.

The processes of assimilation and synthesis between Roman and Teuton are illustrated in the history of the Visigothic kingdom. Settling in Spain and southern France,
the Teutonic Visigoths formed a small ruling class over a
large Romanic population. At first they attempted to preserve their position by resisting any compromise with their
subjects. They spoke Gothic, their subjects Latin. They
lived by the Gothic laws, their subjects by the Roman.

They upheld the Arian religion, their subjects the Catholic. Even intermarriage was forbidden. But the Goths gradually yielded, in spite of the fact that from the mid-sixth century the encroachments of the Byzantines upon the territory of the Goths increased the distaste of the latter for things Roman. Slowly they adopted the Latin tongue, which, for its part, acquired but few Gothic elements. King Receswinth codified the Gothic law along Roman lines. King Reccared, converted to Catholicism after bloody wars between Catholics and Arians, threatened to destroy the kingdom. Intermarriage was finally condoned. By the time of the Arab conquest in 711–713, the Goths had been almost wholly assimilated to Roman culture, the exception being in the realm of law and political institutions, where a synthesis was effected.

Elsewhere, except in England and the Vandal kingdom, the story was similar. The Ostrogoths in Italy imagined themselves Romans striving to keep out those whom they called barbarians and who in fact were their cousins. Theodoric's chief policy, which he called *civilitas,* was a conscious effort to effect a coexistence, if not a union, between Roman and Goth. The barbarians were, as one poet put it, learning to "sound the praises of Christ with a Roman heart."

Gibbon, who regarded the Teutons with no great favor, did not consider the Celts worthy of mention. To the eighteenth-century English mind, the contemptible "Celtic fringe" did not even offer the interest of other barbarians who directly participated in the onslaught upon the Empire. Preoccupied with the decline of the old, Gibbon neglected one of the creative elements of the new.

The Celts, while antropologically of diverse types, enjoyed, like the Teutons, a degree of ethnic and linguistic unity. The Celtic tongues form one of the main branches of the western Indo-European family and are most closely related to the Germanic languages, on the one hand, and to the Italic on the other. The original home of the Celts may have been in *Germania* next door to that of the Italic Latins. The La Tène archaeological period, commencing about 500 B.C., was a period of enormous expansion on their part. Known as *Galatai* as well as *Keltoi*, they left their mark on the place-names of such widely separated places as Gaul, Polish Galicia, Galatia in Asia Minor, and Wales; as late as the fourth century A.D., St. Jerome could detect a similarity between the language spoken by the Asian Galatians and that heard in the neighborhood of Trier in Gaul. The Celtic sack of Rome about 390 B.C. was the last time for precisely eight hundred years that the Eternal City was taken by a foreign enemy. It is a strange twist of history that a people so numerous and powerful, and occupying a rightful place as equals of the Teutonic and Italic branches of Indo-European culture, should have failed so completely to build lasting political institutions. Caught between the growing strength of their Latin and German neighbors, the continental Celts were not so much driven westward as conquered and assimilated. In Caesar's time only Gaul and the Britains were left to them, and when the Roman conquest of Britannia was followed by the English, there remained only the extreme western fringe of Europe in Ireland, in Brittany, and what is now Scotland. Thus were a great people subdued by Romans and Teutons. If one excepts the kingdom of Scotland (and even that was partially English), no Celtic state survived the early Middle Ages.

Yet though the Celts were politically vanquished, they were not without a hand in the building of Europe. Celtic, Latin, and Teutonic peoples were early in contact and exchanged certain vocabularies: Gaelic *fín* derives, as does our *wine*, from the Latin *vinum*, while the classical Latin words for shield, *scutum* (cf. Welsh *ysgwyd*) and sword, *gladius* (cf. Welsh *cleddyf*) derive from the Celtic. The Germanic tongues derive such words as *leather* and *booty* from the Celtic. Celtic place names dot France and the Isles (Lyon-Lugdunum, after the god Lug). The Roman administrative divisions of Gaul, the *pagi* and *civitates,* were based upon the Celtic. One need not descend as far in history as Bernardo O'Higgins, John Kennedy, or Yeats and the "Celtic Revival" to find further Celtic influence. Irish art forms affected English and continental art; Irish myth and magic, like Teutonic, persisted in the rites of peasants and the pages of poets: Merlin, Perceval, and Tristan are Celtic heroes. The Irish land of youth, the Tir na nOg, where live immortal beings under the rule of the gods, still dwells in our imagination: in J. R. R. Tolkien's extraordinary fantasy, *The Lord of the Rings,* the Elves depart the Grey Havens of a dying world to set sail over the sea for Westernesse.

Certain Celtic traits have enjoyed particularly long duration. The Irish have never despised the comforts of the cup, and the poet of the tenth or eleventh century surely did not offend the sensitivities of his race when he prayed, "I should like to have a great pool of ale for the King of Kings; I should like the Heavenly Host to be drinking it for all eternity." [2]

The Celtic influence was naturally strongest in the British Isles. There two waves of Celtic immigration overwhelmed the previous inhabitants, the "Iberian" builders of Stonehenge and other megalithic monuments. The Gallo-Brittonic peoples, the "p-Celts" (e.g., "son of" is *map* in Welsh, but *mac* in Irish) came first both to Britain and to Ireland. They were followed by the Goidelic, or Gaelic, peoples (the "q-Celts"), who settled in Ireland.

[2] Anonymous poet in Kenneth H. Jackson, *A Celtic Miscellany* (London. 1951), p. 313.

The Irish were originally known as "Scots," and modern Scotland was formed only when Irish immigrants mingled with Brittonic, Pictish, and English elements. In Britain the Celts were assimilated after the Roman conquest to the culture of the conquerors, and the British tongues borrowed from the Latin to the point that Professor Jackson describes Welsh as in part a romance language (e.g., Welsh *manach*, "monk," from *monachus*; *pobl*, "people," from *populus*). On the other hand, the vulgar Latin spoken in Britain was modified only in pronunciation by the British.

What little the later Anglo-Saxon invaders borrowed initially from the culture that preceded them they took from the Roman rather than from the British. Even when they later fell under a degree of Celtic influence, it came from the Irish, rather than from the defeated Britons. In the meanwhile, the only considerable contribution to the common culture made by the British Celts was the heresy of Pelagius, the British monk who opposed Saint Augustine on the doctrines of free will and grace; it is symbolic that the Church should have rejected this British doctrine totally. It was only later, when Welsh myths and literature were popularized on the Continent by Breton poets whose ancestors had fled Britain for Armorica in the fifth and sixth centuries and who now returned with the Norman Conqueror, that the culture of the p-Celts was brought into the common treasure house of Europe. The Fisher King has been with us from the time of the Conquest to that of T. S. Eliot and Ernest Hemingway.

The reputation of the Irish has varied with the centuries; frequently, it has not been high. Gerald of Wales in the twelfth century described his Hibernian cousins in terms that would have been favorably received in nineteenth-century Boston: ". . . secluded from civilized nations, they learn nothing, and practise nothing but the barbarism in which they are born and bred, and which sticks to them like a second nature. Whatever natural gifts they possess are excellent, in whatever requires industry they are worthless." [3]

With the Teutonic Anglo-Saxons, the Irish were exceptional among the peoples of primitive Europe in the creation of a vernacular literature. As Kenneth Jackson has remarked, the impression that the Irish were obsessed on the one hand by brooding melancholy and mystical visions and on the other by delightful (or repulsive) fantasies involving fairies and leprechauns remains, like many historical canards, unerased. In fact, ancient Irish poetry is as varied as any other great primitive literature. It is by turns virile and exciting, lively and colorful, delicate and pretty, and piercingly simple.

The Irish heroic tale is as vigorous as the Greek, and what it lacks in subtlety it makes up in picturesqueness. Maine Athramhail's meeting with Loegh and Cú Chulainn is unforgettable and not lacking in the grim humor common to the ninth century and the Grand Guignol. [4] The colorful images are, though deficient in shading, sharp in outline: ". . . [Deirdre] saw a raven drinking the blood on the snow. Then she said to Lebhorcham, 'I should dearly love any man with those three colors, with hair like the raven and cheek like the blood and body like the snow!' " [5] Rhyme, repetition, and alliteration are no less common and no less effective in Irish than in other primitive verse. Image is splashed on image in the manner familiar to readers of the Old Testament, and richness is more in evidence than delicacy. [6] A nobly simple lament, however, is that of Créide for her husband Cáel. [7]

[3] T. Wright (trans.), *Topography of Ireland* (London, 1881); James Bruce Ross and Mary Martin McLaughlin (eds.), *The Portable Medieval Reader* (New York, 1949), p. 412.

[4] Jackson, *op cit.*, pp. 36–38.

[5] *Ibid.*, p. 50.

[6] See, for example, the "Cry of the Garb" in Gerard Murphy, *Early Irish Lyrics* (Oxford, 1956), pp. 119–122.

[7] *Ibid.*, pp. 149–151.

The literature of a people is usually too unique really to export, and Irish literature had no great reception abroad before modern times. Yet, vivid images occasionally flash in continental literature that derive from the Irish imagination, and Bieler [8] cites a number of hagiographical clichés, such as the saint that hangs his clothes upon a sunbeam, as deriving from Hibernian influence.

The Irish made further contributions after their conversion to Christianity by St. Patrick, whose career is somewhat opaque to history, and by fifth-century British Christians fleeing the Anglo-Saxons. The Irish fostered learning in the sixth and seventh centuries when most of the Continent and all of England were practically destitute of ideas, even old ones. Nor were they content to hoard their treasures at home. The Irish have always been missionary-minded—California was an Irish missionary province in the nineteenth century—and from the sixth century onward their exploits were so considerable as to defy even bare cataloguing in this space. St. Columcille and his successors helped to convert Scotland and northern England; St. Columbanus and his followers founded monasteries and schools throughout Gaul, Italy, and southern Germany. Countries as remote as Norway and Iceland, Poland, Bulgaria, and Kiev knew the sound of Irish voices in the period from the sixth to the thirteenth century. Irishmen became bishops and abbots in Germany, Italy, and France, and, as late as 1215, there were twelve Irish monasteries in Germany alone. A seventh-century Irish pilgrim, St. Kataldus, became the patron saint of Taranto in southern Italy; an abbot of Wurzburg even in the twelfth century may have borne the name of McCarthy. Irish scholars like Dungal the astronomer and Eriugena the philosopher were the pride of kings like Charlemagne and Charles the

[8] Ludwig Bieler, *Ireland: Harbinger of the Middle Ages* (London, 1963), p. 110.

Bald. Irish monks, influential at Gorze, Cologne, and other centers of reform activity, assisted in the moral as well as in the intellectual reformation of Europe.

A number of Irish practices, though at first declined, were gradually accepted by the Europeans. The Irish penitential system, encouraging the individuation of ethics, by degrees gained general acceptance in the Church and remains the standard practice today. The sacrament of penance had previously generally consisted of a general confession (cf. the existing *Confiteor* in the Mass) followed by a general absolution. Serious sins were expiated by a severe and public penitence. In the monasteries, however, the long-steady practice prevailed in which the religious, under the strict spiritual guidance of their superiors, exposed their souls privately to a personal confessor. The predominance of the monasteries in Ireland ensured that a formerly strictly monastic institution could become general, and the notion of private confession and private penance became, through the work of the Irish missionaries, a general practice throughout Europe.

The motives of this extraordinary enthusiasm for missionary activity are obscure. Doubtless the scriptural injunction to go forth and preach to all nations encouraged their spirits, but even before their conversion the Irish were journeying, raiding, and colonizing neighboring territories. Where other peoples have placed their paradise in the past (the twentieth century seems to prefer the future), the Irish set theirs in a golden land overseas. A common theme in ancient Irish literature is that of the journey in which the excitement of adventure is tempered by a deep longing for the homeland:

It would be pleasant, O Son of my God, in wondrous voyagings to travel over the deluge-fountained wave to Ireland; to Mag nÉolairg, by Benevenagh, across Logh Foyle, where I might hear tuneful music from the swans. . . .

Away from Ireland sorrow filled me when I was powerful,
making me tearful and sad in a strange land. . . . I have
loved the lands of Ireland (utterance uncomposed): to
pass the night with Comgall, to visit Cainnech—how pleasant that would be! [9]

It is possible that some such pressures as enforced Irish emi-
gration in the nineteenth century operated in the early
Middle Ages as well: Bieler suggests that internal quarrels
in the Irish church may have induced members of the defeated party to leave. Historians can only guess at the hidden factors of famine and feud that may have impelled the
ancient Irish, Goths, or Vikings to abandon their pristine
homes. Toynbee observed that frontier peoples, faced by
greater challenge, are often more vigorous than those more
safely situated. Norman Cantor modified this notion in a
manner that fits the Irish situation more exactly, describing the "colonial phenomenon" that induces fringe groups
to prove their allegiance to a civilization with more fervor
than those who, having tasted its fruits the longer, enjoy
their flavor the less. Doubt is permissible. The missionary
contribution of the Irish, and of their Anglo-Saxon successors in the *peregrinatio,* is so much greater than that of
other fringe peoples like the Slavs or Scandinavians as to
suggest the need for further explanation. It may have been
the longing for a beaker of the warm south, or the urge of
a peripheral people to seek the centers of their civilization,
or the desire to see for themselves the lands that produced
the classical treasures they so admired, which made the
Irish respond to the apostolic call with more enthusiasm
than did others. In any instance, the *peregrinatio* became a
distinctive Irish supplement to the ascetic triad of poverty,
chastity, and obedience.

Whatever the reasons for their initial victorious enthusi-

[9] Anonymous, *ca.* 1000, in Murphy, *op. cit.,* pp. 67–69.

asm, and however long the Irish presence remained on the Continent, their vigor eventually waned, while their culture was either finally assimilated by the now dominant established culture or in part cut off from Europe by an isolation imposed by the English. In the ninth century the terrible Norse invasions weakened the Irish spirit at home. A long series of events undermined Irish influence abroad, from the Synod of Whitby in 663 or 664 when the English church opted for Latin practices to the triumph of Benedictine monachism over that of Columban, to the capture of the leadership of the great reform movement by the Roman church. The arrival of Henry II in Ireland in 1171 to supervise the establishment of English rule marked the beginning of a period of seven and a half centuries when the Irish were systematically excluded from wealth, influence, and education in their own country. Irish cultural eminence had been terminated, and, though Irish missionaries and scholars continued to appear in numbers on the Continent, it was as representatives of the Roman, rather than of a distinctive Irish, church that they came.

The elements of Western civilization, then, are Teutonic and Celtic as well as Hellenic and Jewish. But at what time did this common culture, the product of assimilation and synthesis, emerge? We all know that the Antonines are ancient Romans and the Carolingians medieval Europeans, but where is the line of demarcation between ancient and medieval to be drawn? Gibbon accepted, as did most historians before this century, the date 476 as that of the fall of Rome.

Beginning with Pirenne in the 1920's, twentieth-century historians, in their insatiable lust for revision, have offered numerous alternative suggestions. The famous Belgian suggested that it was the eighth century that witnessed the final economic collapse of the Roman world and the end of what culture could rightly be called Roman. It now seems more accurate to describe the crucial eighth century as an epoch, not of collapse, but of commencement. It was the end of the period of transition from Roman to medieval that had begun with the third century and the beginning of what C. Delisle Burns calls the "First Europe."

By the fourth century many of the elements of the new common culture had been assembled, and the processes of assimilation and synthesis were already at work among Ostrogoths and Visigoths before the eighth century. But it was that century, over which two great figures, St. Boniface at its beginning and Charlemagne at its end, tower like the pillars of an arch, which witnessed the culmination of these processes. As Charlemagne created the distinctively medieval empire, Boniface created the distinctively medieval church of northern Europe, and both Charlemagne and Boniface were products of a fusion of Celtic and Teutonic with Latin culture. If the third through the seventh centuries were a period when the synthesis was being gestated, the eighth was the period when it was born.

The eighth century witnessed an extraordinary quantity of events of general importance. By 704 the Arabs had completed their conquest of North Africa, wresting from Christendom one of its wealthiest and most advanced provinces; by 711 they had entered the western gate of Europe at Gibraltar, and by 713 they had effected the conquest of Spain. In 733, having penetrated as far as the Loire, they were finally defeated at the Battle of Tours by Charlemagne's grandfather, Charles Martel. At the other end of the Mediterranean in 717–718 they were hammering at the gates of Constantinople; their defeat there secured the eastern bulwark of Christendom for five centuries. At last, in the second half of the century, the massive Muslim advances ceased and afforded respite to Christian defenses. The accession of Leo III the Isaurian to the Byzantine throne in 717 heralded not only the outbreak of bothersome schism over iconoclasm but also an effective administrative reorganization that lent new strength to the Empire. Meanwhile, the establishment of the Abbasid caliphate in Baghdad in 750 was the cause of two significant events, a revolution that added to the internal unity of that empire and the establishment of a rival caliphate at Córdoba by the Umayyad enemies of the Abbasids. As a result of this foundation, Córdoba became one of the intellectual centers of the world. One year after the establishment of Abbasid rule in Baghdad, the Moslem rout of the Chinese at the Battle of the Talas River (751) expelled that power from central Asia and effected a break of long duration between Christendom and the Far East.

Economically, the century witnessed the continued decline of specie, the last occidental gold coinage for five hundred years, and the emergence of an economy that was, if not entirely "natural," at least gravely deficient in media of exchange. The silver penny came to be the only coin minted in the West. In religion, the mission of St. Boniface, seconded by the efforts of Pepin the Short and Charlemagne, began a movement of intellectual and spiritual enthusiasm that slowly came to dominate the life of the Church. At the same time the foundations of medieval religious dissent were laid, as new varieties of moral heresy arising from reformist enthusiasm or from ignorant eccentricity replaced the old theological heresies of the past. It was in this century too that the linguistic frontier between Germanic- and Romance-speaking peoples was firmly fixed.

At the beginning of the century, pulled away from its

Roman roots and buffeted by the assaults of external enemies, western Europe badly needed to find a new unity. In
the Church, the authority of the Eastern emperor was immeasurably weakened, while that of the Frankish ruler was
not yet firmly established. Ecumenical councils seemed to
be Eastern affairs, and there were no great theologians to
lead the West. The papacy, since the days of Gregory the
Great at the beginning of the seventh century, had experienced a deplorable decline in power and prestige. The
sources of tradition were difficult to discern and the means
of implementing it elusive. The Church suffered grave dis-
unity and decay. St. Boniface described the situation to
Pope Zachary in 742:

> Know, Holy Father, that Carloman, the ruler of the Franks,
> summoned me to him and ordered me to call a council in
> that portion of the Frankish realm under his jurisdiction.
> He told me that he would reform and revive the discipline
> of the Church, quite neglected these sixty or seventy
> years. . . . The Franks have not held a council for more
> than eighty years. They have no archbishop, nor do they
> respect the canon law of the Church. The bishoprics have
> usually been given over to avaricious laymen or exploited
> by an adulterous and unworthy clergy for secular pur-
> poses.[10]

Politically, the order of the Roman Empire had yet to be
replaced with any comparable dominion. In Italy, Lombards, Byzantines, and papacy quarreled one with the
other; Scandinavia, the lands of the western Slavs, and
much of Germany were disorganized. The Frankish kingdom had lacked cohesion since the death of the Merovingian Dagobert in 639. The British Isles were divided between Celts and Anglo-Saxons, and each lacked a united
kingdom. In Spain a few petty Christian chiefs in the
north were all that remained to resist the Muslim power

[10] Michael Tangl, *Die Briefe des heiligen Bonifatius und Lullius*
(Berlin, 1919), no. 50.

that dominated the peninsula. Culturally, the process of union begun earlier by Theodoric and Clovis had yet to be consummated. Europe was in need of unification, and in the eighth century it first found the means to achieve it.

Unification proceeded less by means of action exerted from the center than through the passive attraction it exerted upon the periphery. The three centers of power in Christendom in the eighth century were the imperial court at Constantinople, the papacy, and the Carolingian ruler of the Franks. The power wielded by the Byzantine emperor in the West was in any event debilitated, especially after the Lombard conquest of Ravenna in 751, but even the two other powers sought less than they were sought after. The popes between Gregory the Great and Gregory VII did little, for example, to initiate missionary activity or even to control it once it had been begun. Missions like those of Willibrord to Frisia or of Cyril to Moravia were conceived independently of the pope, and though they obtained the stamp of his approval and access to his advice, they were otherwise little in his debt. The Frankish rulers, at least before Charlemagne, also proved but passively interested in the missionary movements that affected them so deeply, nor was their response to the opportunity offered them by the papacy to conquer the Lombards immediate or even swift. Among the forces of unification must be reckoned the natural drive to extend power, nostalgia for the imperium, and even the ideal of a united *societas christiana*. But these urges, even the pragmatic ones, were not as strong at the centers of power as they might have been. Rather there was a general tendency inward from the periphery, as if the critical point had been passed when the inertia of centrifugal forces was overcome by the mass represented by the desire for unity.

The creation of the common culture was made the easier by the elimination of certain political forces. The deepen-

ing chasm between the Eastern Empire and the West rendered impossible a united Christendom, yet paradoxically
this itself encouraged the unity of the West by eliminating
an unassimilable element. Through the combined, though
not the united, forces of papacy, Lombards, and Franks,
the Italian peninsula was emptied of Byzantine power, except in the extreme south. The papacy now ceased to place
the Byzantine emperor's head upon its coinage and eventually employed in its documents the regnal year of the
king of the Franks instead of that of the emperor of the
East. The elimination of Byzantine rule in North Africa
by the Arabs earlier in the century helped ensure the future exclusion of Byzantium from the West. Other par-
ticularist elements were also eliminated. The Muslim conquest of Spain removed the Visigoths from the picture.
The Mozarabs (Spanish Christians under Muslim rule) retained much of their identity and even, isolated from the
rest of Christendom, enhanced their peculiarities, but
when the Iberian peninsula was again restored to Christian
rule, it was readmitted to the common culture on that culture's own terms. The liquidation of the Lombard kingdom by Charlemagne in 774 removed the only other political entity besides the insular Anglo-Saxon kingdoms; the
Franks, partly through effort, but mainly through default,
found themselves masters of the West.

The eminence of the Franks as leaders of the new Europe had been achieved in spite of formidable obstacles,
some self-inflicted. Since the death of King Dagobert, the
Frankish kingdom had suffered disunion in three ways:
first, the German people whom it held in vassalage on its
eastern frontier reasserted virtual independence; second,
the kingdom itself was subject to division and dissension
owing to succession laws that obliged a king to divide his
kingdom among his heirs; and third, the Merovingian dynasty proved increasingly incompetent. It was owing to

the vigor of the Carolingians that this seventh-century fragmentation was reversed in the eighth. The process of unification began in 687 when, at the Battle of Tertry, Pepin II of Herstal, the Austrasian mayor of the palace, defeated his Neustrian colleague and established his authority over all the Franks. It was continued when the prestige of Charles Martel confirmed the Carolingians in this authority and when, in 751, Pepin III the Short, Charlemagne's father, assumed the royal dignity. The process culminated with Charlemagne, whose every policy was directed at establishing conformity. He subdued and forcibly Christianized the German pagans on his eastern borders and even established a tenuous suzerainty over some of the Slavic peoples beyond. His intention in all this is revealed by his biographer, Einhard, who tells us that the purpose of his war against the Saxons was "that the Saxons, united with the Franks might be made *one people with them*." [11] He endowed his kingdom with as efficient and centralized an organization as had existed in the West since the days of the Caesars.

While the ruler of the Franks found his power enhanced, so did the bishop of Rome. After the death of Gregory the Great in 604, the popes enjoyed little power in Italy and less influence north of the Alps. Between the demands of the Byzantines and the depredations of the Lombards, the seventh-century papacy found itself unable to realize St. Gregory's ambitions for a Europe led by Christian Rome. In the eighth century this situation was transformed. The see of Peter passed in 715 to the first of a series of able popes, Gregory II. He and his successors proved able to derive great profit from the fortune that came their way. Here the expansion of the Arabs again aided the process of unity, for it removed from effectual influence three of the five traditional great sees, Antioch, Alexan-

[11] Einhard, *Vita Karoli*, ed. Louis Halphen (Paris, 1923), p. 26.

dria, and Jerusalem. None but Constantinople remained to challenge papal authority and, if that one see refused to submit, it enjoyed no influence in the Occident.

In 716 St. Boniface, the English missionary, set foot upon the Continent for the first time. Boniface, acting upon his own initiative, though with the consent and approbation of the pope and the Frankish ruler, effected between the papacy and the Frankish throne a close alliance that was sealed when, with the permission of Pope Zachary, the Frankish bishops anointed Pepin king. This was the first significant case in which a Western monarch was anointed by a clergyman, and the event symbolized both the intention of the principals to imitate the Hebrew custom and restore the Kingdom of David and the increasing influence of the Church in the affairs of the state. The papacy now possessed political and religious leverage north of the Alps as it had not done since the day of Gregory the Great. The popes did not hesitate to press this advantage as best they might. Though Gregory III called in vain upon Charles the Hammer for help against the Lombards, Zachary and his successors found in Pepin III and Charlemagne invaluable allies against Byzantines and Lombards. With Frankish help and aided by the forged Donation of Constantine, the dominion of the papacy over central Italy, begun by Gregory II, was consolidated by the end of the century after Pepin and Charlemagne had made "donations" of their own. Papal power having been reestablished, papal theory began to revive; it is difficult to imagine the theoretical claims of Nicholas I in the ninth century or of Gregory VII in the eleventh without the pragmatic foundations laid by Gregory II, Boniface, and Charlemagne in the eighth.

At the same time, the alliance between the papacy and the Carolingians promoted a practical and theoretical union of throne and altar that had enormous implications for both, particularly for the altar. No society before our own has seriously considered the possibility, let alone the desirability, of a separation of church and state. It was taken for granted from the time of Constantine that Christianity and the Empire were indissolubly connected. The decay of imperial authority in the West from the fifth century, however, made this of little consequence. Popes, it is true, were, until the eighth century, frequently at the mercy of the Byzantine emperors, but even this had little effect upon western Christendom north of the Alps. From the reign of Pepin the Short onward the Frankish monarchy, developing similar "caesaropapist" notions, exercised increasing control over the Church. Pepin called councils with as much confidence as if he had been pope, and his assemblies legislated for religious as well as for secular matters. Charlemagne showed as much readiness as Constantine to direct not only the administration, but also the doctrine, of the Church. At the Council of Frankfurt in 794, which he had summoned, he dared pass judgment upon decisions of an ecumenical council (II Nicea, 787) already approved by the pope, as well as to preside over the condemnation of the Adoptionist heresy.

With the growth of feudalism, promoted by the introduction of the stirrup into Europe and the expansion of mounted warfare in the early part of the century, secular influence in the Church was not limited to the highest levels, but spread downwards even to the smallest and most remote parishes. So pervasive was it that a recent historian of the Church has described this period of ecclesiastical history as "the Church in the hands of laymen." It was in reaction to the enormous moral and political implications of this situation that the great papal revolution of the eleventh century occurred.

There was assimilation and synthesis in more purely religious matters as well. The conversion of the Lombards to

Catholicism in the latter half of the seventh century put an end to the Arian threat to theological unity, while the evangelization of the pagan Germans completed the great task of uniting the people of western Europe under the cross. The Slavs and Scandinavians remained pagan, but the conversion of Germany permitted a share of evangelical energy to be diverted from *external* missionary work to *internal* missionary labors, to projects of reform and standardization. The mission of Boniface was thus aimed not only at the conversion of pagans but also at the effective submission of northern Europe to Roman practices. Boniface extended and improved the organization of the Church under the papacy, and the moral and intellectual reforms he promoted also encouraged the establishment of common practices and customs. The Anglo-Saxon church had a specially close relationship with the papacy; witness the practice of sending a yearly tribute to the pope in the form of "Peter's Pence."

The sundry liturgies that until the eighth century had competed with one another were reduced to one when Charlemagne's adviser Alcuin composed one based on that approved at Rome but containing elements of other traditions as well. His production was so successful that it forms the basis of the *missale romanum* now in use. It was in this period, too, that the Irish custom of private penance gained general acceptance. The life of the secular clergy was regularized by Bishop Chrodegang of Metz, a follower of St. Boniface, who ordered the clerks of his cathedral to live by a semimonastic rule based upon that of St. Benedict. This successful experiment, which, by grafting together the secular and religious lives, achieved wide currency throughout Europe and helped begin the long line of vigorous clergymen of the world, of whom St. Dominic is perhaps the best known. The diverse monastic orders yielded to standardization shortly after the turn of the ninth century when Benedict of Aniane, a protégé of Charlemagne and his son, Louis the Pious, enjoined the Benedictine Rule upon all the monasteries in the Frankish kingdom.

Minor contributions of the English to the continental synthesis included the propagation of libraries, the establishment of confraternities and chantries, and the introduction of certain fasting regulations.

On Christmas Day, 800, exactly one week by our reckoning before the end of the eighth century, the process of unification received its apotheosis. On that day, before the crowds gathered to give thanksgiving in the basilica of blessed Peter the apostle in Rome, Pope Leo III placed the imperial crown upon the brow of Charlemagne. Whether the event was planned by Charles, by Leo, or by both is not within the province of this chapter. But here, in the space of one morning, the achievements of the century were summarized. The Teutonic monarch wore upon his brow the imperial crown of Rome. Continuity with the coronation of Pepin was preserved as the liturgy intoned was a Romanized version of the Frankish one used at the earlier event. The pope, anointing Charlemagne with holy oil, recognized the imperial right to direct the Church and to foster the movement of reform, even as the emperor had earlier confirmed the dignity of the pope. The task of unification which at the beginning of the century had been undertaken by a missionary from the far Isles now passed to the care of the imperial Charlemagne. The West had found its political center.

Forces of intellectual unity were also at work. At the Carolingian court, Teutons and Celts, imitating the ancients but in fact producing new creations, expressed their ideas in Latin verse. Charlemagne became a Virgilian hero, and bucolic Aachen, when it was not the "seat of David," became the second Rome!

It exceeds my power [modestly declaimed an anonymous
poet around 800] to describe the most just King Charles,
the chief ornament of the world, the delight and the pride
of his people, the esteemed head of Europe, most excellent
father, hero, Augustus. Powerful is he in the possession of a
city where the second Rome is rising in new flower, its
great towers reaching high, its lofty domes touching the
stars. Noble Charles stands remote upon a tower, directing
the work and planning the high walls of the future Rome.
Here he disposes the forum, there the sacred senate.[12]

The biographer Einhard wrote in slavish imitation of
Suetonius and other classical writers, as well as of Christian
hagiographies, but Bede and Paul the Deacon, while draw-
ing upon classical models and standards, produced more
original works of history. In the "Franco-Saxon" school of
Charlemagne's time, Byzantine art influenced Irish, Irish-
English, and English-continental art. The script upon
which our own lowercase letters are based is a continental
one, developed at the scriptoria of Corbie and Tours, but
the abbreviations used in this Caroline minuscule were insular in their derivation. Charlemagne's establishment of a
palace school and his encouragement of others in every diocese was a great step toward the improvement and standardization of education, although the program was never
fully implemented.

The Anglo-Saxons were among the most prominent of
the forces promoting the development of the common culture. So ubiquitous did Anglo-Saxon churchmen become
that they eventually aroused resentment. With characteristic continental disregard for distinctions among things
insular, Frankish monks, complaining about the visit of
the Anglo-Saxon Aigulf to his countryman Alcuin, ex-
claimed: "This Briton or Irishman has come to see the

[12] F. J. E. Raby, *The Oxford Book of Medieval Latin Verse* (Oxford,
1959), p. 89.

other Briton who lies within. O God, deliver this monastery from these Britons, who all come to this man like bees returning from every direction to their queen!" [13]

The English church was of just the syncretic nature to make the Anglo-Saxons the logical standard-bearers of the common culture. Irish missionaries, among them Aidan, Cedd, and Chad, had converted much of northern and central England, imparting a Celtic flavor and establishing a great center of learning at the Holy Isle Lindisfarne off the coast of Northumbria. At the same time, the Roman church, represented by the St. Augustine whom Gregory the Great sent to evangelize the English in 597, had extended its influence from Canterbury over southern England. A century later, the see of Canterbury was strengthened by the arrival of Theodore of Tarsus who, with his assistant Hadrian, there established a cathedral school that became the fountainhead of English learning. Theodore was Greek in origin, and at Canterbury English scholars mastered Greek, if not proficiently, at least as well as anywhere else in the West. Thus, the Teutonic Anglo-Saxons were exposed to all the other elements of synthesis, Latin, Greek, and Celtic.

The famous Synod of Whitby in 663 or 664 contributed immeasurably to the process of synthesis. There King Oswy of Northumbria, having heard St. Wilfred argue for the practices of the Roman church and defeat St. Colman's defense of Celtic practices by forcing him to admit that Christ had bestowed the keys upon Peter rather than upon Columba, declared that henceforth his kingdom should worship after the manner of the bishop of Rome. This spelled the triumph of Roman over Celtic Christianity throughout England. The Synod of Whitby was a triumph

[13] *Vita Gregorii abbatis Traiectensis* c. 4, *Monumenta Germaniae Historica*, SS., XV, 71, quoted by Wilhelm Levison, *England and the Continent in the Eighth Century* (Oxford, 1946), p. 169.

of unity over particularism. The triumph, however, was less a crushing repudiation of the Irish than an invitation to join in the process of synthesis. The significance of the synod has often been misinterpreted. Toynbee, convinced that the Celtic church was the embryo of a "Far Western Civilization" that might have developed its own identity, believed that Whitby was a major factor in procuring its abortion. But the differences between the Roman and Celtic churches have been greatly exaggerated; they were certainly not sufficient to constitute the Irish a separate civilization. Bede himself, eager to enhance the dramatic effect of his narrative, may have overstated the disagreement and its consequence.

It must be remembered that the Christianity brought to Ireland from Britain in the fifth century was Roman, that the Irish church was in close contact with the Continent until the beginning of the sixth century, and that even after the conquest of most of Britain by the pagan Anglo-Saxons, Irish communication with the Continent, though impeded, was not interrupted. The Irish continued to frequent the Continent and to enjoy influence down into the late Middle Ages. Further, though it is true that Irish practices differed from Roman, these differences were not, even for a theologically minded age, essential. Irish theology and liturgy were not significantly different from Gallo-British. The Irish emphasis upon the monastic and eremitical life, though peculiarly strong, was nothing repugnant to Roman Christianity. The Irish church, though its organization was largely monastic, did not, as some careless writers have implied, lack bishops entirely. The points actually in dispute were a difference in the monastic tonsure, a difference in the way of calculating the date of Easter, a possible difference in baptismal practice, and the custom of some, though probably not many, of the Irish clergy of permitting women to distribute the chalice in communion. Of these momentous differences the most hotly disputed was that of the reckoning of Easter. The sort of effect the Synod of Whitby really had is best illustrated in the fact that in the half-century following King Oswy's decision the Celtic communities themselves in Scotland and northern Ireland accepted the Roman calculation of Easter. Whitby was not a repudiation of, but an invitation to, the Irish. That it was an invitation accepted is witnessed by the subsequent persistent devotion of Ireland to the Holy See.

Though St. Colman had suffered humiliation at Whitby, there is no indication of continuing hostility between Anglo-Saxon and Irish in England. Aldhelm, the most noted English scholar of the end of the seventh century, first studied under an Irish teacher at Malmesbury before concluding his studies in Greek and Latin at Canterbury. Aldhelm's writings always retained a strong Celtic flavor, as did many other compositions of the eighth century, notably Felix' life of Guthlac. The influence of Irish art and calligraphy is evident in English manuscripts. The Celtic atmosphere lingered at Lindisfarne (cf. the "Lindisfarne Gospels") though Celtic prelates had departed.

The most important lesson taught the English by the Irish was the ideal of *peregrinatio* or holy wandering. The first great English missionary, St. Willibrord, was born about 658 and studied as a child at Ripon, probably under St. Wilfred, the victor of Whitby. Had Whitby produced unquenchable hostility between Englishman and Celt, Wilfred's pupil would scarcely have elected to complete his education in Ireland, but this is in fact what Willibrord did. "Because he had heard that schools and learning flourished in Ireland, he was encouraged further by what he was told of the manner of life adopted there by certain holy men," [14] among whom were two Anglo-Saxons, one of them being Egbert, a bishop in the Irish church. In Ireland Willibrord imbibed the missionary spirit and in 690 took ship for pagan Frisia accompanied by eleven apostles (if Alcuin may be trusted) in imitation of St. Columban's own emulation of the Master. Having preached there to an audience that did not prove wholly sympathetic, Willibrord visited Pepin of Herstal and Pope Sergius I in order to enlist their aid. The pope, approving his work, bestowed the Roman name of Clement upon the Irish-trained Englishman. Willibrord-Clement now returned to Frisia where he enjoyed moderate success in Christian eyes, crowned, rather than spoiled, by his eventual martyrdom at pagan hands.

His successor in the continental mission was Winfrith, who also received from the pope a name, Boniface, more grateful to Roman ears. Though Boniface, unlike Willibrord, never studied in Ireland, he was brought up in Devon, a region only recently conquered from the Celts by the Kingdom of Wessex and which lay on the borders of the still independent British Dumnonia. There was a large British population in Devon, and the church of Wessex, though Roman, had always been in close contact with the Celts. Aldhelm's career is evidence of how close his relationship could be. Boniface's own literary style was influenced by Aldhelm's and has an occasional Celtic savor. In 716, when Boniface first grounded his boat on Frisian sands, he gazed eastward into a still half-wild continent peopled by pagans, heretics, schismatics, and by an ignorant and disobedient clergy. When he returned to Frisia after many journeys to meet his martyrdom at Dokkum in 754, he left much of Germany converted, organized into

[14] Alcuin, *Life of Saint Willibrord*, in, C. H. Talbot (ed.), *The Anglo-Saxon Missionaries in Germany* (New York, 1954), p. 5. See Levison, *op. cit.*, pp. 45–69.

dioceses, and dotted with monasteries. He had established a Frankish monarchy under a new dynasty dedicated to the cause of reform and reconstruction and a papacy immeasurably strengthened by its alliance with the Franks. And he had begun a movement of moral regeneration and educational improvement which, encouraged and implemented by the Frankish rulers, became for four centuries the greatest dynamic force in western Europe.

Boniface, like Charlemagne after him, always kept foremost in his mind the need for unity. "I, Boniface," he swore to Gregory II in 722, ". . . will not agree to anything opposed to the unity of Universal Church, no matter who should try to induce me, but I will maintain complete loyalty to you and to the welfare of your church." [15] It was owing to his deep realization of the need for unity as well as to some degree of rigidity in his character, rather than to any ancient hostilities provoked by the Synod of Whitby, that he was led into conflict with the Irish clergy in Germany. In some instances the Irish urge to roam had resulted in the arrival of improperly trained priests in Europe, and Boniface attacked the "false doctrines" of these unfortunates with indignation. His intolerance toward opposition to his grand scheme occasionally led him into injustice fired by fanaticism, as when he attacked the Irish bishop of Salzburg, Fergil or Virgil. Virgil had certain unusual ideas as to the existence and nature of the antipodes, conceptions that Boniface violently condemned as heretical. It is perhaps not being too uncharitable to the memory of the great saint to consider it probable that Boniface's outrage was the result, less of a scientific and theological controversy whose import his temperament would have been unlikely to understand, than of his anger at Virgil's resistance to his plans for the reorganization of the Bavarian church.

[15] Tangl, *op. cit.*, no. 16.

Boniface's character was not without its defects, but it was nonetheless the character of a great man, perhaps one of the greatest in occidental history. His vision was of a western Europe united in a common Christian culture under the leadership of the Frankish king and the bishop of Rome. The programs of few statesmen have enjoyed so complete a success.

The first fruits of the cultural seeds sown by Boniface were the "Carolingian renaissance," the intellectual burgeoning centered at the court of Charles the Great and his successors. The Carolingian renaissance was both a cultural synthesis and the first sign of the new creativity that followed the establishment of the common culture. To the court of the Frankish king came the English Alcuin, the Visigothic Theodulf, the Lombards Peter of Pisa and Paul the Deacon, the West-Frankish Modoin and Angilbert, and the East-Frankish Einhard. There the children of the nobility learned to read like Romans and fight like Franks. Charlemagne "wanted his children . . . first to be instructed in the liberal arts, to the study of which he also applied himself; then, when his sons had attained the proper age, he had them taught to ride in the Frankish fashion, to wield arms, and to hunt." [16]

So assiduously did the ancestrally barbarian scholars of the court seek to create a "second Rome" that they not only emulated Roman verse but assigned one another classical names like Horace, Homer, and Pindar. Charlemagne, remembering that he was the heir of the Hebrews, chose the name David. Yet the Carolingian scholars did not stop at the imitation of the ancients, nor were they paralyzed, like some of their Renaissance counterparts, by a slavish regard for classical learning. Their productions, sometimes stale and imitative, were often fresh and new, the begin-

[16] Einhard, *op. cit.*, p. 58.

nings of the brilliant creativity of the later Middle Ages, a creativity that became possible when through assimilation and synthesis a common culture had been established and peace restored to a fragmented society. The period from the eighth to the eleventh century was one of youth and vigor. Even the coronation of Charlemagne in 800 was not only a summation of the past, a synthesis of old elements. Charlemagne's new dignity was not merely the combination of a Teutonic sceptre with a Roman diadem. Whatever contemporaries thought it, it was in reality a new institution, a new creation, something the like of which had never before been seen in East or West.

Any century is a century of decision, but the eighth was more decisive than most. Thanks to the general desire for unity, thanks especially to the two great figures of the century, Boniface and Charlemagne, the fabric of society, rent in the third century, was rewoven in the eighth. The pattern was new, however, and in it one can for the first time discern the configuration of our own civilization.

Our civilization is the child of that of Greece and Rome. Yet it might never have been much more than an imitation or at best a continuation, had Celt and Teuton not challenged, modified, and transformed it. This is our debt to them, that without them we would not be ourselves.

IX

MUTATIONS IN ART

Albert Hoxie

GIBBON, in his monumental work, never discusses art as such. Indeed, the few references that touch upon it at all are singularly unilluminating and are confined to such matters as a condensed version of Procopius's description of Justinian's building of the great church of Santa Sophia in Constantinople. Gibbon's only reference to Ravenna in terms of art is limited to stating that Charlemagne removed columns from there to be used in his buildings at Aachen; he makes no mention whatsoever of that city's famous mosaics. Gibbon's interest in Santa Croce in Florence is limited to the persons buried in it, rather than the building itself or the works of art contained within it. In his autobiography, his most notable statement on art is some praise of the church of St. Sulpice in Paris for its proportions, a reference to its neoclassic facade. Consequently, the basic question in regard to Gibbon and art is why he should so rigorously have ignored it.

An educated and cultured man, Gibbon had been exposed to the views of art then current and, more particularly, to the English attitudes. Moreover, his concepts about art were closer to those of the English gentlemen who considered the Grand Tour a part of their education than to the interests and theories of the artists of the time such as Reynolds.

Among the visual arts, it was architecture that primar-

ily engaged the attention and interest of English gentlemen. It was the one field in which they actively participated, not only as patrons in the building of great houses,
but also as designers and collaborators, the most obvious
instance in the eighteenth century being Lord Burlington.
Knowledge of architecture was eminently a proper pursuit
for these gentlemen; and it is notable that Gibbon's few
references to art are specifically to architecture.

The period in which Gibbon was preparing for and beginning his great work in England was the age of Adam. It
was strongly neoclassic in nature; and, though Walpole
had already built his neogothic Strawberry Hill, such evi-
dences of the coming Romantic Age were still eccentric
sports rather than belonging to the mainstream of accepted principles. Propriety is the basic point of view. A
building should properly reflect the position of its owner,
and it should be properly proportioned in the relationship
of part to part and of part to whole. Moreover, the parts
should be distinct and stated with clarity. Any decoration
should not only be properly classic in nature, but should be
used to clarify the various parts, never to obscure them. It
is, perhaps, worth noting that, in those instances where a
church forms a part of the general building program centered on a great house, the church is always well subordinated to the house, given some dignity of treatment, but
suggesting clearly that it is the place of business of the
local rector rather than the house of God.

The essence of the great house lay in its exterior and in a
suite of state rooms. All other elements are subordinated,
and the plan is dictated far more to the proper effect of
these elements than to any convenience. Proportions are
determined by them, and symmetry is essential, sometimes
resulting in windows having no relationship whatsoever to
the rooms behind them where those rooms are unimpor-
tant to the planning. There are instances where, in the

lower-ceilinged servants' quarters, a window covers two floors, lighting the ceiling of one room and the floor of the one above. The point is that exteriors are of the utmost importance and take precedence as architecture over interiors, except for the suite of state rooms.

To the English gentleman, then, architecture is the primary art; and the house, not the church, is the center of his attention. The arts of painting and sculpture are clearly subordinated to this primary interest. They are the proper ornaments of a gentleman's house. To this end, a steady stream of art works poured into England; but the English of the eighteenth century purchased in accordance with clearly defined standards of taste. They were not, with rare exceptions, very adventurous collectors. Classical statuary and paintings by approved masters were the rule.

The eighteenth century, however, was extraordinarily cavalier, to our eyes, with works of art. Classical sculpture was regularly restored before it became a fit ornament for the house of a gentleman, and the restoration was extreme. It meant not only the addition of lost limbs and heads, but also resurfacing to give the admired, sleekly polished surface. Men such as Thomas Jenkins ran complete workshops in Rome which transformed fragmentary originals into properly surfaced and impeccably completed ornaments for the English trade. Restoration was not, of course, any innovation of the eighteenth century, nor peculiar to the English trade. Important works had long been restored in Rome, frequently incorrectly as in the case of the famous Laocoon, and by artists of the stature of Bernini in such works as the Ludovisi Ares. However, the English passion for a complete and proper work was notable.

Painting was treated quite as cavalierly as sculpture. It was conceived to be an ornament fitted to the wall. Perhaps the most notorious examples of the mistreatment of paintings occurred in the Imperial Collections of Vienna, where masterpieces by Rubens were sometimes cut to a new size, had sections folded under, or were enlarged by stitching on new sections of canvas thereby continuing the painting in order to bring it to the desired size for a new wall position. Another obvious example is the fate of Rembrandt's so-called "Night Watch," which had more than two feet cut from one side and a smaller strip from the other when it was moved to a new location. Contemporary works were ordered by the size to fit into specific locations or to match existing works.

That recognized works of art could be subjected to such extraordinary treatment is conceivable only when they are considered as a decorative adjunct to architecture and subordinate to it. The museum mind had not yet come into being, in spite of the numbers of great collections already formed.

To these basic English attitudes must be added the fact that the British had had a relatively brief and timid baroque experience with figures such as Wren and, above all, Vanbrugh; but it did not take root in England and was rejected by the eighteenth century. Rococo was doomed in England by the failure of the baroque there and, with a few exceptions, exists only in some types of ornament and in the lightening of Burlingtonian classicism into that of Adam. Gainsborough, whose feathery brushwork is in the rococo tradition, needs only to be placed beside Fragonard to see how deeply he is chastened by the English taste.

In painting and sculpture, as a whole, the English patron desired propriety, clarity, and nobility. Though they were already collecting works by Claude which were full of atmospheric light, it is notable that they collected works by Canaletto and Pannini in vast quantities, while rejecting the contemporary works of Guardi. Preference was for clarity of detail rather than for the impressionistic glitter of light and air found in the Guardis. Propriety of proportion and idealization of the figure within a measurable and clear space pattern was the very essence of art; and the English gentleman had a supreme faith in his own taste and knowledge of what art should be and was. There were clearly established standards. What fell outside of that was not art.

Gibbon was unquestionably aware of these absolute standards which established what was art and what was not. He is also one of the outstanding examples of the English gentleman's abhorrence of "enthusiasm" or zeal. It is precisely this distaste for "enthusiasm" which made the baroque despised as excessive and which was bound to cast into the outer darkness along with baroque all forms of art which were expressionistic in nature and which distorted form and space for the purpose of expression. Such forms were non-art.

It is easy for us, living in a world of the most violent artistic turmoil, to realize that a highly sophisticated age can reject accepted forms and formulae and revolutionize the most basic concepts and definitions of art. The problem of what is art and what is non-art, or even if non-art is itself a legitimate concept, is one of the major battle-grounds of our own time. It has developed in us a whole new vision, an understanding of, and a deep interest in, periods of art which quite literally did not exist as art to the age of Gibbon. It seems most likely that Gibbon ignored the art of the era he wrote about at such length quite simply because in his eyes it was not art at all. Non-art was not a subject worthy of his pen.

The period of which Gibbon writes does, of course, see just such a drastic change in style. It is an age that abandons the basic concepts and principles of Classicism in favor of expressionism developed with great stylistic diversity in the various parts of what had formerly been the relatively homogenous artistic domain of the Roman Empire.

This classical style, which Gibbon accepted as being the measure of art, was unique in the ancient world in several respects. It alone had concerned itself with the problem of working out canons of ideal beauty for the human figure; and it alone had dealt with the problem of realizing an illusionistic space within which the figures might exist. Indeed, it carried illusionistic reality further than any prior style in all respects. Under the Roman Empire, this style became the official banner of the Roman Imperium, carried everywhere within the confines of the Empire. Everywhere on the periphery of the Empire, however, reminiscences of older styles remained unforgotten, continuing to affect the official style in Egypt, Gaul, and Syria.

These older and alien styles all had some points of common reference. Notably, they were expressionistic rather than idealistic; and, since none of them had been interested in illusionistic space, they were more interested in frontality and more inherently two-dimensional. Frontality, along with an expressionistic emphasis on the eyes, was especially notable in cult statues since only this position suggested a direct communication between the image and the communicant. Even within the classic style, frontality, though without the emphasis on the eyes, had been maintained in the major cult images.

When the classical style began to disintegrate in the third century, the older styles exerted the major pressure in that disintegration. On all sides of the Empire, certain aspects of the pressures were the same. All acted in favor of expressionistic distortion, frontality, and the abandonment of illusionistic space effects. Though the multitude of local styles that arose in the artistic revolutions of the third and fourth centuries took recognizably different paths, all shared those qualities and thus operated to destroy the basic qualities of the classic style.

This does not mean that the classic style disappeared overnight or, indeed, at all. It was far too powerfully entrenched and too omnipresent an influence. Time and time again it would regain its old power and exert its spell over the minds of men to create that long series of so-called renaissances until it again ruled so supreme that to Gibbon there was no other true art. Our subject here, however, is not the perseverence of classicism but the artistic revolution and the appearance of those new styles so rigorously ignored by Gibbon.

The one art in which the break is least evident and which continues straight on from the second century in a steady line of development is architecture, the one area where we might expect Gibbon to show some real interest. Unfortunately, Gibbon's orientation is toward western Europe, the very area where the barbarian invasions disrupted and then destroyed architectural progress. Gibbon did not personally know the architecture of the Eastern Empire and always wrote of that empire with the basic assumption of its hopeless decadence. Even without those factors, however, architecture from the second century onward was moving steadily away from the classic principles that Gibbon accepted as basic to art.

Roman architecture was clearly, from the age of Hadrian onward, developing along lines analogous to the baroque. Having conquered the engineering problems involved in building a great, open, vaulted space, it began to center its interest on interior space rather than on external proportioned clarity. The Pantheon, built under Hadrian, is just such an example. The relationship of the exterior portico to the circular building behind it has always been slightly awkward and somewhat disturbing, though in its original condition, now vanished buildings that surrounded the circular portion would have masked that problem. There has never been any question, however, about the triumphant success of the Pantheon's spatial interior. The essence of the building lies there. Though Gibbon never says so, there is a very good chance that he may have felt that very space to be "enthusiastic" and quite out of any proper proportion to the human body.

Hadrian's villa would certainly have displeased Gibbon, even when it stood whole and perfect. Enormous and incredibly diffuse in organization, it spread tangentially in all directions. It had no major facade and lacked even any clear axis to control the diffuse parts. Made up of a loosely connected series of self-contained parts, it was always the interior structuring of courts and rooms which dominated the design. The layout must always have been bewildering and full of baroque surprises. Order and clarity are alien to its very concept.

The same basic architectural ideas are continued in the third century in such famous works as the Baths of Caracalla. Though there the ground plan has very strict symmetry, the planning is based on the interior spaces involved. Its facade can never have been noble; and its roof line was a fantastic jumble of vaults and terraces. Moreover, its interiors were not only a series of vast spaces, but were encrusted with an enormous variety of colored marbles and mosaics which must have sacrified clarity of organization to the expression of a multicolored, shimmering splendor of highly impressive but confusing spaces with extremely varied light effects. With its marbles stripped away, leaving only the huge jumble of brick walls and broken vaults, it is highly problematical whether Gibbon would have considered it architecture at all, certainly not proper architecture.

Byzantium, and Islam after Byzantium, were to carry on these concepts of the vaulted space and the primacy of the interior over the exterior. Justinian's architectural triumph, the church of Santa Sophia in Constantinople, remains just such a vaulted space, its great dome hovering 180 feet above the floor, as Gibbon mentions. But Santa Sophia never had a facade to match or even to suggest its interior. Exterior views of it are confusing and relatively unimpressive except by sheer bulk. Inside it is again the expressive elements of light and color and space which dominate. The huge, golden dome floats above a circle of light from the forty windows that pierce the base of the dome, denying its mass and substance, a clear example of enthusiasm and impropriety.

Smaller Byzantine churches, such as San Vitale in Ravenna, present the same improprieties. From the exterior, San Vitale is a most unimpressive brick building, and its original main entrance lay off axis. Inside, it is designed as a highly complex and sophisticated spatial architecture, the central space being lobed to mold an undulating space, further confused by calculated lighting effects and the shimmering colors of the mosaics that still line the choir. Gibbon does not even mention its existence. Why its mosaics must have seemed non-art to him is a problem to which I shall return.

The easiest monument in which to see the stylistic revolution of the Late Antique is the Arch of Constantine in Rome. Erected in some haste between the years 312 and 315, the arch utilizes sets of reliefs from three second-century monuments of Trajan, Hadrian, and Marcus Aurelius alongside reliefs made for the arch, thus immediately juxtaposing the two styles. Architecturally, it belongs to the new baroquizing style with its boldly projected, freestanding columns that serve as bases for freestanding figures of barbarians at the attic level, thereby breaking up the simpler cubic forms of earlier arches into greater complexity with more play of light and shadow.

In the sculptured panels, a variety of changes are easily visible. The very technique of carving had altered from the elegant and refined, illusionistic and idealized realism of the Hadrianic rondels in favor of a coarser handling in which folds are reduced to gouged lines and proportions are changed to a stocky, rather flattened awkwardness. The handling of the sculptural forms is, indeed, so summary that Berenson dismissed the work as a travesty on older forms perpetuated by craftsmen rather than sculptors. Of equal importance to the handling of the stone itself, however, is the new spirit that appears most clearly in such a relief as that of Constantine Speaking to the People of Rome.

In this relief, the easy balance of the older reliefs is abandoned in favor of an absolute symmetry. The blocks of persons representing the people fill the two ends of the long relief. The rostrum of the Roman Forum occupies the exact center, and the Emperor, now minus a head, occupies the center of the rostrum, flanked by equal groups of notables on either side. There is no attempt at any realism of space. The arrangement is purely hierarchic: the Emperor in the center, nobles flanking him, the populace flanking them at a lower level. Separate figures are not individualized. They exist as symbols of groups in a world dominated by the Emperor. The shift from individualization to hierarchy and from reality to symbol is to be at the very heart of the stylistic revolution.

These radical changes have an involved and complicated background, parts of which can only be guessed at now. It is notable, however, that the Roman tradition of the realistic portrait, which survived into the third century with such examples of "baroque realism" as the famous head of

Caracalla, underwent a change later in the third century
to the so-called Soul Portraits, where the eyes turn upward
as though inner-directed, and vigor gives way to uncertainty. The next stage is the clear freezing of the imperial
portrait into a self-contained symbol of imperial majesty,
obvious in the famous head of Constantine once in his basilica in Rome. All this reflects precisely the alterations in
the position of the Emperor through the desperate years of
the third century to the hierarchically removed Sacred
Majesty of Constantine.

The development of expressionistic detail at the expense
of realism and the development of symbolism in the figure
at the expense of realism also take place in the third century, almost certainly under strong influences from the
eastern Mediterranean, especially from Egypt, where both
these concepts survived from their Pharaonic past in spite
of the elegant Hellenism of Alexandria. An easy example is
the famous group in porphyry of the Tetrarchs, now built
into a corner of San Marco in Venice, traditionally
brought there from the East. Dating from the late third
century and representing the Tetrarchs of Diocletian's
time, the figures are static, awkward, with large heads, not
individualized, but with a sharp emphasis on the eyes. The
two points expressed in the work are the detailing of the
military dress and the amity between the two pairs expressed in the embrace. To the age of Diocletian, no ideas
were more welcome than those of military protection and
of amity, rather than civil war, between the rulers. The reliefs sacrifice every other point to the clarity of those.
Thus they become symbolic representation.

The frontality that is so marked in the Constantinian reliefs had been sliding into Roman sculpture along with the
development of the emperor cult. Augustus, in the reliefs
of the Ara Pacis, moves in profile, merely the first of the
procession. In the triumphal reliefs on the Arch of Trajan,

however, the chariot with the figure of the Emperor begins to swerve frontally though no other elements in the relief break the illusionistic space. By the time Septimius Severus erected his triumphal arch in Leptis Magna, the chariot turns completely to allow the figure of the Emperor to be seen fully frontally at the expense of the total disorganization of the space concept. From that it is only a short step to the complete frontality of the Constantinian reliefs, and the illusionistic space of classicism exists no longer.

Another element in the stylistic revolution is the flattening of sculptural form. A comparison of the famous portrait of Augustus from the Prima Porta with one of the consular statues of the fourth century in the Capitoline Museum shows that both have basically the same position, and that the changes are all in favor of creating a two-dimensional effect in a freestanding work. The raised arm that moves forward so commandingly in the Augustus has moved straight to the side in the Consular figure and no longer commands in actuality but simply raises the symbol of office. The draperies, which bulk so effectively in the Augustus and which do so much to define his existence in space, have in the Consular statue been developed into a series of planes emphasizing verticals and horizontals, denying validity to any except a strictly frontal view. The Consular statue would, in fact, be quite as effective as a relief. The history of sculpture as it moves out of the Late Antique into the Byzantine style will be precisely this. Sculpture in the round will almost disappear in favor of the relief and two-dimensionality. Plotinus in the third century is already speaking in favor of two-dimensionality as opposed to three-dimensional realism.

One of the most debatable elements in the reliefs of the Arch of Constantine is the extraordinarily summary quality of the carving itself, a point often tactfully ignored. It appalled Berenson in his notorious small book on the arch, which infuriated art historians by the manner in which it treated the monument as a kind of hideously incompetent death knell to classicism without granting any virtues to the work, a point of view which I suspect Gibbon would have endorsed wholeheartedly. That the arch has other values and is a milestone in the creation of a new style is unmistakable; but Berenson has a very real point, which cannot be dismissed simply.

There is some background to this kind of summary technique, though most of the evidence lies in the field of painting rather than in that of sculpture. As far back as the frescoes of Pompeii, there exists a style that is not monumental, building solid forms in an understandable spatial relationship, but is highly impressionistic: small scenes dashed on the wall in large, visible brushstrokes that give no more than essential elements without attempt at detailing. Attempts have been made to posit this as a popular style as opposed to a more formal aristocratic or court style, an attempt made difficult, if not impossible, by the appearance of both styles in the same building. However that may be, it is the summary and impressionistic style that dominates catacomb paintings. The subjects are reduced to essentials, and spatial reality is hardly a factor. How far this style had progressed and whether it did, in actuality, have a clear-cut sculptural counterpart is problematical.

There exist a few fragments of Christian sarcophagus reliefs, earlier in date than the Arch, which show precisely the same carving technique that appears in the Constantinian reliefs and which are closely related to them. Nonetheless, the summarily gouged lines in the Constantinian reliefs seem a remarkably close parallel to the fresco technique; and, in both, the presentation of symbol is preferred to the graces and finish of more realistic works. It has, indeed, been suggested that the carvers of the Constantinian reliefs were Christians rather than the foreign artisans posited by Berenson. Gibbon, I fear, would have found the distinction unimpressive.

Nonetheless, the coarse technique moves in the same direction as the other elements in the reliefs, away from reality and idealization and toward symbol and two-dimensionality. Moreover, it is easy to see in our own contemporary arts that in an age of stylistic revolution artists can and do feel revulsion toward slick finishes and techniques and may develop intentional crudities of proportion and of execution as an essential element in breaking with older styles. One must be wary of any and all assumptions in interpreting such periods.

The squat proportions and the coarse technique were to be dropped in the eventual formation of the developed Byzantine style, which reached its first great flowering in the sixth century under Justinian. The other elements present in the Constantinian reliefs, however, all form basic elements in the Byzantine style: the frontality, the hierarchical arrangements, and the generally expressionistic tone of the whole. There were, of course, clear classic survivals in art all through this period, and classicism was to stage repeated revivals in one form or another throughout the Middle Ages; but that side of the story is being deliberately omitted here.

The developed Byzantine style is, above everything else, a Christian style and the first to be wholly so. It faced up to and resolved the basic problems confronted gropingly by the artists of the catacombs and of the Constantinian reliefs, that of creating new forms to embody new ideas and new ideals, radically different from the humanistic philosophies and religion of the Classic Age. To do so it had to find a type of form which would emphasize the ideal of a Christian heaven, divorced from and different in character from earth and earthly humanity, not simply an idealization of that humanity.

To see the difference one must hold in mind the appearance of a Byzantine church of the most fully developed eleventh-century type, such as the church at Daphni or the one at Hosios Lukas. In both, the architecture is completely internalized, having extremely simple brick exteriors as opposed to the lower interior parts being sheathed in marble and the upper parts shimmering with golden mosaics. The churches are domed, and the entire scheme of decoration is both hierarchic and highly intellectualized. In the central dome, the highest portion, floats the figure of Christ Pantokrator with angels, seraphim, and cherubim. In the second zone of the apse is the Virgin; and in the area of the dome pendentives are pictures of the Twelve Great Feasts, the key passages in the Life of Christ: the Annunciation, the Nativity, the Baptism, and so on. Beneath that zone lies the zone of the intercessors, the saints and martyrs who are the intermediaries between the congregation and God. The lowest zone is that of the congregation, earth.

The figures themselves have undergone expressionistic distortion. Long and slim, they stand frontally and weightlessly against their shimmering golden backgrounds, two-dimensional though suggesting the forms and articulation of the body, symbols of human beings removed into a realm where earthly space, and weight, and dimension no longer operate. Above and beyond any other single feature, one is inevitably aware of the direct and sober gaze of the emphatic eyes.

The almost infinite complexity and intellectuality of this highly sophisticated style can barely be suggested here. Only a few aspects, at best, can be pointed out. One such is the extraordinary effectiveness of the use of the golden mosaic backgrounds. The earliest of the surviving great Christian mosaics used a blue background, seen at its most exquisite in the little mausoleum of Galla Placidia in Ravenna. It expresses a clear interest in creating an effect of a vast space and of a heavenly sphere; and, indeed, the effect is so successful that one feels immediately that one has entered a space larger than that enclosed by the brick walls of the exterior, a different realm, intensified by the fact that the mosaics are not made up of tesserae of a uniform blue, but of a whole series of blues which operate together to create a vibrancy that destroys the sense of any enclosing wall. Blue continues to be identifiable, however, as the sky color of our earth.

The shift to the use of gold seems to be based on the identification of the presence of God with light: "I am the Light of the world." The gold reflects, gathers up, and emanates its own light. It no longer suggests sky space, but the space of heaven, light filled, light emanating. Moreover, in the best examples, the thousands of tiny tesserae are laid into the wall most carefully so that they point downward toward the viewer and are set, not flatly, but at constantly varying, slight angles to one another. Any slight movement on the part of the viewer brings different tesserae into focus, and the result is a soft shimmering, never a flat glare. The radiance is ever moving and changing. Walls and space itself are alike dissolved in this radiance. Contrary to the theorists of a generation ago who praised mosaic, as opposed to illusionistic frescoes, for its preservation of the integrity of the wall, no frescoes have ever so totally dissolved walls into heaven as do the Byzantine mosaics.

The effectiveness of weightless two-dimensionality in symbolizing a removal from the sphere of this world is too obvious to require elaboration. The importance of the expressionistic emphasis on the eyes may be stressed, however.

It is not a meaningless feature of the style; and it combines with frontality for its effect. The eyes are clearly felt to be the organ of communication between the congregation and the sacred figures. Proof of this is found in those scenes where evil appears, in the form either of the Devil or of Judas. Notably and uniquely in these figures, the heads turn away so that the eyes may not seek communion with the congregation. Another clear proof lies in the habits of the Egyptian hermits who took over the ancient Egyptian tombs for habitation. Surrounded by paintings of the ancient gods, they rendered them impotent, not by hacking them off the walls, but by scratching their eyes out. It is the Evil Eye, not the evil mouth or hand, which is to be feared.

The refinement of the crude hierarchical quality of the Constantinian reliefs into the sophisticated hierarchicalism of the developed Byzantine style is the perfect reflexion of the Byzantine court, as well as of the Church. Christianity had, of course, developed a hierarchical church system even before its official recognition; and the court of the emperor had undergone an equal change under Diocletian with the full blossoming of the emperor cult. When the court became Christianized, the emperor cult continued, only now in Christian guise. The palace becomes the Sacred Palace with its regiments of ceremonial costumes and orders of officials. The peculiar synthesizing of the emperor cult and of Christianity is seen clearly when Constantine lays out and builds his new Christian capital at Byzantium. There he erects a tall column bearing a statue of himself; and at its base he places an altar holding Christian relics, so that the celebrant there simultaneously worships the Christian God and the deified emperor.

The grip that the developed Byzantine art style held on the Byzantine imagination can nowhere be seen more in-

tensely than in the way the style invades life itself. The
emphasis on the idea as opposed to reality, on symbol in
preference to fact, becomes a part of both church and
state ritual. In the church, priestly vestments are now cut
and designed to fall in flat planes, shimmering with their
own golden radiance, designed to attempt to turn corporeal bodies into two-dimensional images. Moreover, the
same style of cutting robes to fall into heavy, flat planes is
the style of the imperial court dress. Both the multitude of
imperial portraits surviving and the unique example of the
Sicilian coronation robes, Byzantine in both style and man-
ufacture, exhibit the same interest in two-dimensionaliz-
ing reality. The epitome appears in those recorded imperial
receptions of foreign ambassadors by Byzantine emperors
in which the emperor simply stands in the hall of the
Sacred Palace, arrayed in his radiant, flat planes of clothing, motionless and unspeaking. It is his minister standing
beside him who speaks to the ambassadors and hears them
for as long as the audience lasts, which, on some occasions,
amounted to hours. The emperor had become an icon, the
living parallel to the saints in the churches.

The Byzantine is the greatest and the most completely
conscious of the artistic styles that grew out of the artistic
revolution. It is seen at its best in its homelands of Asia
Minor and the Balkans. Both Egypt and Syria developed
variations that reflect, in part, the nationalistic tendencies
of those areas; but, in both instances, the Islamic conquests
crushed a full development. The Coptic style tends to continue the squatter forms of the Constantinian period and,
existing in frescoes rather than mosaics, has a more rugged
quality, along with an enormous charm, in the many examples of Coptic textiles which survive.

Syria, always very open to influences from the Parthian
East, continues the highly frontal, expressionistic style to

be seen early at Palmyra and in the Parthian palace at Hatra. It also takes over the interest in overall, symmetrical design, the so-called carpet patterns.

Islam, developing in an area that had no strong artistic background on which to draw, frankly derived its early art styles from those it found in the conquered countries: Byzantine, Coptic, and Syriac, using artists of all those areas. Since the Islamic religion did not accept the picturing of the elements of its faith in human form, however, its art became purely decorative. It is true that Ommayad frescoes surviving in the desert palaces show the human figure, but these seem to occur only in the baths and thus mirror the downgrading of the figure. The surviving parts of the great landscape mosaics that decorated the mosque at Damascus are Byzantine in workmanship and design, but represent ideal park landscapes uninhabited by human beings; and in every inch the surviving exterior parts of the great desert palace at Mshatta are covered with a luxuriant relief of plant life inhabited by birds and animals. All this is frankly decorative, basically symmetrical, and already moving toward the geometrical abstractions that form so large a part of Islamic art. The arts are clearly subordinated to architecture and serve to ornament it.

This brings us back to Gibbon, who, as I have already suggested, would share such a view of the relative position of the arts. Such work as that at Mshatta would have been anathema to Gibbon. Ornament to the classic eye should be used to demarcate the parts of the architecture, to clarify. The ornament of Mshatta, flooding the entire surface, tends only to obscure the basic architecture. He would have considered this an overzealous "enthusiasm" for decoration in its own right.

As for Byzantine art, the eighteenth century simply dismissed it as "primitive," by which was meant incompetent. Though English travelers were already going to

Greece to study the antiquities, they uniformly ignored the Byzantine remains as uncouth. They had no understanding of its sophistication or of its intellectual subleties. To an eye tuned to classicism, its two-dimensionality seemed only a lack of ability to project a proper sense of volume, its frontality seemed awkwardness, its heavenly space simply a failure to understand the laws of perspective, and its expressionistic distortions another proof of incompetence.

One example will suffice to indicate the unintelligibility of Byzantine concepts to the Western eye, conditioned by Renaissance art. The one omnipresent example of a baby in Byzantine art is, of course, the Christ child who is always portrayed in the proportions of a small man. It seems never to have entered the eighteenth-century mind that, with both plenty of real babies around and an infinite number of surviving classical amorini as prototypes, this distortion might be intentional. The Byzantine artist is, of course, seeking to divorce the Christ child from the human baby, to emphasize the fact that this is not just any baby, but the Christ child. The distortion is the very symbol of that idea, one far more deeply Christian and religious than all the highly idealized babies in the works of Raphael, which glorify an ideal humanity and mother love, inevitably a more palatable concept to modern tastes than that of the dematerialized Mother of God and the Christ. The true meaning of the Byzantine form, however, would probably not have rendered it any more attractive to Gibbon.

Western Europe during the early Middle Ages saw no true equivalent to the rise of the highly sophisticated Byzantine style. The barbarian hordes that poured into the devastated Western lands brought with them an artistic style of their own too greatly at variance from the classical style either to appreciate or to assimilate classicism easily. Theirs was an ornamental rather than a monumental style.

Too little settled to have developed much sense of architecture, their art was primarily based on the ornamentation of portable objects: jewelry, clothing, hangings, the smaller articles of furniture. The style itself was semigeometric, using interlace patterns, but also full of extraordinarily dynamic animal forms, highly distorted and expressionistic. The human figure that occupies the heart and center of classic art has no place in the art of the barbarian tribes.

Even the Gauls of France, who had been highly Romanized in the course of the centuries, had a background of dynamic art forms in which animal life played a major role and where a certain harsh crudity in sculpture persisted under the classic superstructure and which produced monsters of far more genuinely terrifying aspect than any of the chimeras or medusas of the classic age. Under the pressure of the invaders, their art forms easily reverted to nonclassic style.

The history of artistic styles in the West is far more obscure and various than that of the eastern Mediterranean. Nothing survives in an absolutely pure form. The barbarian style itself was not suited to a full expression of the ideas of the Christianity that the Germans so quickly adopted as a religion. As a result, there is an uneasy attempt, on the one hand, to cling to some elements of the classic past along with strong waves of Byzantine artistic influence, the Christian style par excellence, while retaining elements of their native styles. Only the Celtic style, as developed in Ireland and later in Anglo-Saxon England and exported from there back to the Continent, saw anything like a full and fairly autonomous development.

Before looking at that, however, it is worth noting that the influence of the barbarian style had a marked influence in Italy itself. The Goths, with their capital in Ravenna, had tended to take over the early Christian, semi-Byzantine style and artists they found in Ravenna. The Lombards did so to a far lesser degree. Starting perhaps—the datings remain highly problematical—in the seventh century, a new element appears in a large series of ornamental reliefs in Italy, which have been referred to as being of the "Lombard style," though many of them seem totally unconnected with the Lombards. Most of these were altar screens, altar panels, and sarcophagus panels, all sharing the same tendencies.

The barbarian style was already two-dimensional, ornamental, and basically geometrical, but not symmetrical. The area in which it could be expected to have an impact was on just such reliefs, shallow, ornamental, nonfigurative. Moreover, the earliest Christian iconography had drawn very heavily on the animal world for symbols of Christian ideas. Classical ornament, where nonfigurative, had been strictly symmetrical and elegantly proportioned. Those are the elements that disappear in the new style, whether "Lombard" or not.

It begins in small ways: a panel made up of repeated small elements that look symmetrical superficially, but which, upon examination, prove to have a number of small, almost casual deviations from symmetry. A tendril hooks up into one panel alone, or one cross deviates. It would look like sheer carelessness, and was long dismissed as such, except that this type of carelessness can occur easily in painting, but not in a piece of laborious marble sculpture, otherwise highly finished and polished. Such deviations tend to grow and increase in obviousness until such a work as the famous Theodota relief, where a perfectly symmetrical and standard Ravennate pattern composed of two peacocks flanking a fountain, inexplicably has a large plant form tacked onto one end of the relief, totally destroying symmetry and proportion. Even today, the eye tends to try to ignore the presence of the plant form as an unwelcome intruder into a familiar scheme. Yet it is deliberate.

The barbarian style may well represent an artistic rebellion against the tame symmetry of the classic ornament, easily paralleled in contemporary art concepts. The direction the rebellion takes, however, is in line with the dynamics of the barbarian style. Both the Franks and the Visigoths produced works of art which were too uneasy an amalgam of classic and Byzantine influences grafted onto the barbarian stock to develop into a powerful and individual style. However charming the Visigothic reliefs on Santa Maria Naranco and San Miguel de Lillo are to contemporary eyes, they retain a tentative quality too uncertain not to collapse under the impact of foreign styles. Even the Merovingian manuscript style with its compulsive fascination with fish and birds as decorative elements disappeared under the impact of the more sophisticated Carolingian style.

It was in Ireland that the barbarian style developed forms powerful enough to absorb and to use outside influences without being overwhelmed. Typically, its masterpieces are to be found in small objects: in manuscript illumination with those supreme masterpieces, the Book of Kells and the Lindisfarne Gospels, and in metalwork, such as the Ardagh Chalice and the Tara Brooch. In these works, complex interlace patterns in endless variety are carried to the ultimate. Moreover, dynamic asymmetry is carried to an anticlassic perfection. Wherever the human figure appears in the manuscripts, however, it is clearly based on imported works, though the Celtic style flattens it to a degree beyond the Byzantine and subjects it to distortions that are less deliberately expressionistic in intention than a process of forcing it into design patterns not evolved from the human figure. Moreover, in the famous series of "carpet pages" and "cross pages," the absolute symmetry of the small elements has always suggested the Middle Eastern patterns, probably filtered to the West through Syriac productions. Nonetheless, in Ireland these importations are not simply crudely imitated, as they are in Visigothic work, where the door jambs of San Miguel de Lillo are roughly enlarged copies of a Byzantine ivory diptych. In the Celtic style, the foreign elements are regularly assimilated, transmuted, and made into something new which remains thoroughly Celtic.

Notably, the Frankish and Visigothic works are local styles. The Celtic style, carried into Anglo-Saxon England and thence to the Continent in the great missionary ventures of the Celtic group, was sufficiently formulated and powerful enough to survive the moves and to maintain itself on the Continent to become one of the strands from which Romanesque was eventually to be woven.

Every element in the barbarian style doomed it to extinction in the eighteenth century. Its finest works were viewed as craft articles rather than as art. Its nonhuman bias and its dynamic asymmetry appeared as misguided incompetence. The eighteenth century in its more venturesome aspects of the proto-romantics was evolving an interest in Gothic, but not even they make any mention of the Romanesque. Indeed, it is the early nineteenth century that sees the ruthless demolition of two of the mightiest and most imposing Romanesque churches of France, Cluny and the great Pilgrimage church of St. Martin at Tours. Under such conditions, Gibbon could not be expected to be aware of the existence of such works or to classify them as art.

Today, we are in a vastly different frame of mind. Appreciation of Romanesque art and adulation of Ravenna are de rigeur. The monuments left from the Dark Ages of the West are cherished and restored and studied. Two-dimensionality, frontality, abstract pattern, and expressionistic deformations have once more become the essence of art. One sees them as such in the arts of any other age or climate; and, again, the idealized, humanistic perfections of the classic style have become a bore in artistic circles, and neoclassicism a bad joke. It is useless to be pejorative of Gibbon for seeing with eighteenth-century eyes. If he failed to appreciate the art of those ages, he simply eschewed all mention of it. He did not fall into the greater error of condemning it.

CONCLUSION:
THE TEMPLE OF JUPITER REVISITED

Lynn White, jr.

*T*HIS SYMPOSIUM has been a prism of three faces: each in his own way, and never with equal emphasis, the contributors have discussed, first, what really took place (as we today view these matters) in late Antiquity and the early Middle Ages; second, Gibbon, and why he thought what he thought; and third, ourselves, and why we think about these events as we do. Since more has been said about the first two than about the third, at the end we should try to redress the balance by pondering ourselves and what we can learn about ourselves in weighing Gibbon and his problem.

Gibbon records his moment of truth on October 15, 1764, as having occurred in what was once the Temple of Jupiter. Despite his intensive study of Roman antiquities, he was wrong: St. Mary's in Aracoeli rests on the site and incorporates the remains of the Temple of Juno Moneta where the ancient Roman mint had been secure within the citadel. The shrine of Jupiter was on the other side of the Campidoglio, on the slightly lower eminence of the bi-corned Capitoline. The blunder is worth noting not merely for the sake of sweet pedantry but also for its symbolic value: like so many of Gibbon's errors it affects his magnificence in no way. Surely we Californians who have composed this symposium, dwelling in a state where possessions are dominated by the Visigothic law of community property between husband and wife, should easily award to Jupiter at least half ownership of the Aracoeli. Essentially, it is neither new facts nor more careful appraisal of facts known to the later eighteenth century which compels us to disagree with Gibbon's perspective and judgments: it is our different mode of vision.

Indeed, many of the new facts have been discovered not primarily because they were sitting waiting to be seen but because recent generations have found eyes to see them. Gustave von Grunebaum and Miriam Lichtheim have rightly emphasized that most of the basic documents for an understanding of early Islam and of the Monophysites were simply not available to Gibbon. Jeffrey Russell noted that Gibbon scarcely mentions the Celts. Yet surely the great surge of Islamic, Syriac, Coptic, and Celtic studies, and much else, is not accidental: it has occurred because phenomena and attitudes which to an educated Occidental lacked significance or merit in 1764 have now gained power to stir our minds and hearts.

That it is less new facts than new ways of looking at things which separate us from Gibbon is made clear by the case of Byzantium. As Speros Vryonis points out, Gibbon knew a high proportion of our present major sources for medieval Greece; and this is not surprising, since the transplanting of Byzantine intellectual culture to the West by refugees fleeing the Turks coincided with the emergence of the printing press. Yet even Gibbon's genius, vast learning, and Olympian sense of humor failed to reveal to him the absurdity of his view of Byzantium; for surely Constantinople's life span from A.D. 330 to 1453 is the most prolonged and resilient "decadence" in the annals of our race. One is tempted to quote to Gibbon the deathbed apology of Charles II to his courtiers: "Gentlemen, I am an unconscionable time dying, but I hope you will excuse it."

Not merely new erudition, but, above all, new eyes:

these make the difference! Doubtless our own age commits its distinctive atrocities, but today we can only be appalled at the blindness, the insensitivity, of the Enlightenment to all that did not harmonize with its rather narrow gamut of values. In 1745, when Gibbon was eight years old, Frederick the Great of Prussia, needing stones for building Sanssouci, destroyed the surviving masonry temple of the medieval pagan Wends. Shortly after Gibbon wrote his history, the Book of Kells, the culminating work of Irish illumination, was rebound so nonchalantly that the binder sliced off sections of the designs while trimming the edges. And, as Albert Hoxie mentioned, Cluny, the greatest of Romanesque churches, secularized by the French Revolution, was being destroyed piecemeal for road metal even as late as the 1820's, to the point where only one proud transept survives. Gibbon, I suspect, could not have understood our modern recoil from such deeds any more than a medieval bishop or a Barbarini pope could have comprehended both Gibbon's and our own reaction to their inveterate habit of quarrying Roman structures to build contemporary shrines and palaces. Gibbon is more akin to the historical attitudes of the centuries before him than he is to ours. The selective vandalism that earlier ages wreaked upon monuments considered obsolete was based on an absolutizing of values. And surely Gibbon was an absolutist: to his way of thinking the reigns of the Antonines were the Golden Age of mankind; all subsequent changes were deplorable; if, recently, Europe had regained a decent level of civilization, it was largely because of the restoration of classical tastes. As a result of this intense and dogmatic historical selectivity, Gibbon mutilated for his own purposes all that did not please his sensibilities. To say this is not to derogate his greatness: after all, the maker of many a masterpiece has cannibalized the past.

The thing that chiefly distinguishes us from Gibbon and

from all his predecessors is that we have substituted affirmative faith in the pluralism of values for the old faiths in
exclusive sets of values. It is possible—indeed it is necessary
—for us today to enjoy not only the Laocoon and the Blue
Boy but also a Byzantine ivory, Norse jewelry, a Benin
bronze, and a Melanesian mask. Humanists steeped, like
Gibbon, in the classical tradition of absolutist values sneer
at our current attitude as muddleheaded eclecticism, cultural drift, psychic spinelessness. The judgment is not
merely too harsh: it is blind. Pluralism insists on the spiritual necessity not only of judging one's own active relationship to everything in reach, whether it be a work of
art, a political system, or a religious belief: pluralism also
lays upon us an obligation of understanding from the inside even, or especially, the things we do not like. It is permissible not only to condemn headhunting but also to support the police in discouraging it; nevertheless, we have a
supplementary responsibility, an engagement as human
beings to try to comprehend why our fellow human
beings, the headhunters, approve headhunting.

The gulf between Gibbon's mentality and our own is
bottomless because it involves two contrasting approaches
to human phenomena and therefore to self-understanding.
The change in the meaning of the word "anthropology" is
a symbol and also a symptom of what has occurred to our
mode of thinking during the past two centuries. "Anthropology" in Gibbon's day still meant a branch of theology
dealing with the nature and destiny of man; and, despite
his skin-deep allergy to religion, Gibbon's bones remained
theological. The word "anthropology," in its modern sense
of a detailed empirical effort to understand the immense
diversity of mankind's cultures as expressions of human
needs molded by an infinite variety of ecologies, time se-
quences, and diffusionary processes, first emerges in English from the 1870's onward. Similarly, the term "ecology,"

for a key concept in modern thinking about all life, including our own, is not found in English until 1873. Clearly, during the past century we have been developing intellectual instruments that are entirely novel and that profoundly separate our mental processes from those of Gibbon.

Specifically, how does our pluralism, our anthropology, affect our view of what happened to the later Roman Empire?

First of all, we have detribalized Gibbon's view. To our eyes it would seem that the very title of the *Decline and Fall* reflects a western European parochialism. Earlier than the thirteenth century the Byzantines were not aware that they were declining and falling. On the contrary, while they treasured the remains of their pagan Greek past, the new dispensation of Christ so ably described by Gerhart Ladner seemed vastly preferable, and their zest in it produced a glittering new art, new poetry, and new scholarship, not to mention a vast network of commerce and an amazingly stable and sophisticated governmental system. Nor were the Muslims conscious of being victims of a decline and fall. Quite the reverse: the faith of Muhammad released new energies in all the peoples it touched; it was the catalyst in the emergence of a novel culture extending from the Atlantic to the Hindu Kush which was a source of pride to those who shared it. As for the western part of the Roman Empire, that is, north of the Mediterranean and the Ebro, Gibbon's view was more accurate: the decline was steep, the fall bruising, and many contemporaries were painfully aware of it. But geographically this amounted to only about one-quarter of the former Roman Empire; it was probably the part most thinly populated; it was certainly the region most recently and precariously civilized. The wintry experience of a few provinces should

not provide the name for an era when the lands of more
ancient culture were passing through a spring and summer.

Since the days of the Hebrew and Greek historians,
ethnocentrism has been so commonly the tacit assumption
that it can scarcely be considered a vice in Gibbon in 1764.
Nevertheless, from the standpoint of the later twentieth
century it invalidates his entire structure of interpretation.

Indeed, a whole new pattern of history has been emerging. To Gibbon, who accepted the ancient Greeks as his
peers, the more recent Near East, whether Christian or
Muslim, seemed entirely alien. Yet recently a San Franciscan husband and wife of education and sensibility had a
very different experience which symbolizes our present
view of things. They started westward on a leisurely trip
around the world. They saturated themselves in the treasures of Japan, then of the peripheral Chinas which they
were permitted to enter; afterwards, of Cambodia, Java,
Thailand, Burma, and India. Then they stood before the
columns and stairways of Persepolis and said, "We're
home!"

They were correct. In the landmass of the Old World,
civilization first sprang up in three widely separated, although not unconnected, areas: the Yellow River valley,
the Indus-Ganges valleys, and the Fertile Crescent of the
Near East, extending from Iraq through Syria into Egypt.
It is to this third species of culture that, in its farthest extension, we Californians belong, as my San Franciscan
friends spontaneously recognized. What we call "ancient
history" is the study of the process by which the Near
Eastern culture spread west to embrace the Greeks, who,
with Alexander the Great, lashed back and half-Hellenized
the parent culture; then how Rome entered the circle of
civilization, unifying the Mediterranean and applying at

least a veneer of higher culture to lands north of the Alps, while failing to subdue its rival, but sister empire, Persia, or to extend its sway to South Arabia which, since at least the days of the famous Queen of Sheba, had been integral to the Near East.

The centuries that we label "Middle Ages" mark a regrouping and vast expansion of the forces within the cultural complex extending from Baluchistan to the Atlantic. Three cousinly cultures emerged from late Antiquity, each emphasizing one ingredient of that cosmopolitanism. In the Aegean and Anatolia a revivified Greek world went on to new triumphs and extended its influence over millions of eastern and southern Slavs hitherto outside the pale of civilization. A revived Near East found its rallying cry in Islam and provided a realm of common assumptions extending from Portugal to Turkestan. In the West, after agony, the Latin way of life was diffused to Celts, Germans, Scandinavians, and western Slavs. The Middle Ages are a period, east and west, of differentiation, of firming up, and of notable geographical outreach by a closely related set of cultures which were all phases of the single great and ever changing civilization originally stemming from the Near East. With our present anthropological approach, we can see what Gibbon could not: that Muslim, Byzantine, and Frank were astonishingly alike, united by far more than separated them.

We have returned, indeed, to the contemporary medieval view. St. John of Damascus in the eighth century, and Dante in the fourteenth, were quite correct in considering Muhammad not as the founder of a separate religion but rather as a schismatic rending the unity of the Church, the seamless garment of Christ: Islam, after all, is a Judeo-Christian heresy. Throughout all the segments of the Middle Ages men were asking the same basic question: "What is the relation of reason to revelation?" It is no accident that the intellectual processes of scholars, whether they spoke Greek, Arabic, Hebrew, or Latin, were dominated by Aristotelian methods; and that whenever they wearied of Aristotle many of them turned to Platonism, if not to Plato himself. It astonished no one in thirteenth-century Paris that the primary goal of Thomas Aquinas was to refute the philosophical position of Ibn Rushd, a Spanish Muslim who died in Marrakesh. Writing in 1122–1123, the German Benedictine monk Theophilus, without affectation, included in his treatise on craftsmanship the arts of Greece, Russia, Arabia, Italy, France, and Germany: these were within his natural horizon. Even medieval anti-Semitism had common elements everywhere: as our UCLA colleague Moshe Perlmann has recently shown, a major point in Muslim polemic against the Jews was their failure to recognize Jesus as a prophet.[1] In this context the Crusades become less an Herodotean confrontation of East and West than a series of civil wars for the control of shrines sacred to all factions. And, as in most civil wars, the mayhem eventually became impartial, culminating in the Christian looting of Christendom's greatest city, Constantinople, in 1204. Moreover, the common belief that the Near East was effectively unknown to the West before the Crusades is nonsense. St. Jerome's Latin gazeteer of biblical geography—there was no work of equivalent prestige in Greek—so interested Westerners in the Holy Places that through the centuries they had gone to Palestine in larger numbers than the Greeks. Moreover, before the First Crusade there were considerable groups of Westerners living in the major cities of the Levant.[2]

[1] Samau'al al-Maghribī Ifḥām al Yahūd, *Silencing the Jews*, ed. and trans. M. Perlmann (New York, 1964), pp. 42–44.

[2] S. Vryonis, "Problems in the History of Byzantine Anatolia," *Ankara Üniv. D.T.C. Facültesi Tarih Araştirmalari Dergisi, Cilt I., Sayi l den ayribasim* (1963), p. 119 n. 21, observes that in 1071, in the Syrian city of Edessa, well east of the Euphrates, there were 1,000 Latins in a total population of some 35,000.

Nor was cultural diffusion entirely from east to west. Chess entered Christian Europe through Spain about A.D. 1000, and for some two hundred years was played with identical rules from Iceland to the Indus. In the thirteenth century, however, the Westerners began tinkering with the game, and thereafter all modifications of it in the Near East can be traced to European influences.[3] To offer another random example, from the eighth century onward the Franks developed a method of mounted shock combat superior to that used by Byzantines and Muslims. This led to gradual modification of arms and armor in the West and diffusion of the new forms eastward. By about A.D. 1000 the old round shield had been elongated by Westerners into a kite shape to protect the left knee of the rider. This is found in Byzantium by 1066 and in Cairo by 1085.[4]

These are not items of great significance in themselves, but they point to a kind of symbiosis by the three great segments of the medieval world which we have begun to recognize only recently. Much remains to be ascertained. Philip Levine uses palaeography in a most original way to illuminate the transition from Latin pagan to Latin Christian culture. There is a mutation in handwriting around the year 800 which raises problems in the relation between the Franks and Byzantines. In the later eighth century, first at the Benedictine abbey of Corbie and then at St. Martin's of Tours, a radically new shape of letters developed which is essentially the one in which this book is printed. The novel script had great advantages: it could be written and read more rapidly than the old style; it was more compact and thus saved parchment. Within a few decades it had replaced most of the older ways of writing

[3] H. J. R. Murray, *History of Chess* (Oxford, 1913), p. 394.

[4] L. White, jr., "The Medieval Roots of Modern Technology and Science," in *Perspectives in Medieval History*, ed. K. F. Drew and F. S. Lear (Houston, 1963), p. 22 n. 3.

in the West. In the early ninth century exactly the same sort of change occurred in Greek handwriting. Since the Carolingian and Byzantine empires were in constant contact and bilingual persons were not infrequent—indeed, we are told that Charlemagne could understand spoken Greek—it is absurd to think that no one in the educated classes of Byzantium had knowledge of the revolution in book production which was sweeping the Latin regions. While specific evidence is lacking, it is probable that the Greek minuscule was directly inspired by the Carolingian minuscule, the ground having been prepared for the change by a shift in both regions from the reed pen to the quill pen which seems to have begun in the sixth century.

To those still dubious of the functional unity of medieval East and West and contemptuous of chessmen, shields, and the nibs of pens as proper subjects for humanistic study, let me offer a loftier order of thinking deliberately cultivated by my colleague Gustave von Grunebaum to redress the imbalance at the University of California, Los Angeles, created by my peasant mind. In an astonishing study [5] of the comparative development of religious emotion in Islam and in Greek Christendom, he has identified a shift of focus from the majesty of God to the beauty of God, which appears in the Greek Church about A.D. 1000, which is decisive for the mood of Islamic orthodoxy by the end of the eleventh century, and which, in the West, is clearly visible in St. Anselm and dominant in St. Bernard. Once more, documentation of direct connection between these three closely analogous changes in styles of piety is elusive. But the observed phenomena are scarcely to be brushed aside as mere coincidence. Any explanation, whether diffusionary or derived from social psychology, establishes, at the most intimate level of cultural life, a

[5] "Parallelism, Convergence, and Influence in the Relations of Arab and Byzantine Philosophy, Literature and Piety," *Dumbarton Oaks Papers*, XVIII (1965), 91–111.

unity of the three geographic segments of the Middle Ages which Gibbon would scarcely have been prepared to recognize.

The title of Gibbon's work assumes a "Fall," a decisive end of Antiquity. The substance of his book contradicted its title by demonstrating a continuity of Antiquity with Byzantium which had implications that Gibbon could not accept: they violated those sensibilities of the eighteenth century which Andrew Lossky has expounded to us; they would have destroyed the choreography of Gibbon's great historical masque.

In 1937 the Myth of the Fall was metamorphosed by the admirable Belgian historian Henri Pirenne, who insisted that Mediterranean culture remained unified until the end of the seventh century when the Islamic conquests isolated the West, forced it back upon its own resources, and thus provided the basis, north of the Alps, for a new kind of "Western" civilization. The scholarship of the past quarter-century has largely destroyed Pirenne's fertile hypothesis, but it has no more dimmed esteem for him than criticism of the *Decline and Fall* has altered admiration for Gibbon. But we must note that there is in Pirenne a residuum of Gibbon's tribalism: he is really interested in the *West*, and the trauma of the early medieval West compels him to think in terms of general catastrophe, a "Fall." Today, with the detribalization of history, we Occidentals feel less psychic need of cataclysmic interpretations of history. Our phrasing of "Decline and Fall" is "The Transformation of the Roman World," some of the transformation having been wretched and some magnificent.

In addition to detribalizing Gibbon's view of history, our pluralistic anthropological way of thinking has also democratized it. This second change may be even more drastic than the first.

Edward Gibbon came of the English gentry and was

proud of it. He habitually wore the sword that was still the sign of the aristocrat, even though, as one unkind observer remarked, he never drew it. Gibbon's inherited class presuppositions were confirmed by a classical education saturated with elitist values. In Gibbon's concept of history, the top few of mankind are all that count: I see no evidence that he had interest in, or even any abiding compassion for, the mass of the common people. Certainly he did not ascribe to them a dynamic role in history.

We are changing all that. Beginning in 1776 our Western culture, and more recently, by mimesis, the non-Western cultures, have been passing through a series of democratic revolutions. The first phase was political. Today, at least in the industrialized nations, we have supplemented a degree of political democracy from which Gibbon would have recoiled with an economic democracy which would have been unintelligible to him. Now, on the basis of our ancient and lavish inheritance of aristocratic culture, we are advancing to the third and most difficult stage of the democratic revolution: the creation of a democratic intellectual culture. The realization that the mute millions have in fact been historically creative is essential to this process, and it greatly alters our perspective on what happened to ancient Rome.

One of the unusual aspects of Mortimer Chambers' chapter is his insistence on the overwhelmingly rural nature of Greco-Roman society. It is rare to find an historian of the ancient world writing in these terms: the *polis*, the *civitas*, was the essence of that *civilization* which is by etymology the condition of existence in a city, as *politics* is the social metabolism of the *polis*. Yet it is a safe guess that the productivity of ancient agriculture was so low that it took some nineteen people living directly on the land to produce a surplus to support one living in a city.

Thus envisaged, the higher levels of ancient culture are

seen to have suffered from great fragility. Such culture was, in effect, confined to the cities, which were small organisms of sophistication floating on an ocean of rural barbarism. The vast majority of men did not share the benefits of urban life and were hostile to cities as centers of parasitism, oppressing the countrymen. Most people would feel no stake in the city or loyalty to it. The psychological relation of the ancient city to its huge rural matrix was insecure.

And what if agrarian productivity dropped because of warfare, plague, drought, or foul weather? The surplus of food was terrifyingly slender at best; even a slight decline might imperil the existence of the urban population. Prolonged scarcity would whittle away the size of cities and their cultural vigor not only because of a reduced food supply but also because the failure of agrarian sales to the cities would cut down rural purchase of articles made by urban craftsmen. Thus commerce in staple goods would fail; trade would become a matter of luxuries for the very rich. At last even the civil and military authorities would begin to retreat from the decaying cities to seek an agrarian base where food could be assured by closer supervision of its production and collection.

This is the disintegrative pattern that can be traced from the time of the great plague under Marcus Aurelius in A.D. 166, the effects of which were compounded by the prolonged military anarchy of the third century. By the end of the third century the social, economic, and, to some extent, the cultural state of the western, and especially northwestern, provinces of the Empire was beginning to foreshadow that of the early Middle Ages.

To understand why the same crises did not produce the same disasters in the Near East one must invoke the concept of the "critical mass." Let us suppose that two American cities, one twice the size of the other, maintain sym-

phony orchestras. If the population of both cities were cut
in half, one city would probably be forced to abandon its
orchestra: the other, despite difficulties, could probably
continue its musical tradition. In the western Roman Empire there was only one large city, Rome itself, with an
incredibly parasitic population sustained by the taxes of
the rest of the Empire and by free distribution of grain
brought from Egypt, Tunisia, and Sicily—a rabble that
shrank quickly when the *annona* dwindled. In contrast,
the great arc of the Near East, from Egypt northward
through Syria, Anatolia, Thrace, and Macedonia, supported a fairly dense agrarian settlement built up over
millennia, and this population served both as food source
and as market for the manufactures of a chain of great
cities extending from Alexandria in the south to Thes-
salonika at the head of the Aegean. From the late second
century onward, great misfortunes afflicted the East as
well as the West; yet it would seem that, save exceptionally
and locally, sufficient population and productivity were
maintained in the eastern countryside to support a critical
mass in the cities, and thus to permit continuity in the cultural tradition. The hero of the late Roman Empire and
the early Middle Ages is the peasant, although this cannot
be discovered from Gibbon.

In the northwestern provinces of the Empire, the peasantry sustained production less effectively than elsewhere.
The Germanic invasions of the West were more disturbing
than those of the Orient: the long rhythms of plowing,
sowing, and reaping were broken so often that the already
scanty population fell to the point where cities lost the
critical mass essential to urban culture, save possibly in the
Po Valley, Provence, and along the coasts of southern Italy
which were closely tied to the Near East. But the chief reason for the failure of the reduced peasantry of the northern regions of the Empire to produce the necessary surplus

was that the agricultural methods at their disposal were defective in relation to northern climates and soils.

In prehistory the type of agriculture which had developed in the Near East was introduced to northern Europe. Its basic tool was the scratch plow drawn by two oxen. Only half the arable land was planted each year; the other half was left fallow to regain its strength. After the autumn plowing, the seed was scattered and the harvest was gathered in the early summer. This is basically the system still used all around the Mediterranean and deep into the Near East. It is well suited to the light soils of those regions and to the concentration of rainfall in the winter. The scratch plow does not turn a furrow, but merely disturbs the soil. Cross-plowing is required, and the pulverizing of the soil both preserves the scanty moisture and brings fertilizing subsoil minerals to the surface by capillary attraction.

In the north, however, this scheme was not operable except in well-drained sandy or chalky soils of low fertility. Thanks to the perpetual boreal drip, the problem was not how to preserve moisture but how to get rid of it. The rich soils of the north were alluvial: mostly heavy clays which the Mediterranean scratch plow could handle only with difficulty. To repeat: everywhere and at all times the urban culture of the ancient world was sustained by a pathetically slender margin of agricultural surplus which could vanish quickly in the face of many different kinds of crisis. In the northwestern provinces the higher culture was particularly fragile because imported methods of farming had never been adapted to a radically different climate and set of soils. This failure is central to our understanding of the lack of resilience in the West, as compared with the East, from the third to the eighth centuries.

Jeffrey Russell has correctly told us that the eighth century marks a new beginning in the West, and I would un-

derscore Warren Hollister's insistence that improved agriculture north of the Alps and the Loire was integral to the
rebirth of the Occident. The Romans had experimented
with new types of plows suited to the heavy northern soils:
naturally these required more draft power than the scratch
plow, and Pliny tells us of an eight-ox wheeled plow used
in the Alpine region. Nevertheless, we know from Virgil
that this wheeled plow had a curved pole; it was not, therefore, so stout and efficient as the typical medieval wheeled
plow which had a quadrangular frame. Indeed, for all their
intelligent gropings, the Romans never managed to produce an agricultural system well suited to their northern
provinces.

The breakthrough seems to have come in the sixth century when the heavy plow of the northern Middle Ages appeared in Slavic lands. Perhaps it came from Central Asia:
the word "plow" is an etymological mystery, being neither
Slavic, Romanic, Germanic, nor Celtic. The new type of
plow was known in the Po Valley by the later seventh century and among the Rhineland Germans by the early
eighth. I recall Dr. Hollister's remarks about the modification of field shapes and soil drainage made possible by the
new method of plowing, and the development, in the
north, of so-called open fields. Finally, in the later eighth
century, we find the earliest evidence, between the Seine
and the Rhine, of the three-field system which added a
spring planting to the older autumn planting, an innovation made possible by the summer rains of the lands north
of the Alps and the Loire. Thus, by the eighth century the
peasants of the old northwestern provinces of the Roman
Empire were rapidly developing an entirely novel type of
agriculture, no longer imitative of the Mediterranean system but now intimately designed to suit the northern soils
and climates. It turned out to be an agrarian pattern con-

siderably more productive, in terms of human time and labor, than that of the Mediterranean region.

But more was involved than improvements in plowing and planting. In Antiquity the raising of cattle and of cereals seem normally to have been separate operations. One of the most important aspects of the early medieval agricultural revolution in northern Europe was the development of a type of farming which combined herding with grain production. The symbol of this new system is the scythe, the haymaking tool. Roman scythes exist, but are remarkably rare; they increase in Merovingian times, and by about A.D. 800 Charlemagne is trying to rename July the "Haying-month." Under the old plan, cattle usually browsed on the wasteland and thus their droppings were lost. Now, under the new open-field system, they were pastured, whenever possible, on the fallow or on the stubble after harvest, thus leaving their droppings to enrich the next year's crops. Moreover, systematic haying and stall-feeding began to produce the big manure piles which for the past millennium have been status symbols among the northern European peasantry, and with justification.

Roman farmers were by no means uninventive. In Gaul they developed an ingenious grain-harvesting machine consisting of a flat row of double-edged knives on a wheeled frame which was pushed by an animal; the heads of grain were cut off and fell into a trough between the wheels. This was a good laborsaving device, appropriate to a purely cereal agriculture. But it wasted the straw. As soon as the combined herding and grain-growing pattern developed, straw was too valuable to be lost, and the Gallo-Roman harvester became obsolete. The new system was notably more productive than the old: cattle and sheep ate what had been waste material, thus providing meat, dairy products, wool, and hides while their manure fattened the fields for the plow. And from the sixth century onward it was a new and more efficient plow that was beginning to turn the furrows of the northern fields. North of the Alps the agricultural surplus rose; a firmer basis than Antiquity had known was laid for urbanism and a culture of cities. Charlemagne's age shows the new vitality; the destructive waves of Viking and of Magyar invasions in the ninth and tenth centuries masked the effects of agrarian advance; but, by the end of the tenth century, the shape of a new Europe is clearly visible.

Henri Pirenne observed that the most significant fact in European history is the transfer of Europe's center of gravity from the Mediterranean to the great northern plains where it remains. Pirenne rightly identified the period of this seismic shift as the eighth century. Its essential cause, although Pirenne held other views, as Warren Hollister has indicated, was the emergence north of the Alps of a larger and more stable agricultural surplus than could be achieved in the Mediterranean area. The hand of the peasant on the plow was guiding the course of history.

But was it in fact those stupid rustics who made such epochal improvements? Gibbon would have doubted it. Wasn't it really the learned abbots and bishops who were trying to increase the revenues of their lands? We may be sure that not only the upper clergy but also the secular aristocrats were quite aware that their well-being depended upon production: as the centuries pass we find them increasingly authorizing the cutting of forests and draining of swamps to expand the plowland. But there is no scrap of evidence that any cleric or lord ever proposed an improvement in agrarian technology. It is beside the point that manuscripts of the old Roman agricultural writers were fairly common in medieval libraries: perusal of them would lead only to agricultural conservatism, not progress.

When in the thirteenth century new agricultural treatises begin to appear, they are trailing the peasant, not leading him. Walter of Henley, for example, is quite deceived about the relative advantage of the horse over the ox as a plow animal, yet every peasant who could afford it had been shifting to the horse for two centuries past, at least on the Continent.

There is no virtue in romanticizing the peasant or artisan and his works and days: the lower classes of all ages would seem to have been as well endowed with Original Sin as were their social betters. Nevertheless, if we are to discover the history of mankind, and not merely the history of the very thin and friable upper crust of mankind, we must broaden our researches to include the anonymous and faceless mass of men. Were they in fact anonymous? They had names and knew each other by them. Were they faceless? No more than we, or Gibbon. It is not their defect but our ignorance which has put them beyond our historical horizon.

Our jargon about "Movements," "developments," and the like must not entice us into historical animism; all history is in fact a matter of persons. One of the most important "developments" of the early Middle Ages was a new capacity for utilizing horsepower far beyond the Roman level. One of the items in this sequence occurs toward the end of the ninth century, presumably somewhere between Germany on the west and central Siberia on the east: somebody shaped up iron horseshoes and nailed them to the hooves of a horse. Historical movements do not hammer nails. It had to be done by an individual; and he was a bold man. Even if he had the horse thoroughly trussed, he was risking the ruination of a valuable piece of property. The experiment worked, and within a few years nailed horseshoes were being used very widely in moist northern lands where the hooves of horses soften easily and are abraded by steady work. The fact that horsepower remains today in engineering a standard theoretical measure of the rate of work is a symbol of the historical impact of our unknown inventor.

Let me summarize. The pluralism that increasingly has come to dominate the minds of Western men since Gibbon's day has given us both a new vision of the unity, and a new reverence for the diversity, of mankind. More intensive study of the East Asian and Indic cultures has put our own Western civilization into perspective to the point where we now envisage it as the present stage of what started out as the culture of the Fertile Crescent of the Near East. In this pattern of thinking, the political disintegration of the Roman Empire is a sign of vitalizing differentiation into the three great medieval subcultures of Byzantium, Islam, and the Franks, each of which achieved a peculiar magnificence and immensely expanded the geographic area that may be called civilized.

Second, our pluralism has embraced the common people within the scope of history. Although there is emotion in it, this is not sentimentalism; we have simply found that the activities of the upper classes alone do not account sufficiently for the observed facts. To be historians of any society we must be historians of the whole of that society, including the lower orders. Gibbon neglected this dimension of his problem. Consequently he failed to understand that differences in the effectiveness of agrarian methods largely account for the anemia of the northwestern provinces of the Empire and for the resilience and recuperative forces of the rest.

There is a widespread impression that in our age the humanities, that is, the study of the human phenomenon, are stagnant and that the natural sciences alone are surging ahead to new levels of truth. Yet our kind of history is as

far advanced over Gibbon's as the present nuclear physics
is over Newton's superb formulations. And the study of
history, like that of physics, continues in rapid flux.
Doubtless no living physicist is Newton's equal in genius,
yet physics today is immeasurably enlarged. No historian
of the later twentieth century can fail to be awed by Gibbon's acumen and grandeur. Yet, as history, his work is almost unbelievably obsolete, save for antiquarian details. It
is today a proper object of historical study, a magistral artifact of the eighteenth century, like the *B Minor Mass*. As
for ourselves, we are on the way toward producing a history of the globe, and of all mankind.

185–186; of Merovingian Gaul, 188–189
Gracchi, 30
Gratian, 206, 208
Gregory II, 253, 254
Gregory VII, 83, 251, 254
Gregory of Nazianus, 128
Gregory of Nyssa, 128
Gregory the Great, 85, 174, 194, 195, 196, 199, 203, 204, 250, 251, 253, 254, 259
Grotius, Hugo, 6

Hadrian, 42, 46, 272, 274; villa of, 273
Hannibal, 48
Heliogabalus, 63
Helios, 50
Hellenism, medieval, 92–118
Helvétius, Claude, 15, 18
Henana, 133
Henry II, 247
Heraclius, 93, 104, 138
Hercules, 55, 56
Herder, Johann Gottfried, 7, 155, 171, 172, 173
History: European, classification of, 1–2; classicist view of, 5; Montesquieu's view of, 9; "scientific" method of, 12; Gibbon's system of, 22–24, 24–25, 60, 302; Niebuhr and, 41–42; melancholy element in, 60; Byzantine, 117; concerns of eighteenth century about, 162; forces of, 171–172; modern approach to, 175–178, 294, 302; ancient, defined, 297; of Middle Ages, 297
Homer, 10, 61, 116, 234
Horace, 227, 228
Hottinger, J. H., 155
Hume, David, 14, 18, 23, 155
Huns. See Barbarians
Huzaya, Joseph, 133
"Hymn to Paradise," 130–131

Ibas, 132
Iberia, 107 n. 21
Imperium Galliarum, 33
Indicopleustes, Cosmas, 109–110
Indus-Ganges valleys, 296
Ireland. See Celts
Ishāq, Hunain ibn, 142
Isidore, Bishop, 195, 196, 199
Isis, 48, 50, 51, 68
Islam, 147–178, 295; Gibbon's view of, 149–168, 295; Arabic role in Middle

Ages, 155, 162; conquests of, 157; character of Muhammad, 157–159, 163, 164; extent of Muslim Empire, 161; and Arabic civilization, 162–167; and Gibbon's world, 169–170; modern approach to study of, 170–178, 297; early art styles of, 284
Istanbul, 109
Italy, 107 n. 21

Jackson, Kenneth, 242, 243
Jacob of Edessa, 142
Jacob of Serugh, 135–136
Jannābī, 156
Jerome, St., 187, 196, 197, 198, 219–221, 240, 298
John, St., 69, 70, 71
John of Damascus, St., 297
John of Ephesus, 137, 138
John of Tella, 137
Johnson, Samuel, 14
Julian of Halicarnassus, 136
Jupiter, 47, 55, 56; temple of, 3
Justin I, 136
Justin II, 138
Justinian, 93, 100, 104, 121, 136, 266, 274, 279
Juvenal, 213

Kant, Immanuel, 8
Kells, Book of, 293
Kenneshrin, 137, 142

La Bletterie, 24
Lactantius, 56, 217
Latin tradition, 206–231; and Christian victory over Roman paganism, 206–212, 216–225; and Latin literature, 209, 210, 211, 212, 213, 227; role of schools and continuity of, 209, 216, 217; and palaeography, 211–212, 215, 228, 299; and editorial activity, 213–214, 226, 227; and Church fathers, 217–225; influence of Cicero on, 218–221; Jerome and, 219–221; Augustine and, 221–225; preservation of, 224–225; and barbarians, 225–226; culmination of, 228–229; and Church institutions, 229–231
Latouche, Robert, 190
Lausanne, 11, 13, 14, 17
Law, William, 19
Leclercq, Dom Jean, 79
Leibniz, 174